LEGAL INTERVIEWING
AND
COUNSELING:
A CLIENT-CENTERED APPROACH

By

DAVID A. BINDER

Professor of Law, University of California, Los Angeles

and

SUSAN C. PRICE, Ph.D.

Assistant Clinical Professor, Neuropsychiatric Institute,
University of California, Los Angeles

ST. PAUL, MINN.
WEST PUBLISHING CO.
1977

Binder & Price Leg.Interview & Counsel MTB

6th Reprint—1986

To Melinda.

*

PREFACE

We would like to begin by saying a few words about learning to be an effective legal interviewer and counselor. In our view, in order for a lawyer to develop proficiency in interviewing and counseling, a number of things must occur. Initially, one needs to gain an understanding of the objectives of legal interviewing and counseling and the factors which motivate clients to participate fully in these processes. Additionally, one needs exposure to basic interviewing and counseling techniques. Finally, one needs the opportunity to practice using the basic techniques under circumstances in which feedback about effective and ineffective performance is available. In short, interviewing and counseling cannot be learned solely through intellectual mastery of a set of materials. What is required is familiarity with basic concepts and techniques and *then* constructive feedback regarding the utilization of these basic concepts and techniques.

This book represents an effort to provide a description of the objectives of the legal interviewing and counseling processes, the forces which motivate clients to participate in these processes, and the basic techniques which are needed to successfully achieve the goals of legal interviewing and counseling. Our intention is that this book will serve as a foundation in a course where the student will have an opportunity to practice the techniques we have described and to receive constructive feedback about the student's actual performance.

The process of interviewing and counseling, like any process involving human interaction, is very complex. In an attempt to make this complex process comprehensible, we have done several things. First, we have suggested that it can be helpful to think of the highly fluid lawyer-client dialogue as consisting of a number of somewhat discrete stages or steps. Second, we have attempted to provide some rather precise techniques which we believe can facilitate the lawyer-client dialogue. We have not contented ourselves with merely suggesting that lawyers achieve abstract goals such as "building rapport" and "helping clients find solutions." Instead, we have attempted to describe through detailed case examples certain specific techniques which a lawyer can consciously employ in order to reach these abstract goals. Third, we have limited the description of the interviewing and counseling processes to cases falling within the context of litigation. Thus, we have not attempted to describe lawyer-client interaction in planning situations such as the preparation of a will, the formation of a corporation, the preparation of a buy-sell agreement, etc.

PREFACE

Most law students have their initial interviewing and counseling experience in clinical programs where the cases typically involve litigation rather than planning. Although there are similarities in all legal interviewing and counseling, we believe that it is most helpful and least confusing to focus a beginning text such the kinds of interviews in which most students are actually involved.

Finally, a few words of caution are in order. Our approach of suggesting that lawyers think of the fluid process of interviewing and counseling as consisting of discrete stages or steps and our detailed descriptions of specific techniques should not be taken as absolute. Our intention is to provide general models which can be used as a foundation for learning to become an effective interviewer and counselor. The models are intended to serve as basic guidelines, as a way to begin. The models should not be seen as rigid formulas from which no deviation will be permitted. Anyone who slavishly attempts to always break interviewing and counseling into the steps we have described or who attempts to use, in a "cookbook manner," the skills we have presented, will soon find that relations with clients lack the warmth and spontaneity which any good relationship requires. Although we believe our models provide a useful foundation which is applicable in a wide range of situations, there will be many instances in which modification will be called for. In short, to become fully proficient, the lawyer will have to learn a basic approach and, at the same time, retain sufficient flexibility to modify that approach to meet special circumstances.

DAVID A. BINDER
SUSAN C. PRICE

Los Angeles, California
September, 1977

ACKNOWLEDGEMENTS

Many people have helped us in the writing of this book. We would especially like to thank Herbert Morris who read early drafts and encouraged us to continue; William Klein whose detailed comments and suggestions were enormously valuable, and whose efforts went far beyond the call of duty and friendship; Paul Bergman and Kenney Hegland whose feedback and suggestions greatly improved this book; Paul Boland whose development of interviewing and counseling training exercises helped us and our students learn a great deal.

Our thanks also to Kenneth Graham, Arthur Rosett, and Gary T. Schwartz for their valuable comments on various portions of the book.

We are also grateful to the instructors and students in the UCLA Law School Clinical Program who, over the past several years, have attempted to apply our various models and techniques as part of their clinical work and who have provided us with a great deal of constructive criticism. Our thanks therefore to Paul Bergman, Paul Boland, Kenney Hegland, Robert Mann. Also, thanks to Judy Bakal, Dawn Friedman, Ronald Marks, and David Pettit, as well as numerous law students at UCLA.

Additionally, we would like to thank Charles McCreary for developing the consultation program between the UCLA Neuropsychiatric Institute and the UCLA Law School. Without his concern for developing innovative programs between psychology and law, we would never have begun this book. Also, we would like to thank Charles McCreary and Robin Drapkin for their feedback and suggestions on the text.

Special thanks go to Karen Lee Patterson, who served as our research assistant. Thanks also should be given to Dennis Patrick for his research on client-centered decision making.

Most of all, we would like to thank Melinda for her knowledge of English grammar, constructive criticism, emotional support, and wonderful dinners, all of which helped us survive and actually enjoy writing this book.

*

TABLE OF CONTENTS

CHAPTER ONE.   LAWYER–CLIENT INTERACTION: AN OVERVIEW
(Page 1)

CHAPTER TWO.   MOTIVATION WITHIN THE INTERVIEW

CHAPTER THREE.   ACTIVE LISTENING

TABLE OF CONTENTS

CHAPTER FOUR. QUESTIONING

CHAPTER FIVE. ASCERTAINING THE CLIENT'S PROBLEM AND LEGAL POSITION

TABLE OF CONTENTS

TABLE OF CONTENTS

CHAPTER EIGHT. THE NATURE OF THE COUNSELING PROCESS

CHAPTER NINE. CONDUCTING THE COUNSELING PROCESS

TABLE OF CONTENTS

CHAPTER TEN.   COUNSELING DIFFICULT CLIENTS

CHAPTER ELEVEN.   REFERRING A CLIENT TO A MENTAL HEALTH PROFESSIONAL

†

LEGAL INTERVIEWING
and COUNSELING:
A CLIENT—CENTERED APPROACH

Chapter One

LAWYER–CLIENT INTERACTION: AN OVERVIEW

This book concerns the ways in which lawyers might interact with clients in order to help clients solve problems. The specific focus of the book is upon lawyer-client interaction within the context of dispute resolution cases.[1] Within this context, the book will examine the tasks which lawyers must perform, and the skills which lawyers should possess in order to be effective legal counselors.

Traditionally, lawyer-client interaction has been described under the labels of "interviewing" and "counseling." Interviewing has been defined as the task of gathering information, while counseling has been defined as the task of formulating solutions.[2] Before deciding whether these definitions are useful, we will provide an overview of what lawyers and clients generally discuss during the course of a dispute resolution case. That is, within the litigation context, we will describe what clients typically request from lawyers and what lawyers typically do in their direct dealings with clients to fulfill these requests.

We will begin the overview with a description of what is usually involved in a dispute resolution controversy. Generally, a dispute resolution case involves an existing or potential controversy about what legal obligations, if any, have arisen as the result of some past occurrence. Typically, a plaintiff contends that as the result of some previous incident (the sale of merchandise, the firing of an employee, the robbery of a store), the defendant is now obligated to take certain further action (the payment of money, the rehiring of an employee, the paying of a fine). In response, the defendant contends that no such obligation exists. Usually the defendant bases his/her

---

1. In Chapter Seven, there will be a brief description of how the lawyer might proceed to obtain information from witnesses.

2. H. Freeman & H. Weihofen, Clinical Law Training—Interviewing and Counseling 8 (1972).

contention on one or a combination of the following: (a) the incident did not occur as the plaintiff contends, (b) even if the incident did occur as the plaintiff contends, the law imposes no obligation of the type sought by the plaintiff.

When the dispute resolution client enters the lawyer's office, the client will usually have two basic questions in mind: (1) what *can* I do, legally and practically, about the problem which has arisen from my conflict with X concerning transaction Y?, and (2) what *should* I do about the problem? For example, when a potential plaintiff consults a lawyer about what can be done to collect an unpaid debt, the person will usually wish to know: (1) as a legal matter, and as a practical matter, what can be done, and (2) from among the alternatives that are available, which would be best to choose? These two questions will usually exist regardless of the extent to which the client (plaintiff or defendant) may have already formulated tentative answers. Some clients will have a fairly sound idea of what rights the law provides or what obligations the law imposes in cases of their particular type. For example, some potential plaintiffs in a defective merchandise situation will know that basically the law provides that someone in their circumstance may either affirm the transaction and sue for damages or return the merchandise and cancel the transaction. Further, some clients, regardless of their understanding of their basic legal rights and obligations, may have a fairly good understanding of the general courses of action open to them. For example, they may know that in their situation the basic options are litigate, settle, or forego litigation.[3] The credit manager of a large corporation, for example, will usually be quite sophisticated in this regard. When clients have a basic understanding of their rights and the solution options open to them, they may enter the lawyer's office with a fairly well-formulated plan of action in mind. Nonetheless, these clients, as well as most other clients, will usually be asking the lawyer to help them undertake, at least to some degree, a consideration of the questions of what can and should be done in light of the situation.

To assist the client in answering these basic questions, the lawyer will usually begin by obtaining a general idea of the nature of the client's problems. Thus, initial lawyer-client interaction usually focuses on problem identification. What is it that is causing the client to ask "What can and should I do?" In this initial discussion, the lawyer usually obtains general information about (1) the nature of the underlying occurrences which have caused the client to seek legal assistance, (2) the basic difficulties which now confront the client as the result of the occurrences, and (3) the results the client desires. "I've been in an automobile accident, and now my insurance company is threatening to cancel my car insurance. Can I stop them from

3. In Chapter Ten, we will discuss how a lawyer might proceed should the client ask only whether or not a proposed course of action is lawful. See p. 201 infra.

doing that?" "I was fired because my supervisor didn't like black people, and now I can't get a decent job. Can I make the company rehire me?" [4]

In dispute resolution cases, there usually can be no meaningful evaluation of what avenues of approach are available, let alone which should be adopted, until there first has been an analysis of the client's legal rights. Where the client stands legally as of this moment is the crucial question. The answer, of course, can be obtained only after the lawyer has learned how the "past" transaction, from which the client's problem springs, "in fact" took place.[5] The law fixes the rights of the parties only when the actual facts have first been determined.[6] Therefore, in a dispute resolution case, once there has been a general identification of the client's problem, the interaction between lawyer and client usually focuses on factual investigation. The lawyer attempts to gather information about the underlying facts comprising the "past transaction." To accomplish this task, the lawyer will ask the client, and often third persons, how the underlying transaction actually occurred. For example, in the case of the alleged discriminatory firing, the lawyer will discuss with the client what occurred to cause the client to conclude that he was fired because the supervisor disliked blacks.

When this task of gathering the initial information about the underlying transaction has been completed and the information has been evaluated in light of the applicable law, the lawyer and client will usually begin to address directly the questions of what can and should be done. On the basis of the lawyer's evaluation of the client's probable legal position, there will be a consideration of whether litigation or some other action will best resolve the client's problems. To accomplish this consideration, the dialogue between the lawyer and the client will typically shift to the activities of: (1) identifying potential alternative solutions, (2) predicting the probable positive

---

4. The language used by clients often will not include the specific questions of "What can and should I do?" Nonetheless, experience dictates that although many clients do not articulate these two questions, they are almost always present to some degree. If the client in the insurance cancellation case were pressed to explain what was meant by the phrase "Can I stop them from doing that?", it will usually become apparent that the client is asking, at least to some extent, both "What can I and should I do?" Similarly, the client in the discriminatory firing case certainly does not simply want to know whether or not under the law the company must rehire him. He will also want to know what can be done to bring about a re-

hiring, and probably whether or not he should follow whatever course of action is available. Moreover, if there is more than one avenue of approach available, he will probably wish to know which alternative he should choose.

5. In Chapter Four, we will briefly discuss the issue of the extent to which an individual has the capacity to accurately perceive, recall, and report what has been observed. See p. 48 infra.

6. For an excellent discussion of the process by which the law fixes the rights of parties, see J. Frank, Courts on Trial 5–61 (Atheneum Ed. 1949).

and negative consequences of the adoption of any specified solution, and (3) weighing each solution against other available solutions in order to decide which solution seems most appropriate.

If the initial decision is to enter litigation, the lawyer will then begin, through formal and informal means, to conduct pretrial discovery. Part of the informal discovery will usually involve further meetings with the client to obtain additional information about what occurred in the underlying transaction. As the discovery progresses, the additional information which the lawyer gains will confirm or modify his/her initial evaluation of the client's legal position. As a result of these re-evaluations, as well as various procedural and tactical maneuvers undertaken by the adversary during the course of the pre-trial stage, the lawyer will have still further meetings with the client. These meetings will be for the purpose of considering whether the initial decision to enter into litigation should be abandoned in favor of another alternative such as settlement.

When the lawyer-client dialogue turns to the possibility of adopting a course of action other than that which was initially selected, the basic inquiry usually remains the same, "What can and should be done?" As in the conference resulting in the initial decision to litigate, the conversation between the lawyer and client will, in light of the most recent evaluation of the client's legal position, again usually turn to: (1) identifying potential solutions, (2) predicting probable positive and negative consequences, and (3) weighing potential solutions with their respective advantages and disadvantages one against the other.

Before concluding this description of lawyer-client interaction during the process of solution formulation, one further point might be made. Whether the solution formulation discussion focuses on an initial decision to litigate, or a subsequent decision to abandon litigation, the discussion usually requires more information than was gathered in order to appraise the client's legal position. To consider what alternatives are available, and the respective advantages and disadvantages of each, much more information will usually be needed. For example, in considering the advisability of a proposed settlement, information about the client's financial position may be needed. If the litigation is likely to involve substantial attorney fees, can the client afford the litigation? Similarly, if the litigation is likely to be prolonged, there may be a need to consider the client's physical and emotional condition. Can the client endure the strain of a four-week trial? Moreover, what about the effect on the client's life situation —job, family relationships, etc.?

Accordingly, when the lawyer and client come to discuss what course of action should be followed, the lawyer-client dialogue will not be confined solely to the formulation and weighing of alternatives. To determine what consequences may result from adopting a given course of action, information gathering, the activity which dominated the early phases of the lawyer-client interaction, will continue to be essential. Information gathering, therefore, will usually occur simultaneously with, and as an essential part of, the solution formulation process.

Given the foregoing overview of typical lawyer-client interaction in dispute resolution situations, what about definitions of the terms "interviewing" and "counseling?" The definitions we will adopt accord fairly closely with those which are traditionally given.

"Interviewing," as used in this book, refers to lawyer interaction with a client for the purpose of identifying the client's problem, and for the purpose of gathering information on which a solution to that problem can be based. Given the nature of problems which typically arise in the dispute resolution context, interviewing will usually involve gathering data about the following: (1) the nature of the client's problem, (2) the client's legal position, and (3) during the course of solution formulation, the probable consequences of adopting litigation or some other course of action to resolve the problem.

"Counseling," as used in this book, refers to a process in which lawyers help clients reach decisions. Specifically "counseling" refers to a process in which potential solutions with their probable positive and negative consequences are identified and then weighed in order to decide which alternative is most appropriate. Given the nature of problems which typically arise in the dispute resolution context, the basic question to which this process will usually be applied is whether the client's problem should be solved through litigation or through some alternative such as settlement.

We have, for the purposes of clarity, provided separate definitions for the terms "interviewing" and "counseling." However, as the previous discussion suggests, interviewing and counseling are not always independent activities. Interviewing is a process which occurs both independent of, and as an essential part of, the counseling process.

At this point, we will conclude the overview and commence a detailed examination of lawyer-client interaction. The examination will begin with an analysis of client motivation to participate in the interviewing and counseling processes.

Chapter Two

MOTIVATION WITHIN THE INTERVIEW

MOTIVATION TO ACT

In the remaining chapters of this book, we will discuss a variety of specific techniques which can be used in legal interviewing and counseling. In setting forth this range of techniques, our goal will be the development of (1) a repertoire of interviewing and counseling skills, and (2) an ability to analyze the extent to which each specific technique may be effective in facilitating the interview. In discussing the effectiveness of the various techniques, we will frequently address the subject of the usefulness of the techniques in stimulating a client's willingness to participate fully in the interviewing and counseling processes. The purpose of this chapter is to set forth some basic theoretical concepts about human motivation upon which our subsequent analysis of the efficiency of specific techniques will be based. Our pedagogical notion is that if one can begin with some general understanding of human motivation, one may more readily understand our subsequent analysis of why particular techniques are likely to encourage full client participation.

To accomplish the goal of providing a general understanding of human motivation, we will begin with an elementary explanation of human behavior. We will then examine the concept of human motivation as it applies more specifically to the context of legal interviewing and counseling. In setting forth some general theoretical concepts about human behavior, we shall not attempt the appraisal of any particular psychological theory, nor shall we rely on any particular theory of human motivation. Rather, we shall limit our discussion to a few generally accepted, broad-based concepts about human behavior. Though these concepts are basic elementary ones, we believe, for the reason set forth above, there is value in articulating them.

Human beings have a variety of needs. These needs have been variously described, and there exists no precise agreement about their exact nature or number.[1] In general, needs can be divided into two broad categories: (1) physical needs and (2) psychosocial needs. Physical needs are often called primary and include the need for food,

---

1. For a description of some of the various theories regarding the nature of human needs see: R. I. Evans, Carl Rogers The Man and His Ideas 3–8 (1975); R. C. Bolles, Theories of Motivation (1975); D. McClelland, Studies in Motivation (1955).

shelter, sex, etc. These needs are inborn and common to all people, although the particular ways in which they are satisfied are learned and consequently show tremendous variation.

Psychosocial needs are often referred to as secondary. These needs are learned through an individual's association or affiliation with a particular society and culture. Included among these secondary needs are the desire for love, status, recognition, etc. Attempts to enumerate all psychosocial needs and to arrange them in a hierarchy of importance have produced little consensus. Secondary needs vary greatly from one society to another. In addition, they find unique organization and expression within each individual.

Although there is little agreement as to the precise nature of the psychosocial needs, there tends to be universal agreement that these needs, in combination with the primary ones, profoundly influence patterns of thought, attitude, and behavior. In general, a person acts (or refrains from acting) primarily to fulfill one or more primary or secondary needs. Thus, motivation to act exists principally when the person perceives (either at a conscious or intuitive level) that his/her conduct will satisfy one or more such needs.

Though these needs serve to energize and direct (motivate) human behavior, the individual is rarely aware of their presence or the influence they exert. The needs are usually experienced in the form of feelings. Typically the feelings involve some sort of discomfort [2] accompanied by a desire to find relief.[3]

Needs exist contemporaneously and are often in conflict. For example, a client, John Bridgeport, has consulted you regarding the subjects of divorce and bankruptcy. He is a former aerospace engineer who has been unable to find employment for the past six months. His house and his car are about to be foreclosed, and his wife is threatening to leave him because of their impoverished state. The local high school district has offered him a janitorial job on the swing shift. The job pays fairly well, but Mr. Bridgeport is in doubt as to whether or not to accept it. Though the income may indeed be sufficient to save his material possessions and his marriage, his needs for self-respect and esteem may not enable him to accept the idea that he is working as a "janitor."

When needs are in conflict, motivation to act will likely exist only when the individual feels that a course of action will satisfy one or more needs without unduly interfering with others. Thus, only when the individual perceives overall gain in terms of need satisfaction, will there be sufficient motivation to act.

2. The discomfort can appear in any number of forms—e. g., fear, dissatisfaction, anxiety, etc.; the intensity will vary from minimal to extreme.

3. There are theories of motivation which postulate that not all behavior is motivated by a desire for relief from discomfort. See A. Maslow, Motivation and Personality (1970).

The hypothetical concerning Mr. Bridgeport points to another aspect of needs which bears explicit mention. As has been frequently noted, some of the strongest needs which an individual experiences have to do with feelings of self-esteem and self-regard.[4] As a consequence, there will be many situations where the individual will choose a course of action which produces little material satisfaction over a course of action that is materially beneficial. The individual's need for self-respect is often of greater importance than whatever needs may be satisfied through material gain.

MOTIVATION IN LEGAL INTERVIEWS

Given that people generally act or refrain from acting in order to satisfy their needs, what might motivate clients to participate in, or withdraw from, the interviewing and counseling processes?[5] Clients will usually have a general underlying motivation to participate in the interview. Typically, clients seek out a lawyer because they believe that speaking with a lawyer can provide a solution to the problem at hand. Whatever needs can be satisfied through a resolution of the client's problem can perhaps be met by conversing with the lawyer.[6]

However, even though the dialogue between the lawyer and the client may be buttressed by an underlying motivation to communicate, the interviewing and counseling processes will usually be fraught with motivational difficulties. Frequently, full participation may be contrary to certain client needs. From a psychological perspective, clients will often have needs which will be undermined if all relevant information were disclosed. For example, a client's need for self-esteem may motivate a client to withhold information if providing all relevant data means disclosing that he/she was "at the scene" because of participation in a homosexual affair. Similarly, need for self-esteem may prevent a client from disclosing that a principal reason for considering dropping a lawsuit is that attorney fees can no longer be met because of foolish gambling losses.

Usually, it will not be possible for a lawyer to analyze precisely what specific needs may be blocking full client participation. Though the lawyer may recognize that the client is not fully and freely participating in the interview, the lawyer generally will not be able to determine precisely what psychological needs account for the client's reluctance. In general, lawyers lack the training to uncover and re-

4. R. Kahn & C. Cannell, The Dynamics of Interviewing 40 (1957) [hereinafter Kahn & Cannell].

5. Unless otherwise noted, this discussion of client motivation is equally applicable to witnesses.

6. Often this underlying motivation is not present in witness interviews; typically, a witness has no problem which can be resolved by conversing with a lawyer. In Chapter Seven, there will be a more detailed examination of techniques for interviewing witnesses who are not motivated to converse with the lawyer.

solve an individual's underlying psychological needs and conflicts. The process of uncovering unmet needs and conflicts is most appropriately undertaken by a trained mental health specialist.[7] However, without getting into the realm of deep psychological analysis, we believe lawyers can develop some expertise in dealing with needs that typically block motivation for full participation in the interview. There exist some identifiable psychological factors which commonly inhibit client participation, and other psychological factors which, when appropriately brought into play, tend to satisfy or overcome those factors which inhibit participation.

Our premise is that if lawyers are aware of these common psychological factors, they will be able to effectively motivate full client participation. Lawyers will often be able to achieve this goal even though they will usually be unable to analyze the specific needs of their clients. Thus, with knowledge of these general factors, we believe lawyers will usually have a sufficient basis for employing interviewing and counseling skills to meet the psychological needs of their clients. Therefore, rather than attempting to provide a framework for focusing on, and analyzing, each individual's unique configuration of needs, we will provide a general list of the common psychological factors which tend to inhibit and facilitate full participation. With an understanding of these factors and their potential motivational effects as a background, we believe lawyers can then move on to learn how to successfully employ specific interviewing and counseling techniques.

The most common psychological factors that operate to create or, conversely, to interfere with client motivation during an interview have been variously described.[8] We will discuss these phenomena in two groups. Group one contains "interfering" or "inhibiting" factors. These are factors which commonly arise during an interview and which the lawyer must overcome if he/she is to stimulate maximum client participation. Group two contains "positive" or "facilitating" factors. These are factors which the lawyer can introduce into the interview both to overcome and to prevent client unwillingness to participate.

Inhibitors

In the "inhibitor" group, seven factors bear mention. Though each will be discussed as separate phenomenon, they are not mutually exclusive. Each factor often combines or intertwines with other inhibitors. The seven factors do not, of course, represent all the phenomenon that may inhibit the flow of information from client to law-

7. There are some authors who believe lawyers can be trained to engage in a fair degree of psychological analysis. See A. Watson, The Lawyer in the Interviewing and Counseling Process 153–154 (1976) [hereinafter Watson].

8. R. L. Gorden, Interviewing Strategy, Techniques and Tactics 70–95 (1969) [hereinafter Gorden]; Kahn & Cannell supra note 4, at 45–53.

yer. The factors analyzed are some of those that most commonly operate to block communication in a legal interview. They are factors which operate across a wide range of client personality types.

Of the seven factors, the first two—ego threat and case threat—play the most pervasive role in blocking full communication.

Ego Threat

People tend to withhold information which they perceive as threatening to their self-esteem. When individuals evaluate themselves, or are evaluated by others, in a positive manner, they tend to feel comfortable and confident—they tend to feel good about themselves. Since positive evaluations develop feelings of self-esteem, people are motivated to maintain or seek out positive evaluations. However, people often have negative feelings about their past or anticipated behavior. Their feelings can range from mild embarrassment to strong feelings of guilt or shame. When asked questions which call for revelation of the conduct, they are reluctant to respond. They believe that revealing the conduct will cause the listener to think negatively about them. A truthful response poses a threat to their self-esteem; it is therefore "ego threatening."

For example, a lawyer is consulted by a businessman of relatively high regard in the community. The man claims he was fraudulently induced to invest in a large real estate venture. Though quite experienced in business matters, the man had neglected to make any investigation of the venture before parting with his money. He had simply relied upon the smooth talk of the person who presented him with "the deal." When the lawyer inquires about the man's knowledge of the venture at the time the investment was made, the man is reluctant to admit that he knew nothing. He believes he was stupid and naive. Additionally, he is afraid the lawyer will think him stupid and not much of a businessman if he admits he knew nothing about the venture when he made his investment. Similarly, a client who is discussing the advantages of proceeding to trial may be reluctant to reveal that a major advantage the client sees in continuing the case is that it will cause the adversary great financial and emotional discomfort. The client is ashamed to admit a principal motive is that of revenge. The client believes the lawyer will view him/her as an unconscionable person if the true motive were revealed.

The problem of ego threat sometimes does not involve the lawyer but rather is focused on a fear that the information may become public and thus lower the client's esteem in the eyes of others. Thus, a client may admit an "extramarital affair" as long as he/she believes it will be kept from family members.

Case Threat

A second major factor tending to block client communication is "case threat." The client believes revealing the sought information will be "harmful to the case." A criminal defendant fails to disclose that he was near the scene of the crime. He believes revealing the information will cause the lawyer to disbelieve him and thereby to lose interest in the case. Alternatively, the defendant may believe that to tell his lawyer will be tantamount to having the fact come out at trial. Perhaps both thoughts are present.

In some instances, data may be considered both ego threatening and case threatening. Thus, a criminal defendant with a past record may fail to reveal its existence because he is ashamed, and because he believes that if the lawyer knew of the record, the lawyer would not pursue the case diligently.

Case threat can be operative with both clients and witnesses. To the extent a witness identifies with a side or a party, the witness will to some degree be subject to the phenomenon of case threat. Thus, in a will-contest case based upon the decedent's alleged insanity, a close relative of the contestant may be reluctant to reveal to the proponent's lawyer facts indicating the decedent was competent.

Role Expectations

Most people have a set of beliefs about what kind of behavior is appropriate within the confines of particular relationships. For example, most people think there are certain ways one should or should not behave when interacting with parents. Similarly, most people have beliefs about how children should relate to adults. Whenever a person interacts with another individual whom the person sees as falling within a particular category, beliefs about appropriate behavior often unconsciously come into play and modify behavior to conform with the beliefs. We have labeled beliefs about what constitutes proper behavior as "expectations." Since the expectations pertain to relationships between persons fitting into specified categories, we have labeled the entire phenomenon "role expectations."

Role expectations develop from a variety of sources, from both actual and vicarious experience. Family, friends, associates, news media, institutions, etc., constantly deliver messages about what constitutes appropriate behavior when one assumes a particular position. In short, role expectations are learned or shaped by life experiences.

In our society, people are frequently taught that in role relationships one person will assume a position of authority or leadership. Therefore, when people initially enter into a particular relationship they often expect to be in either a dominant or subordinate position. If one is a parent one expects to dominate; if one is a child, one expects to be dominated. If people are teachers, they often see their students as occupying subordinate roles. Again, these beliefs develop unconsciously from years of cultural infusion. Undoubtedly, people might be better off if they saw more relationships as involving shared responsibility, but the fact is that frequently they do not. Rather, they see relationships in terms of dominant and subordinate positions.

When a client enters a lawyer's office, the client will frequently have a set of expectations about what constitutes appropriate "client behavior." The expectations will vary from client to client; not all clients will have acquired their expectations from the same learning sources. In many instances, the client will think of the lawyer as being in a position of authority. In such situations, the client may be somewhat reluctant to communicate fully. There may be a belief the lawyer knows what subjects deserve inquiry and what subjects do not. If a topic which the client feels important is not discussed, the client may often assume either consciously or intuitively, that the topic is not a significant one. Other clients may have an opposite set of beliefs, perhaps based on the idea that insofar as gathering the facts is concerned, the lawyer's primary function is to listen. After all, the lawyer wasn't there when it happened and therefore ought to withhold any analysis until the facts are out.

The closer the client's expectations come to either extreme of the dominate-subordinate spectrum, the more difficulty the lawyer may encounter in developing full information. The subordinate client must be motivated to talk much more freely; after all, even the most brilliant lawyer will not be able to think of all the questions necessary to bring out everything that occurred. Where the client's expectations tend toward domination, the client must be provided with the impetus to speak about topics of interest to the lawyer as well as to the client. What the client sees as important is often not legally salient. Further, even though the client may discuss some relevant data, the client will often omit other important information.

Etiquette Barrier

A fourth interfering phenomenon can be called "etiquette barrier." [9] Often an individual has information that he/she will freely provide to some persons but not to others. Thus, there are things that women tell women but not men; that blacks tell blacks, but not whites; students tell students, but not teachers. Information is perceived to be appropriate for peers, but not for those in other groups or roles. Loss of self-esteem is not involved. Rather, the client desires to avoid relating data which the client believes will be shocking, embarrassing, or discomforting to the lawyer.

For example, Sgt. Robert Henderson is the investigating officer assigned to the Linda Murstein murder. In the course of the investigation, Henderson learns that the deceased had been sexually assaulted and savagely mutilated in her vaginal area. In discussing the results of the investigation with the deputy district attorney, Elizabeth Mullian, Henderson is reluctant to reveal the details of the mutilation. Though Henderson has had no difficulty discussing these facts

9. This term is borrowed from R. L. Gorden. See Gorden, supra note 8, at 76–78.

with other male police officers, he feels it is somehow inappropriate to relate this kind of information to a woman. Sexual mutilation of a female is simply not a subject that a man discusses with a woman; the subject would be too disgusting or distressing to her.

Sgt. Henderson's reluctance springs not from anything he knows about Ms. Mullian. Rather, the reluctance stems simply from his belief about what is properly discussed with a woman. Where a lawyer senses a client may find a topic to be "taboo," the lawyer must convey the idea that the topic is open for discussion. If the lawyer does not take the initiative in granting permission, the client will usually continue to withhold the data.

Trauma

This phenomenon occurs when a person is asked to recall an experience which evokes unpleasant feelings. There are many events in which people experience negative feelings such as fear, anger, humiliation, or sadness. When they are asked to recall these events, they often tend to re-experience these feelings. As a consequence, most people are motivated to avoid thinking and talking about unpleasant past events. For example, a mother being interviewed about a beating administered to her child by a baby-sitter may be reluctant to talk about the incident; the mother may want to avoid re-experiencing the anger, frustration, and sadness which the incident caused her. A potential plaintiff in an automobile accident may have a reluctance to talk about the details of the incident for the same reason.

Perceived Irrelevancy

This inhibitor does not involve any feelings of discomfort or threat. The feeling involved here is one of "there is no reason" to provide the sought data. There is nothing to be gained or accomplished by providing the requested information.

An interview of a parent accused of child abuse provides an illustration. Those who have worked in the area of child abuse have observed that battering parents are frequently individuals who have very few and infrequent social contacts.[10] A lawyer for a parent accused of child abuse may therefore wish to develop information about the nature and extent of the client's social contacts. However, to a parent faced with the accusation of child abuse, questions about the general nature of the parent's social activities are quite likely to seem irrelevant. The questions are not concerned with the relationship between the parent and the child. They seemingly have nothing to do with the case. As a consequence, there is little motivation to provide a detailed response.

10. C. H. Kempe & R. E. Helfer, Helping the Battered Child and His Family 208, 272, 275 (1972).

Greater Need

The last of the phenomena on our inhibitor list is "greater need." The situation is characterized by the client having a need or desire to talk about a subject other than that which is of immediate interest to the lawyer.[11] As a consequence, the client cannot concentrate on the lawyer's topic, and full and accurate information is not forthcoming. For example, an incarcerated defendant concerned primarily with bail or O. R. release will often not be able to turn full attention to questions relating to the underlying charge. Similarly, a tenant threatened with eviction may be more concerned with when and where he can move than with inquiries related to a potential "habitability defense."

In these situations, the lawyer's questions are not perceived as irrelevant or in any sense threatening. Rather, the client is simply concerned with a subject which, while perhaps secondary to the lawyer, is primary to the client.

Facilitators

There are five principal phenomena which lawyers can draw upon to motivate full participation. As in the discussion of "inhibitors," the treatment will be confined primarily to describing the factors. A discussion of the techniques by which these phenomena may be put into use is reserved for subsequent chapters.

Empathetic Understanding

This factor is mentioned first for the purpose of emphasis. Our experience is that far too few law students and lawyers are aware of the enormous extent to which communication can be opened up through the effective use of empathetic understanding.

There are limited opportunities in our society to actually express one's thoughts and feelings to someone who has the ability to (1) listen, (2) understand, and (3) at the same time not judge. People on the receiving end of a communication are usually too busy to really listen, and too interested in themselves to avoid responses that include the listener's "own two cents." The "two cents" will appear in a variety of forms. Advice on how to handle the situation is one typical response. "Don't worry. You'll feel less angry as time goes on." Analysis of why the feelings have arisen is another common listener reaction. "You probably feel angry because you feel you should have seen through that smoke screen." When this kind of advice-giving or analysis occurs, the individual often has little impetus to continue the conversation. There is little point in expressing your ideas and feelings if all you get in return is lay psychoanalysis or advice on how to change or ignore your feelings.

---

11. Sometimes the phenomenon is present in the form of the interviewee wishing to do anything other than talk. A potential witness busy with his/her work is an obvious example. For a discussion of competing time demands, see Gorden, supra note 8, at 117–118.

However, in the presence of someone who exhibits non-judgmental understanding—a listener who provides empathetic responses—most people will be strongly motivated to continue communicating. Almost without realizing it, people will tend to provide an ever increasing amount of information. Precisely why the presence of non-judgmental understanding results in increased inducement to communicate is not known. However, the fact that it does have this self-propelling effect has been frequently noted.[12]

The opportunities for lawyers to utilize empathetic understanding are endless. Both clients and witnesses are continually expressing their thoughts and feelings about what has or is likely to occur. Clients and witnesses do not simply report previously observed facts. Their communications with lawyers are usually far more complex and may include such diverse matters as: (1) how they felt when an event occurred, (2) why an event occurred, and (3) how they now feel both about what occurred and what the occurrence portends for the future. The following examples are illustrative:

"I remember seeing the gun; I was shocked. John wasn't the type of person who resorted to violence. But there he was with it in his hand.

"When the policeman told me she was dead, I was stunned. The week before she told me she made out a new will, but I didn't attach any significance to it. And now those vicious people wanting to contest the will; they are the ones that must be crazy.

"Now I have to decide whether to accept the $3500. If I don't accept it, I may regret my decision for a long time. On the other hand, if I don't go to trial I may always wonder if I could have gotten a lot more."

Lawyers who develop the ability to demonstrate that they understand both the facts and feelings which are reported will usually become recipients of an ever increasing amount of information.

Fulfilling Expectations

"One of the important forces in social interaction is the tendency for one person to communicate, verbally and non-verbally, his expectations to another person. The second person then tends to respond consciously or unconsciously to those expectations. This may be viewed as one manifestation of the more general human tendency to conform to the group of peers and to the suggestion of higher status persons in society."[13]

When the presence of inhibitors causes a client to feel reluctant to provide information, the phenomenon just described can often be

12. Carl Rogers, Counseling and Psychotherapy 131–151 (1942).

13. Gorden, supra note 8, at 84.

usefully brought to bear. On sensing the reluctance, the lawyer can verbally and non-verbally convey a strong expectation that the sought data should be revealed. In many instances, the individual's need to conform to the lawyer's expectations will be stronger than needs being met by the reluctance to respond. In these situations, the inhibitors will be overcome and the information revealed.

There are two additional points to be made about the phenomenon of fulfilling expectations. First, the phenomenon can be useful in overcoming memory difficulties as well as inhibitors. Second, the phenomenon can be inadvertently employed to create an expectation that the sought data need not be revealed. The following example is useful in considering both points.

Assume a client has indicated that she cannot remember what occurred immediately after the accident. In this circumstance, the lawyer will want to convey the expectation that the client should try to overcome the memory difficulties.

"I understand how hard it is to recall; I've often had that difficulty myself. Often I find, however, that if I concentrate for a while, things start to come back. Why don't you think about it a little more?"

These statements by the lawyer employ two facilitators. First of all the lawyer empathizes; the lawyer articulates that he/she understands the difficulty. But the lawyer does not stop. Rather, the lawyer additionally conveys the expectation that the client direct more effort toward trying to recall what occurred.

Unfortunately, lawyers often do nothing more than empathize with the client's difficulty in remembering. "I understand that it is difficult to remember details of an event that happened so long ago." This kind of statement alone is counterproductive. While the lawyer may be doing a very fine job conveying understanding of the client's dilemma, the lawyer is also conveying the idea that the lawyer no longer expects an answer. Lawyers who want to avoid such a result must go beyond solely conveying empathetic understanding. The lawyer must, as in the first example, add to the understanding a message which conveys the idea "though the task may be difficult, I expect that you will attempt it."

Recognition

Human beings tend to have a need for attention and recognition from people outside their close circle of family and friends. They seem to enjoy feeling important and will seek out the attention and esteem of outsiders. Studies indicate that giving an interviewee "recognition" motivates the interviewee to be more cooperative and open.[14] In situations where the lawyer is not a close friend or relative, the lawyer is in a position to supply "recognition." The task is

14. Gorden, supra note 8, at 86–87.

not difficult. All the lawyer need do is provide the client with direct, sincere praise for his/her cooperation or help. "Your giving me that information is very helpful." "That was very important information you just gave me." "You're really doing a good job of outlining all the consequences of settling."

Altruistic Appeals

There seems to be a human need to identify with some high value or cause that is beyond immediate self-interest. This may be a form of identification with the objectives of some larger group. The group may be real or imaginary, contemporary or not. Altruistic deeds usually increase self-esteem whether or not the person's deeds have been public. This distinguishes altruism from recognition.[15]

Frequently, lawyers employ altruistic appeals when dealing with reluctant witnesses. The following are illustrative:

"As you know, the crime rate in our community is really on the rise. If you can tell me what you know, it will help to make sure we have the right person. I'm sure you want to do your part in helping to make our streets safe.

"If you can tell what you know, then the case will be resolved on the basis of the truth; none of us wants an innocent person to be convicted."

Extrinsic Reward

When individuals realize that certain behavior will be in their self-interest, they are usually motivated to engage in that behavior. This concept is frequently called upon to facilitate communication. The lawyer points out why providing the sought data may be useful in solving the client's problem. Providing the information is shown to be in the client's best interest.

This concept differs from the facilitators previously discussed. The earlier phenomena drew their motivational strength by satisfying the client's psychological needs through the interaction of the interviewing process itself—e. g., empathetic understanding, recognition. The concept of extrinsic reward, on the other hand, draws its motivational force by pointing out how participation in the interview will satisfy needs external to the interview—i. e., through favorable case resolution. It is from this idea of reward outside the interview that the term "extrinsic reward" has been fashioned.

In a legal setting, extrinsic reward is clearly available in the case of clients. Clients seek out lawyers with the expectation that they can provide solutions. So long as the client sees the information requested by the lawyer as relevant to the problem about which advice is sought, the extrinsic reward phenomenon may be operative. Should the client fail to grasp the significance of a particular line of

15. Gorden, supra note 8, at 87–88.

questioning (perceived irrelevancy), the lawyer can utilize the extrinsic reward concept by pointing out how the information sought is relevant. "You want me to call Mr. King as one of your witnesses. Before deciding whether to do that, I want to decide if the jury is likely to disbelieve him because he is a close friend of yours. That is why I am asking you all these questions about how well you know Mr. King."

When the interview involves a non-client, particularly one who is not very interested in the outcome of the case, extrinsic rewards are likely to be absent. A gas station attendant who knows no one involved in a robbery case can gain little or no concrete benefit by talking with the defendant's lawyer about the attendant's observations of the get-away car. However, perhaps the attendant can be motivated through recognition or altruism.

Before concluding this discussion of client motivation, we will provide a summary table of the common inhibitors and facilitators. It will probably be helpful to become fully familiar with the meaning of these terms as they will be referred to frequently throughout the remainder of this book.

INHIBITORS	FACILITATORS
Ego Threat	Empathetic Understanding
Case Threat	Fulfilling Expectations
Role Expectations	Recognition
Etiquette Barrier	Altruistic Appeals
Trauma	Extrinsic Reward
Perceived Irrelevancy	
Greater Need	

Personality Conflicts

In closing this chapter, we wish to mention one further subject. Lawyer-client communications can also be inhibited by a clash of personalities. If the client, for one reason or another, perceives the lawyer as the type of person with whom he/she cannot feel comfortable, or someone who is too aggressive or too passive to effectively handle the case, the client may feel reluctant to participate fully. Similarly, the lawyer may encounter clients who, for one reason or another, seem too aggressive, passive, unscrupulous, or disorganized, and these perceptions may inhibit the lawyer's interaction with the client.

There is no ideal type of lawyer personality—what's pleasing to one client can be abrasive to another. With self-examination and specialized training, lawyers might learn how certain aspects of their personalities come across to most clients. This self-examination and training, therefore, may help some lawyers interact more effectively with their clients. However, no amount of personality restructuring or self-awareness will enable a lawyer to work effectively with all clients.

Although specialized training can probably help some lawyers gain insight into their personalities and those of their clients, this kind of training is usually not available to most law students and lawyers.[16]   Despite this absence of specialized training, we believe lawyers and law students can learn to interact successfully with clients by being trained to relate in an open and supportive manner. In this regard, it is our judgment that if lawyers can learn to utilize the basic facilitators mentioned in this chapter and the basic skills described in subsequent chapters, lawyers will develop the sensitivity and ability to maintain adequate rapport with most clients.

Rather than continuing with any further abstract discussion of motivation and rapport, we will now turn attention to the subject of technique.   As we make this change, our objective is two-fold.   First, we desire to expose you to a range of available techniques.   Second, we desire to develop your understanding of how choices among available techniques can often be predicated upon the concepts of motivation put forth in this chapter.

16.   There are some authors who believe that intensive training in personality analysis should be the cornerstone of any beginning course in legal interviewing and counseling.   See Watson, supra note 7, at 75–93.

Chapter Three

ACTIVE LISTENING

In an interview, the majority of communication from lawyer to client takes the form of questions—Who, What, Where, Why? Our discussion of interviewing and counseling skills, however, begins with an examination of the subject of listening. We begin with this subject in order to stress the importance of being an effective listener. Most lawyers do not do enough listening. They have no time to listen. They are too busy asking too many questions.

It may seem that to listen is a very simple and easily accomplished task. Most people, when told to listen, believe that all one needs to do is to sit back and hear what is said. From the viewpoint of effective interviewing and counseling, this belief is incorrect. First, listening involves much more than sitting back and hearing. Second, listening is not a task easily performed. Rather, it is one which requires enormous concentration and affirmative action.

Before turning to a discussion of listening techniques, we will discuss two points: (1) why effective listening is so important for the accomplishment of the goal of obtaining full client participation, and (2) what it is that lawyers can and should listen for.

In our discussion of factors tending to facilitate communication, we stressed the importance of empathetic understanding. We noted that providing a client with the feeling that he/she has been heard, understood, and yet not judged, often has an enormously facilitating effect. What we wish to stress here is that listening, when properly carried out, is the technique through which empathetic understanding

1. Reprinted by permission of Chicago Tribune—New York News Syndicate.

is most readily communicated to the client. Thus, listening is important not simply to insure that the lawyer hears and understands what has occurred, but also to provide the client with the motivation for full and complete communication.

Given the importance of listening in providing empathetic understanding, what is it that lawyers can and should hear, understand, and accept? Stated simply, what is there to listen for?

When an individual views or participates in an event, the individual typically observes the various details which make up the incident and often simultaneously experiences various feelings about the occurrence. In recalling the event, the individual will, therefore, often describe both the content of what occurred and the feelings associated with the event.[2] Moreover, recalling the event during an interview may trigger still further emotional reactions. "I didn't think about it much then, but now every time I think about it, I get mad." Accordingly, in an interview a lawyer can listen for both *content* and current and past *feelings*.

Clients' feelings may be clearly stated, "I really was disappointed when he didn't pay me," or they may be expressed in a guarded or even garbled form, "When he didn't pay me, I dunno . . . , felt . . . . Oh, well, he didn't pay me back." Regardless of the form of expression, the lawyer who is really listening will hear both the content of what is said—non-payment—and the feelings associated with the occurrence—disappointment.

IDENTIFYING CONTENT AND FEELINGS

At this point, let us examine in more detail what we mean by the terms "content" and "feelings." We will begin with some definitions. Content refers to the time, setting, people, and specific transactions that make up an event. In short, content refers to detailed facts. Feelings refers to the labels a person uses to describe emotional reactions to an event. Words typically used to describe feelings include: sad, angry, anxious, disappointed, frightened, irritated, confused, happy, amused, excited, etc.

Although from a legal point of view the lawyer may be primarily interested in the content of a client's report (time, place, transactions), the lawyer can usually provide full empathetic understanding only if he/she also identifies and responds to the client's feelings. The following examples can be used for practice in identifying both content and feelings.

Client 1:

"My husband and I sat down years ago and wrote a will together, but I guess I never really thought we'd use it. Then

---

2. Indeed, it has been suggested that human beings are incapable of viewing facts without emotion. For a discussion, see P. Rhinelander, Is Man Comprehensible to Man? 48 (1973).

they called to say my husband had had a heart attack at work. He died two days later. When he died, I felt overwhelmed. Lately, I've been worrying about our finances. It's hard to think of money at a time like this, but I feel like I should. I can't sleep at night and I just sit around depressed all day. Other times, when I think about him, I start crying and it seems like it will never stop. On top of all this, the children are saying they are going to contest the will. They've already hired a lawyer. I'm really surprised, I never expected this."

What is the content of the client's situation?

What are the client's past and current feelings?

Client 2:

"Look, believe me, all I did was spank my child. She has always bruised easily, ever since she was a baby. I didn't hit her that hard, really. The next thing I heard was that the Department of Social Services had put my child in a foster home. I was stunned. Those people really scared me. I'm so pissed off. Where do they get off fucking with my life and telling me how to raise my own child? Do you know, they said I abused my child. How can they say that with so little information? And who are they to judge me? I think I spend more time with my kids than anyone else on our block. If I weren't so afraid that they'd take my kids away for good, I'd really let them know what I think about them. Lately I lie awake with splitting headaches worrying about what they're going to do next. How will they decide if they are going to take Amy away from me?"

What is the content of the client's situation?

What are the client's past and current feelings?

Client 3:

"I fell behind two months in my rent because my Welfare checks didn't arrive on time. The manager said I could stay and then pay him next month instead. I felt relieved, but then the guy shows up with an unlawful detainer complaint and says, 'I'm sorry, there's nothing I can do.' I couldn't believe it. What a double-crosser! And how am I supposed to find a place now? Everyone wants a cleaning deposit and first and last month's rent, and I'm completely broke, and he knows it. I'm so angry every time I see him, I just want to punch him out. Much as I'd like to do that, I've restrained myself because I really want to stay, but even if I get the money, I don't know if that bastard will let me stay now that he got this detainer complaint."

What is the content of the client's situation?

What are the client's past and current feelings?

Here is how you might have conceptualized these three cases:

Client 1:

Content: Husband died unexpectedly and wife must assume responsibility for family finances. Children plan to contest the will and have already hired a lawyer.

Feelings: Sad, overwhelmed, depressed, worried, surprised.

Client 2:

Content: Parent is accused of child abuse and child is removed from home, perhaps permanently.

Feelings: Stunned, scared, angry, unjustly accused, anxious, worried.

Client 3:

Content: Impoverished client served with unlawful detainer complaint by manager who promised client could pay rent late.

Feelings: Relieved, angry, betrayed, frustrated.

Having discussed why listening is important and what should be listened for, let us now turn to matters of technique. How does one listen effectively? As a technique, listening can be broken down into two types—passive and active. Though our discussion will involve both types, we will stress "active listening."[3] We do so for two reasons. First, active listening is probably more effective in providing empathetic understanding. Second, the technique, unlike those involved in passive listening, is generally not one used in normal social conversation. As a consequence, it is a technique that will require substantial effort to master.

PASSIVE LISTENING

Silence

Silence is defined here as a brief but definite pause in the conversation. The client makes a statement and then there is a pause, typically two to five seconds, before the client continues speaking. Many lawyers feel uncomfortable allowing a period of silence. They seem to feel that a good interview must have a constant flow of words, and silence is thus a sign of their incompetence in not knowing the right thing to say. To cope with their discomfort, lawyers often ask a series of rapid questions just to keep the client talking. This failure to allow silence can interrupt a client's stream of association and make the client feel cut off or hurried. Effective lawyers will often wait out the pause and allow the client time to reflect be-

3. This term is borrowed from Thomas Gordon. See T. Gordon, Parent Effectiveness Training 49–50 (1970).

fore continuing with the story. Effective lawyers seem to use silence to communicate the message, "I'm listening, go ahead at your own speed."

Non-Committal Acknowledgements

Silence sometimes can have an inhibiting effect on a client. The client may feel anxious, on the spot, and pressured to keep talking if there is no reassurance the client is being heard. To let clients know that the lawyer is listening and taking in what is being said, the lawyer can respond with brief expressions which tend to communicate acknowledgement of the client's content or feelings. These include such brief comments as:

"Oh"

"I see"

"Mm-hmm"

"Interesting"

"Really"

"No fooling"

"You did, eh"

These are considered non-committal responses because they acknowledge that the lawyer is listening without giving any indication about how the lawyer might be evaluating the client's messages.

Open-Ended Questions

Sometimes a long pause can indicate the client has finished with a particular topic. To get the ball rolling again, the lawyer may ask a brief open-ended question—a question which permits the client to continue to respond in a narrative manner. Open-ended questions are discussed in detail in Chapter Four and include such things as:

"What else happened?"

"What other reasons are there?"

"Can you tell me some more about that?" [4]

These techniques—silence, non-committal acknowledgements, and open-ended questions—are basically *passive* listening techniques. They function primarily to give the client space in the interview to freely communicate his or her thoughts and feelings. However, they do *not* tend to communicate that the lawyer truly understands or accepts the client's messages.

---

4. Often, open-ended questions are used interchangeably with directive probes such as "Tell me more about that." This more directive request is general- ly perceived by the client in the same way as an open-ended question. In this book, the two will be treated as synonymous.

ACTIVE LISTENING

Active listening is the process of picking up the client's message and sending it back in a *reflective statement which mirrors what the lawyer has heard.*

Client: "When I asked him for the money, he had the nerve to tell me not to be uptight."

Lawyer: "Rather than telling you about the money, he suggested you were somehow wrong for asking. I imagine that made you angry."

Note the lawyer does not simply repeat or "parrot" what was said. Rather, the lawyer's response is an affirmative effort to convey back the essence of what was heard. It is a response which, by mirroring what was said, affirmatively demonstrates understanding. Further, since the statement only mirrors, it does not in any way "judge" what has been said. In short, it is a completely empathetic response.

The active listening response differs from the passive response in important particulars. By reflecting back what has been heard, the active response explicitly communicates that what the client said was actually heard and understood. Passive responses, such as "Mm-hmm" or "Tell me some more about that," can only imply the lawyer has heard and understood. In contrast, a reflective statement—one which mirrors back the essence of what has been said—constitutes an explicit form of expression, demonstrating lawyer comprehension.

Moreover, insofar as the empathetic ideal of "non-judgmental acceptance" is concerned, active responses are probably more effective than passive ones. Affirmatively demonstrating understanding through the reflective statement probably carries with it a greater implication of non-judgmental acceptance than do passive remarks such as, "Oh, I see," "Tell me more," or "Mm-hmm."

The active listening response can be used to mirror both content and feelings. We will continue our exploration of active listening in a discussion confined primarily to its use in reflecting feelings. We do so for two reasons.

1. Lawyers tend to pay far too little attention to the feelings of their clients. Typically, lawyers somehow see themselves solely as "gatherers of facts." At either a conscious or intuitive level, feelings are perceived as either irrelevant or objects to be removed from the discussion. The elimination is necessary so that a "rational" decision can be made. We believe that the foregoing line of thought must be rejected on two grounds. First, empathy, the real mortar of any relationship, requires hearing, understanding, and acceptance of feelings which are part and parcel of any situation. Stated more pragmatically, we believe one cannot use the strongest of all facilitators—empathetic understanding—without the ability to accept and respond to

feelings. Secondly, the problems people bring to lawyers do not come in nice, neat, rational packages devoid of any emotional content. Problems evoke feelings and any solutions which the lawyer fashions must effectively deal with feelings.

2. The second reason our discussion of active listening will focus primarily on reflecting feelings is that feelings are probably not as easily comprehended as the factual content which they accompany. Therefore, more effort must be devoted to learning to reflect feelings.

Let us turn now to two common problems lawyers can expect to encounter in endeavoring to reflect feelings: (1) Many people do not actually express their feelings. They leave them completely unstated ("How long will the appeal take?") or reveal them only in the form of non-verbal cues—tears, smiles, etc. (2) Often, to the extent feelings are expressed, they are not clearly articulated. Rather, the feelings are stated in very vague terms, "I felt weird." "I felt uptight."

Vaguely Expressed Feelings

When a client expresses feelings in a vague or obscure manner, the lawyer can be most empathetic by reflecting the feelings in a precise way. Specific labeling of the feelings helps the client better understand his/her own emotional reactions. Here are some examples of client statements which are vague, abstract, or general, and responses by a lawyer which attempt to identify and label the specific feelings:

Client: "I felt *bummed out* when I found out she was having an affair with him. I thought our marriage meant something. *I guess I was wrong.*"

Lawyer: "You felt *hurt* and *disappointed* when she told you about the affair."

Client: "*I've felt out of it* ever since I moved to Los Angeles. *I don't have friends* here or even neighbors to talk to."

Lawyer: "*You've felt lonely* and *isolated* since you came to Los Angeles."

Client: "I don't think I want to testify in court. It sounds like a *bad experience*—all those questions, people looking at me—I would probably be *so uptight, I'd say the wrong thing.*"

Lawyer: "*You feel anxious* about getting up on the stand and perhaps *embarrassing* yourself."

Note how, in each case, the lawyer listens to what the client has to say and then attempts to restate in more specific terms what the client is feeling. Take the following cases—what specific feeling might be reflected back to the client:

Client: "When I told him I was going to a lawyer for a divorce, he just looked at me. He looked for a long time and then he left. It was strange."

> Client: "After I was handcuffed, they put me in the back of the police car. They just stood around, laughed, and had a cigarette. I kept thinking, what's going to happen, you know, what are they going to do with me?"

Unstated Feelings

No lawyer's task is more difficult to learn than that of recognizing and reflecting unstated feelings. This is so not because the technique is difficult, but because the lawyer is often not aware that feelings are present or being expressed. Frequently, clients will discuss situations, which, for most people, would be emotionally charged, without ever expressing any emotions. Consider this example. A woman charged with child abuse is recounting to her lawyer her version of how the child came to the attention of the authorities. She has previously explained that the child was injured in a fall.

> Client: I decided to take her (the child) to the County hospital. I had no car, but finally I got in touch with my aunt. She came over about an hour later. The baby kept crying. It took about an hour to get to the hospital.

> Lawyer: Then what happened?

> Client: I told them what happened. They said we would have to wait. It took almost two hours for me to see a doctor. I kept saying my baby was hurt bad, but the people at the desk kept saying it wasn't an emergency. Finally, a nurse came and took the baby. She told me I would have to wait. I couldn't go with the baby.

Without verbalizing any emotional reaction, the client has just described a situation which, for most people, would be extremely stressful. At this juncture, the lawyer has a choice. The lawyer can proceed directly to gather more data. Or, the lawyer may attempt to gather data indirectly by increasing rapport—i. e., providing an empathetic response before asking for more content. If the lawyer chooses the former, the next lawyer response will either be a question —e. g., "What happened next?"—or a reflection of content—e. g., "So they took the baby and left you waiting." If the lawyer chooses the latter, the next lawyer response will be an attempt to identify and reflect feelings—e. g., "I imagine you were very angry and quite worried about your baby."

Once the lawyer recognizes that the client was probably in an emotion-producing situation, the task of recognizing and reflecting feelings can be undertaken. The task involves two steps: First, attempting to identify the feelings, and second, setting forth these feelings in a reflective response—i. e., "I imagine you felt . . .."

Identifying unexpressed feelings can sometimes be accomplished by attempting to place oneself "in the client's shoes." Even if the lawyer has never experienced the client's precise situation, the lawyer can probably hazard an educated guess about how the client felt. Through the lawyer's vicarious experiences (films, books, stories of friends) and analogous experiences (having to wait in an emergency situation of another type), the lawyer should have a reasonably good idea of how the client was reacting. Thus, if the lawyer thinks about "how the client might have been feeling," the lawyer can form a tentative hypothesis about what emotional reaction was present. With the hypothesis formed, it can be put forth in an active listening response.

Consider the following statements and ask yourself what active listening type response the lawyer could use to respond to the client's feelings.

> Client: "When he failed to pay, I sent him two letters. I got no response. I called three times. He was never in. The secretary said he would return the calls; he never did."

> Client: "The bank has been dealing with this corporation for over 40 years. We've always provided all their construction financing. This loan was on the same terms as the previous four loans. Now they say they didn't understand what they were signing."

> Client: "I'd known the old man for 20 years. He was crying. He kept saying, 'I hate to think of dying.' He said, 'I wish people didn't need wills.' Then he signed it."

In each of these cases, the client may have had a number of feelings. The lawyer cannot know which, if any, were the specific feelings. However, by placing himself/herself in the client's shoes, the lawyer can attempt a reflective response. For example, in the second situation, the lawyer might have said, "You sound pretty aggravated." If the lawyer is correct, the client will usually validate the accuracy of the lawyer's statement—"Yeah, I really am aggravated; given how we have helped these people for all this time, I can't believe they are doing this." If the lawyer is inaccurate, the client will usually clarify the inaccuracy—"Well, I'm not aggravated yet, but I certainly am puzzled. What do you think they're up to?" Thus, even if the lawyer's statement is somewhat inaccurate, it can still facilitate communication. It indicates that the lawyer is actively trying to listen and understand and also tends to elicit further clarifying information.

Non-Verbal Expressions of Feelings

There is a second way in which a lawyer may be able to identify a client's unstated feelings. Frequently, the lawyer can gain an impression of a client's feelings by carefully listening to and observing the client's non-verbal cues. These cues are generally of two types—

auditory and visual.[5] Auditory cues include such things as intonation, pitch, rate of speech, and pauses in the conversation. Visual cues include posture, gestures, facial expressions, and body movements such as fidgeting fingers and constantly shifting positions. Some non-verbal cues are quite easily identified: tears typically indicate sadness; wringing hands usually indicate worry; a smile usually indicates pleasure. However, at times non-verbal cues can be quite difficult to detect. The client may be trying very hard to "maintain composure" and therefore inhibit non-verbal expressions. However, the observant lawyer may nonetheless be able to detect some of the client's feelings since the client usually cannot repress all non-verbal expression. Thus, a client may be able to avoid any facial expression but nonetheless be unable to hide body movements, such as drumming fingers or rapid changes in position which belie feelings of anxiety. Additionally, the lawyer may be able to detect inconsistencies between what the client says he/she feels and what the client's body movements suggest the client is feeling. For example, a client may state, "No, it doesn't make me mad" while tightly clenching his/her fists. Or the client may state, "It's perfectly all right with me," in a disgusted tone of voice.

Lawyers may feel somewhat hesitant to identify and respond to feelings evidenced by non-verbal cues. They fear they may make an inaccurate interpretation. There are wide cultural variations in the way people express emotion, and thus it is sometimes difficult to know the precise meaning of a particular gesture or facial expression. Nonetheless, our experience indicates that most lawyers can become fairly accurate in their general observations of non-verbal behavior. For example, by observing changes in the client's behavior, lawyers are often able to realize that a particular subject is in some way troublesome for the client, even though the lawyer may not know exactly why the subject is bothersome. By observing the client, the lawyer can develop a baseline picture of the client's non-verbal behavior. Changes from the baseline behavior can then be noted as they occur during various points in the interview. For example, the lawyer may observe that the client seemed fully involved in the interview, and then when a certain topic was broached, the client no longer maintained eye contact and gave only very brief responses. Or, in recounting an event, the client's speech may suddenly become more rapid and high-pitched as the conversation turns to a particular topic. If the lawyer is observing the client carefully, the lawyer may be able to identify the client's feelings.

It is extremely difficult to illustrate non-verbal behavior through the case examples in this book. We therefore leave the matter of

---

5. For a more detailed discussion of the interpretation of nonverbal behavior, see Ekman & Friesen, *Nonverbal* *Leakage and Clues to Deception*, 32 Psychiatry 88 (1969).

learning to identify and interpret specific non-verbal cues to class-room and field experiences.

Once the lawyer has a fairly good idea of what emotion the client is expressing by the client's non-verbal behavior, the lawyer can then provide a reflective response. As with any reflective response to unstated feelings the lawyer's statement, even if inaccurate, may still serve to facilitate and clarify communication.

Clearly Articulated Feelings

Although clients will often either fail to express their feelings or state them only vaguely, this will not always be the case. Some clients will be very precise in articulating their feelings. As noted earlier, the objective of active listening is to mirror the essence of what the respondent has said. If the respondent has clearly stated his/her feelings, it will be difficult to mirror the essence without, in some measure, "parroting"—i. e., merely repeating. "Parroting," unfortunately, frequently produces a negative reaction. The client's internal reaction is often something like, "Yes, that's what I said, you dummy; I was disappointed." The client's verbal reply, however, is often more polite, "Yes, I really was." But in terms of the self-generating force usually associated with empathetic understanding, parroting responses are usually not too successful. The client usually will do little more than confirm that he/she was heard correctly.

Client:　I was really disappointed when he didn't pay.

Lawyer: It really disappointed you.

Client:　Right.

When feelings are precisely stated, a positive empathetic response may still be possible. Sometimes a client will describe situations which are so common, the client will readily believe the lawyer has been in the same or a similar situation. When the incident being described is of this type, the lawyer can often empathize by directly expressing that the lawyer can understand the client's reaction.

Client:　I was so angry and frustrated when he again refused to go through with the deal.

Lawyer: I can understand how angry and frustrated you'd feel after he did it again.

This kind of response avoids the irritating aspect of being "parroted" and is fully empathetic at the same time.

However, clients will sometimes describe situations which they believe are quite foreign to the lawyer. In these circumstances, if the lawyer asserts understanding of the client's feelings, the client will often view the lawyer as insincere or patronizing. Thus, a poor-ly-educated, unemployed client who states, "I really feel humiliated when I have to talk with the welfare worker about food stamps" will not be likely to believe the lawyer's response, "I can understand how humiliating that can feel."

We would suggest that when a client is clearly articulating feelings about a situation that is likely to be perceived as quite foreign to the lawyer, a reflective response is likely to be taken as insincere parroting. In such a situation, we suggest a passive listening response may be more facilitative.

Non-Empathetic Responses

Often, when a lawyer identifies a client's feelings, the lawyer fails to reflect the understanding non-judgmentally. Consider the following client statement and lawyer responses.

Client:　When I came home, I discovered she had moved out. She took everything. All the furniture was gone; the house was empty. I was pissed.

Lawyer:

No. 1:　I don't blame you.

No. 2:　But I guess after a while you calmed down.

No. 3:　I guess you felt you deserved better.

Lawyer No. 1 has judged the appropriateness of the reaction. Lawyer No. 2 has treated the feeling as irrelevant and shifted the discussion to another time frame. Lawyer No. 3 has played amateur psychologist. He has attempted to analyze the reason for the reaction. None has simply mirrored back what was said—"You were really furious." Consider this further example.

Witness:　Every time I think about that woman rushing over to her child, my eyes get misty.

Lawyer:

No. 4:　I'm sure the feeling will pass with time. Most people who see an accident like this feel that way at first.

No. 5:　That's probably because you think it could have been you and your daughter.

No. 6:　You certainly have a right to feel that way; it was a shocking thing.

Again, the lawyers do not merely reflect back the essence of what was said—"It makes you sad to think about it." Rather, there was advice (Lawyer No. 4), analysis (Lawyer No. 5), and judgment (Lawyer No. 6).

To reflect feelings in a non-judgmental manner requires practice accompanied by constructive feedback. All we can do here is to point up the fact that lawyers often substitute their own advice, analysis, or judgment in place of a simple reflective statement. Consider the following examples and analyze the lawyers' responses.

Client: We had only been married three years. He was only 32 and now he is gone. I can't believe it; he had so much to give, I feel like I'm not in this world.

Lawyer:

No. 1: Don't worry; most people feel that way at first. The feeling will pass with time.

No. 2: It's probably because his death was so unexpected; you had no time to prepare.

No. 3: It's perfectly proper for you to feel that way. Under the circumstances, no one could expect anything else.

DIFFICULTIES IN MASTERING ACTIVE LISTENING

Many lawyers and law students find it difficult to become proficient in the use of active listening. Because they experience discomfort when beginning to use these techniques, they abandon their efforts to perfect their listening skills.

However, most lawyers are able to persevere and master active listening when they realize that their feelings of discomfort are common to many beginners. Consider, therefore, the following statements:

"Feelings are for 'shrinks,' not lawyers."

"I'm afraid we'll get so involved in feelings, we won't properly deal with the legal issues."

"Cases are decided on the basis of facts. Lawyers deal in facts; psychiatrists, psychologists, and social workers deal with feelings."

Expressions such as these typically reflect the assumption that feelings are irrelevant, that feelings have no legitimate place in the rational process of legal analysis. Though the idea that lawyers deal in facts and not feelings may be appealing to some, experience reveals the concept is untenable. How people feel strongly influences the nature and amount of information they provide and the decisions they make.

The belief that feelings are by and large irrelevant to the legal interview may come from a number of sources. For some, the word "feelings" connotes irrationality and triggers the idea that feelings must be avoided so that lawyers can function as they should, i. e., in a rational and objective manner. Another source of the idea that feelings are largely irrelevant may be lack of experience; the individual may have had little opportunity to observe the role which feelings actually play during the course of an interview. Finally, there may be a bit of rationalization at work. Thinking about feelings may generate discomfort. The easiest way to avoid the discomfort is to conclude that feelings are irrelevant. If the rationalization is successful, the discomfort can be put to rest.

For those who are skeptical about the necessity for lawyers to recognize feelings, development of active listening skills will be difficult. These people will have to do more than struggle with the pains of learning a new skill. They will have to undergo the learning process while plagued by doubt about the appropriateness of what they are doing. Experience demonstrates, however, that those who are willing to proceed despite their skepticism often find that active listening substantially enhances their effectiveness as a lawyer.

"I feel empathetic, but I just can't find the right words."

"Reflecting feelings makes me feel awkward."

"It feels so mechanical, reflecting back what they feel."

"When I listen to myself, it sounds so hollow and forced. I'm sure the client will fee that way, too."

Even if one accepts the idea that empathetic listening will help facilitate interviewing and counseling, active listening skills are not easily mastered. Acquiring a new skill is very difficult and feelings such as those expressed above are to be expected. Initially, active listening techniques will seem very awkward and forced. Uncertainty about when and how to engage in the active listening process will result in statements which suggest, by their tone, that perhaps the lawyer does not really understand. However, usually it is only uncertainty which gives the reflective statement a somewhat hollow tone. With practice, the uncertainty generally disappears and the reflective statements flow smoothly and naturally. The individual is no longer "consciously employing a technique" and can now comfortably reflect the feelings which are expressed.

For those who find reflecting feeling quite uncomfortable, we suggest starting the learning process by reflecting only the content of the client's statements. Once one feels comfortable making reflective statements about content, it is usually easier to add in reflections of feelings.

*"There is no way that I can empathize with that * & % #."*

"Look, I just feel phony. There is no way I could say, 'So you felt like you just couldn't stop yourself.' I can't say that; people can control themselves."

"Even if I try to be empathetic, I'm sure my voice will give away the fact that I don't really mean it."

"Acknowledging those feelings makes me feel like I'm condoning that behavior."

"The guy seems so slick that it makes me feel if I respond to his feelings, he'll think I'm weak or just plain foolish."

"She's so aggressive, I feel that if I respond to her feelings, she'll see me as saying it's OK to act out of spite."

It is not uncommon to encounter individuals who tax one's willingness to be understanding and non-judgmental. Many of us find that we are reluctant to help people who have engaged in certain behaviors or who have certain kinds of personalities. For example, some people find that they have little desire to help welfare recipients, bankrupts, tax evaders, child molesters, con artists, rapists, etc. Others find they are reluctant to assist people who have personalities which are extremely passive, dependent, aggressive, manipulative, etc.

When encountering a person of a type that one is reluctant to help, expressions such as "There is no way I can empathize with this person" quickly surface. In some instances, such statements express the thought that the person is so offensive to the interviewer that the interviewer cannot empathize with any feelings the person may have. In other instances, the expression means only that the interviewer cannot empathize with particular feelings. For example, the lawyer cannot empathize with the passions that consumed the child molester but can understand his/her fear of imprisonment.

There is no set formula to be followed when confronted with a situation where empathetic response seems improper, impossible, or at best extremely limited. Lawyers would probably disagree about what course of action would be appropriate. Some would suggest that referral to another lawyer is the only proper solution. Some would suggest that if some empathy is possible, the lawyer may appropriately continue on the case. Other lawyers believe that continued representation is always quite proper. There is a belief that lawyers can adequately employ active listening techniques even though they cannot truly empathize. The belief is that, although true empathy is lacking, lawyers can proceed professionally by reflecting feelings in a way that creates the impression of non-judgmental understanding. For lawyers with these beliefs, such action is the only approriate response of a professional whose job is to represent people in need.

"Most of the time when I use 'active listening,' the client gets too emotional."

"I really feel uncomfortable when the client starts crying."

"I 'active-listened' to his anger and boy, did he get mad; I didn't know what to do."

"I think it might be a good idea, but I'm afraid the client will get so upset he'll fall apart. What'll I do then?"

Responding to feelings often results in an outpouring of even more intense emotions. When beginning interviewers experience this result, they typically feel uncomfortable and tend to back away from the use of active listening skills. There is a concern that the outpouring won't stop; that inadvertently the person has been made to feel worse; or that it is wrong to elicit all this emotion since there is little that can be done to resolve the feelings.

Concerns about an excessive amount of emotion can usually be overcome if beginning interviewers recognize two propositions. First, although the client may express solely negative feelings, the client's overall reaction to the interview may be quite positive. The client has had the opportunity to get "feelings off his/her chest," along with the satisfaction of being heard and understood. Usually this experience will result in a feeling that the interview, as a whole, was quite beneficial.

Second, beginners must recognize that often the best way to alleviate the client's distress is to let the outpouring of emotion continue. The lawyer's continued empathy will usually cause the emotional tide to recede. If lawyers can struggle through their initial discomfort, a task we recognize as difficult, they will generally find that the client regains composure. Thus, if lawyers can, on a couple of occasions, continue to be empathetic despite their discomfort, they will usually experience the success that comes from allowing the client the opportunity to ride out the emotion. With this success, the lawyer will likely experience less anxiety about eliciting and empathizing with intense emotions the next time they arise.

"Active listening is being manipulative."

"Maybe she's not stating her feelings because she doesn't want to talk about her feelings. I don't think I should do things to try to make her talk about feelings."

"I don't think lawyers should manipulate people to expose their feelings—it's an invasion of their privacy."

"Look, I can go through the right motions to make the person believe I feel understanding and supportive, but I'm really just doing it to get the information."

The employment of active listening skills is indeed the use of a technique to gain information. Hopefully, the information is being obtained in order to assist the client in finding an adequate solution to the problem at hand. And, hopefully, this assistance is provided because the lawyer genuinely desires to exercise professional responsibility in a competent manner. Active listening should not be used to probe into clients' feelings for voyeuristic purposes. However, if a lawyer fails to develop full information because of a failure to deal with feelings that were present in the interview, the lawyer usually is not exercising professional responsibility. Since people generally respond fully only in the presence of someone who exhibits non-judgmental understanding, lawyers will generally be unable to obtain full client participation and, hence, satisfaction without some use of this technique.

For those who fear they will be invading clients' rights to keep information to themselves, we can only say, "Rest assured, if the client doesn't want you to know something, the client simply won't tell you."

HOW MUCH ACTIVE LISTENING?

The purpose of the active listening response is to provide non-judgmental understanding and thereby stimulate full client participation. The technique is to be used to help the client feel free to discuss and reflect upon his/her problem in a comfortable and open manner. In short, the technique is to be used to develop rapport.

A client's feelings will typically emerge throughout the interview. When the client is reporting the past transaction from which the problem emanates and when the client is identifying and discussing the potential consequences of proposed solutions, the client's emotional reactions will be continually in evidence. Given this kind of continual emotional presence, how often should the lawyer reflect feelings? Should feelings be reflected every time they seem to emerge? There is no single, right, or easy answer to these questions.

The amount of non-judgmental understanding that will be helpful in developing rapport will vary from client to client and case to case. A client who feels comfortable talking openly about one case may feel much more inhibited in talking about another. For example, a client who feels quite relaxed talking about an action to recover money due on a promissory note may feel quite reticent to discuss matters relating to an impending divorce. Furthermore, while some aspects of a case can be confronted quite readily, other aspects of the case may pose a much greater problem. For example, a client may feel quite comfortable talking about how an accident occurred but quite uncomfortable discussing the nature and the extent of the injuries sustained. The latter may seem to the client as matters appropriately discussed only with a doctor.

To use active listening effectively, the lawyer must employ his/her judgment in gauging the amount of client rapport that needs to be developed. Is the client talking fully, freely, and openly? Are there some matters which obviously bear discussion and yet are being omitted from the dialogue? Is an incident which certainly must have stirred some feelings being reported without any obvious emotional reaction? Even those people who perceive themselves as totally rational and objective experience feelings. They experience feelings even though they may not often discuss them or show them. On occasion, even these "totally rational" people welcome the opportunity to share their feelings with someone who can respond with non-judgmental understanding.

Good judgment must ultimately be relied upon in deciding how frequently it will be helpful to reflect a client's feelings. Hopefully, constructive feedback about performance as an interviewer and counselor, both in simulated classroom exercises and in actual interactions with clients, will prove to be an aid in developing judgment about when and how often to reflect a client's stated and unstated feelings.

We will now conclude the discussion of listening techniques and turn to the more familiar technique of questioning.

Chapter Four

QUESTIONING

To help clients find satisfactory solutions to their problems, lawyers will typically need to gather information about at least three matters: (1) the nature of the client's problem, (2) the facts which comprise the past transactions from which the problem arises, and (3) the consequences which may flow from adopting proposed solutions. To gather full and accurate information, the lawyer will use a variety of questions as well as active and passive listening techniques. In this chapter, we will describe the four major forms of questions lawyers typically use and the advantages and disadvantages of each form. In addition, we will briefly explore the subject of questioning as it relates to a client's ability to accurately perceive, recall, and report what has been observed and experienced.

FORMS OF QUESTIONS

Open-Ended Questions

In general, questions can be classified in terms of the breadth of information they seek to elicit. At one end of the spectrum are those questions which allow the client to select either: (a) the subject matter for discussion or (b) at least that information related to the general subject which *the client believes is pertinent and relevant.* These questions are called open-ended. The following are examples of open-ended questions which allow the client to select the subject matter:

"Could you tell me a little about what brought you here today? [1]

"Is there anything else that you believe is pertinent to this case?"

The following are examples of the kind of open-ended questions in which the lawyer selects the basic subject, but the client determines what information is relevant and pertinent:

"What happened after the police entered the room?"

"Why do you think Ms. Jones is a good mother?"

Note the range of freedom for response that is left to the client. In each of these questions, the client can select whatever data appear to be pertinent. Thus, in the question relating to the police, the cli-

---

1. Again, recall that in this book directive probes or statements such as "Tell me more . . . ." will be treated as synonymous with open-ended questions.

38

ent is free to talk about: (1) a whole range of *subjects*— herself/himself, the police, third persons; (2) a whole range of *activities*—talking, doing, feeling, as well as (3) a whole range of *places* or *objects*—specific rooms, specific physical items. The only restriction the lawyer imposes on the subject matter concerns that of time, "after the police entered the room."

Leading Questions

At the opposite end of the spectrum is the leading question. The structure of this type of question provides all the data which *the lawyer believes is pertinent and relevant*. Indeed, the question makes a statement and, in addition, *suggests* that the client ought to affirm the validity of the statement. Thus, this type of question does more than set forth the relevant data and ask for affirmation. It also suggests what the answer should be. Here are some examples:

"You heard the officer yell 'stop,' did you not?"

"You had at least four drinks before getting behind the wheel, isn't that correct?"

"This is not your first arrest for drug abuse, isn't that correct?"

"You're related to the defendant, are you not?"

These questions are, in reality, nothing more than statements which the client is asked to affirm through an answer which has been determined by the lawyer.[2]

Between the totally open-ended question at one end of the spectrum, and the leading question at the other end, there may be an infinite variety of forms of questions. However, at least two other major types of questions can be distinguished in terms of the scope of information they seek to elicit.

Yes/No Questions

Yes/no questions are constructed in such a way that the client can respond with a simple, dichotomous "yes" or "no."

"Did you know before entering the party that the occupants were selling drugs?"

"Did the police have a warrant when they entered the premises?"

"Have you ever seen that man before today?"

"Did you arrive before 9:00?"

"Did Mrs. Johnson drive you to the hospital?"

2. For a more detailed discussion of various forms of leading questions, see R. L. Gorden, Interviewing Strategy, Techniques and Tactics 212–214 (1969) [hereinafter Gorden]; 3 Wigmore, Evidence 154–165 (Chadbourn Rev. 1970).

Yes/no questions are similar to leading questions in that they severely restrict the range of response. However, they do not suggest the answer in the way a leading question tends to do. Note the difference in these two examples:

"Did you know before entering the party that the occupants were selling drugs?"

"You knew even before entering the party that the occupants had been selling drugs there, did you not?"

Narrow Questions

Narrow questions not only select the general subject matter, but in addition choose which aspect of the subject matter should be discussed. "When the officer entered, where were you standing?" This question does more than limit the subject matter to the time of the officer's entry. It restricts the response to the activity of the client —and indeed to a particular kind of activity—standing.

In restricting the client to discussing that aspect of the general subject which the lawyer has selected, the lawyer has largely decided what information is relevant. The client is asked to put aside whatever notions of importance he/she may have, and adopt the lawyer's priorities.

The following are illustrative of narrow questions:

"How was the officer dressed?"

"What color was the car?"

"How long did it take you to travel from your home to the park?"

"How old is your daughter?"

"Where did the accident occur?"

ADVANTAGES AND DISADVANTAGES OF VARIOUS FORMS OF QUESTIONS

A question's structural form often affects both the willingness of a client to provide information as well as the breadth of the information provided. At varying times during an interview, the lawyer will have different goals or different priorities insofar as developing motivation and information are concerned. In selecting the form of question to be employed, the lawyer must be sensitive to both (a) the breadth of information sought and (b) the extent to which the lawyer must increase the motivation to communicate.

Open-Ended Questions

There are a number of advantages associated with the use of open-ended questions. We will first consider the goal of gathering relevant data. In terms of providing a full picture of what the client has observed, open-ended questions often allow the client to report information that would be lost if the client were forced to recount his/her story solely through responses to narrow questions. Open-ended questions allow clients to report their observations without a great deal of interruption for specific detail. Because clients are permitted to report events in their own terms, clients are given the freedom to recall events without having their normal train of thought interrupted. As a consequence, clients usually can recall matters which would be forgotten if clients were persistently interrupted with questions designed to get at details the lawyer considers important.

Open-ended questions also can help increase clients' willingness to give relevant information. Giving clients the opportunity to tell their stories in their own words permits clients the freedom to select the data which is important to them. Allowing this freedom tends to communicate that the lawyer is interested in the client and that what the client has to say is important. Thus, by asking open-ended questions, the lawyer indirectly provides "recognition" and "empathetic understanding."

This climate of openness and empathetic understanding can also provide an opportunity for the client to get troubling information "off his chest." In this vein, open-ended questions have the advantage of facilitating communication by allowing clients to talk about topics which seem of greatest importance to them. Thus, to the extent clients are not otherwise inhibited, open-ended questions are ones which are most likely to overcome the "greater need" inhibitor.

Open-ended questions can also be helpful in assisting the client to overcome the inhibitors of ego threat, case threat, etiquette barrier, trauma, etc. Often the general subject under discussion will include a specific topic which the client feels reluctant to discuss. When the lawyer senses that this kind of situation exists, the lawyer can begin the discussion with open-ended questions that focus only indirectly on the specific facts that are needed, e. g., "Tell me a little more about what happened." By proceeding in this fashion, the lawyer initially leaves the client free to avoid discussing those aspects of the general subject which the client finds threatening. The client can begin by relating the information he/she feels most secure in providing. Hopefully, as the discussion proceeds, rapport will increase and the client will feel free to ease into the sensitive topic.

If in approaching a sensitive topic, the lawyer immediately focuses on the subject by employing narrow questions, the client may quickly become defensive and supply only minimal, or even false, information. Once inaccurate data has been supplied, obtaining valid information becomes an even more imposing task. The client must now overcome the additional threat involved in admitting initial inaccuracies or falsehoods.

There are, however, disadvantages associated with the use of open-ended questions. These relate both to the relevancy of the information received and the development of client rapport and motivation. While open-ended questions can be useful in drawing out relevant information, they can have a detrimental effect if the client is extremely verbose and has a poor sense of relevancy. The loose structure of the open-ended question allows the talkative client to ramble on and on about topics that are at best only tangentially related to the case.

Additionally, while open-ended questions promote the disclosure of relevant data by perhaps leaving paths of association intact, they often do not elicit sufficient detail. In responding to open-ended questions, people often tend to provide an overview of the transaction but do not provide the minute features necessary for a complete description. Thus, someone describing the activities of an infirm testator signing a will may note that the testator's hand was guided, but is not likely to go into great detail concerning the placement, pressure, pauses, etc., of the guiding hand.

By their nature, open-ended questions leave the client free to select any aspect of the situation he/she chooses to describe. As a consequence, this type of structural form may provide very little memory stimulation—the client must rely solely on his/her own ability to recall the specific details. By contrast, narrow questions tend to provide memory stimulation. By identifying specific actors, actions, or events, narrow questions can cause the client to think back about what has occurred with a specific focus. By narrowing the area for consideration and introducing a specific topic, narrow questions often bring to the surface details omitted from a general narrative. Most people have had the experience of making a response similar to the following: "Now that you ask about other people being present, I do remember someone else. Funny, if you hadn't asked, I would have forgotten about her."

There is an additional reason why open-ended questions often do not elicit detail. In choosing what details will be reported to a lawyer, clients generally report one or both of the following sets of facts: (1) the facts which, in terms of the client's interests, seem important; (2) the facts, which from the layman's notion of what the law requires, seem legally salient. Using these criteria, the client will often not provide all the legally relevant data. Without knowledge of the applicable legal principles, the client cannot understand which aspects of a situation are legally significant. Therefore, when left, through the medium of an open-ended question, to narrate all that has occurred, the client will often omit legally significant detail.

From the motivational perspective, open-ended questions can also be quite discomforting where there is a general reluctance to communicate. If the client has a general reluctance to talk, the lawyer's request that the client be the primary speaker will add to the client's feelings of uneasiness. Thus, the client who enters the lawyer's office unsure of whether or not to tell the lawyer what has transpired is quite likely to feel inhibited by open-ended questions such as, "What happened after that?"

Narrow Questions [3]

The advantages of narrow questions also operate to develop both motivation and information. We will first discuss the use of narrow questions to develop client motivation. Where a client, for whatever reason, feels uncomfortable, the client is likely to provide less than complete information in response to open-ended questions. The client lacks the confidence to tell all that is known, particularly if the subject is experienced as a sensitive one.

The lawyer who senses that the client is avoiding a sensitive topic can use narrow questions in an attempt to overcome the problem. By using narrow questions to avoid the sensitive topic, the lawyer provides the client with a comforting success experience. The client is able to respond fully to non-threatening questions. As a consequence, the client's overall comfort and motivation tends to increase. When the client's comfort has been increased, the lawyer can ease into the sensitive areas with open-ended questions.

Perhaps an illustration of how narrow questions might be used in these situations will be helpful. Mr. Smith has bequeathed all of his property to the university, leaving nothing to Mrs. Smith, his spouse of thirty years. Execution of the will was witnessed by three people, including Mr. and Mrs. Smith's daughter, Darlene. One of the witnesses has predeceased the testator. Mrs. Smith has employed counsel and filed a will contest. Counsel has interviewed the surviving witness other than the daughter. This witness told Mrs. Smith's lawyer that when the will was executed, the testator appeared to be making some damning statements about Mrs. Smith. The witness, however, could not hear precisely what was said in this regard. Mr. Smith and his daughter were talking by themselves in a corner of the room before the will was actually signed. The witness did, however, hear the testator say many loving things about Darlene, to whom the testator had already given a great deal of property.

The lawyer is now about to interview the daughter. He believes that perhaps the testator, at the time of the execution of the will, was operating under an insane delusion with respect to the conduct of Mrs. Smith. Mrs. Smith has told the lawyer that she and her daughter are not particularly close. The lawyer senses that the daughter may be reluctant to get into the details of what her father (the testator) said about her mother at the time the will was executed. The interview is opened with an exchange of pleasantries and some generalized discussion about the testator. When the interview seems to

---

3. The discussion here includes Yes/No questions.

flow into a discussion of the execution of the will, the lawyer senses he does not yet have maximum rapport with the daughter. Therefore, instead of using an open-ended question, "What happened before the will was executed?", the lawyer proceeds with a series of narrow questions. "How many people were in the room when the will was signed?", "Did your father state the document was his last will and testament?", "Which witness signed first?"

By proceeding in this fashion, the lawyer treats the pertinent subject (the execution of the will) when it arises, but avoids the more sensitive aspects of the subject by deferring them until, hopefully, more rapport can be developed.

We have now illustrated how narrow questions might be used to avoid a sensitive topic while at the same time developing rapport. How might this technique be used in the following situations:

(1) In an initial client interview with a client who responds to an open-ended question, "Tell me how I might help you?" only with the response, "It's about my husband. I'm not sure how much to tell you."

(2) In an interview with a witness to a robbery who responds to the question of, "Why don't you tell me what you saw?" with the answer, "Not much."

Insofar as gaining information is concerned, narrow questions have the advantage of eliciting detail. As noted above, open-ended questions ask the client to survey a general topic and choose those aspects which are important to the client. Open-ended questions rely almost exclusively on the client's unaided ability to recall. Narrow questions, however, cause the client to search his memory with very specific topics in mind. The topics are those which have been selected by the lawyer as relevant. The process of focusing on specific topics rather than attempting to recall either the entire event or large portions thereof, can aid the client in recalling specific detail. Since the client is focused on a narrow topic, the client can concentrate on the details.

The disadvantages of narrow questions, to some substantial measure, may seem obvious. In large part, they can be gleaned by looking at the advantages of open-ended questions, and then noting how those advantages will be foregone by the use of narrow questions. However, *far too many lawyer interviews consist almost exclusively of narrow questions.* As a consequence, much information that could be developed is lost. Therefore, we wish to stress the disadvantages of narrow questions. We do so not with the idea of suggesting that their use is in any sense inappropriate. Obviously, a complete interview will contain both open-ended and narrow questions. Rather, we wish to stress the disadvantages of narrow questions with the hope that by doing so, we can develop a sense of the importance that narrow questions be used judiciously.

Let us begin our discussion by pointing out two ways in which narrow questions can inhibit the development of rapport. Clients who are required to explain their situations almost exclusively through responses to a lengthy set of narrow questions, may feel they never had a chance to fully explain what happened. Denied the opportunity to relate the story in their own terms, clients may feel they were never really heard and understood.

A second obvious misuse of narrow questions involves detailed probing before the client is "ready." People will be willing to provide details, particularly about sensitive subjects, only if they feel comfortable in doing so. Therefore, probing too soon, without first having developed a maximum of rapport, may cause the client to feel improperly invaded. A common reaction may be, "It's none of your business."

However, even if the client is fully willing to provide complete information, the injudicious use of narrow questions can, and far too frequently does, prevent the full story from emerging. As noted earlier, many lawyer interviews consist almost exclusively of narrow questions. Several factors undoubtedly account for this proclivity for the near-exclusive use of narrow questions. Let us explain one of the major causes. The cause is to be found in a phenomenon known as "filling." The phenomenon can best be understood by considering some examples.

Take a few moments and think about each of the following situations. In each you will be asked to conduct an interview with the following potential client:

1. A 40-year-old man injured in a rear-end automobile accident.

2. A thirty-five-year-old mother of two children whose husband has just left home.

After having thought about each situation for a few moments— be sure you stop and think about each—ask yourself the following: Right now, without any more description than that given above, do I have a mental picture, albeit somewhat hazy, about:

1. How the accident occurred and what injuries were sustained.

2. The feelings, the desires, or concerns of the woman whose husband just left home.

If you are like most people, in each case you will have a mental picture which includes some or all of the above features. Why? No one approaches a new situation from a totally neutral point of view. Rather, because of prior experience, each person approaches almost every new situation with a certain set of expectancies about what will take place. The slightest clue concerning the nature of the new situation causes the person to unconsciously relate back to earlier experiences with similar situations. These former experiences need not be personal ones but may have been acquired vicariously from books, motion pictures, friends, etc. As the person relates back, he/she unconsciously forms the idea that the new experience will, in many respects, be similar to those of the past. This unconscious idea comes to the person as an expectancy of what will take place and often produces a mental image, albeit a hazy one, of what will occur now. As the person delves more and more into the new experience, the person tends to see more and more clues indicating that what is taking place now is similar to what has taken place in the past. Without realizing it, the person allows the expectancy arising from past experience to become the actuality of present experience. Without the person realizing it, the past experience "fills in" the details of the present experience, forming a picture of what is now taking place. Indeed, people form this picture without ever realizing that instead of viewing a current experience with fresh eyes, they have, in a sense, become a prisoner of their past experience.

This filling phenomenon is often extremely pronounced in lawyer interviewing and counseling. Each jilted, 35-year-old mother of two is *unconsciously assumed* to be, in the main, like each of her predecessors. The general picture is not needed; the lawyer need only ask for some details. The lawyer has heard it all before, though in fact the lawyer may never have heard it even once.

Unconsciously armed with a general mental picture of what has occurred in this divorce, this accident, etc., the lawyer unwittingly allows his expectancy of what is involved to become what the client actually saw or felt. Instead of allowing a narration of the general situation, the lawyer inadvertently resorts to narrow questions. Unwittingly, only this kind of questioning seems necessary. The mental image has provided a general picture of what occurred. Only the details will be necessary to complete the picture. The details are most expeditiously gathered through a series of narrow questions.

As lawyers listen to what clients have to say, lawyers cannot help but develop expectancies of what is to come next. Mental pictures will form. The human mind works in this fashion; nothing can be done to change that. However, lawyers can become aware that the filling phenomenon is taking place. They can realize the mental image is forming and prevent themselves from becoming its victim. They can do so by making sure that the interview involves a comprehensive attempt to determine what transpired. Such an effort will be one that involves much more than a series of narrow questions eliciting only the details the lawyer believes to be important.[4]

---

4. For an extremely interesting discussion of the filling phenomenon, see R. Buckout, *Eyewitness Testimony* 231 Scientific American 23, 24–27 (1974).

Leading Questions

The principal disadvantages of leading questions are fairly obvious. By their very nature, leading questions suggest an answer and therefore probably increase the likelihood of distortion. Distortion is particularly a danger where the client is *unsure of the answer*. This is especially likely when the subject under discussion poses a "case threat." To the extent that a client feels rejection of the suggested answer will lower the lawyer's perception of merit of the case, the temptation to go along with the suggestion will be almost overwhelming.

There are, however, instances in which a leading question is more likely to obtain correct data than is any other form of question. Under the following circumstances, a leading question is likely to elicit accurate information from a client: The information is clearly known to the client; the client is inclined to withhold the information because to report it would be to admit the client had engaged in a violation of some generally accepted norm of behavior; the norm which the client has violated is one which the client accepts as valid, or at least the client believes the lawyer accepts as valid. Under these circumstances, a leading question may lead to accurate information if it suggests a violation did occur and the lawyer already expects that it did.[5]

Kinsey recognized the value of using leading questions in these circumstances when obtaining data about sexual behavior.[6] Respondents were not asked if they ever engaged in particular kinds of sexual activities. Rather, questions were basically posed in the following form: "When did you have your first homosexual experience?", or "How frequently do you engage in oral sex?", etc. The theoretical advantage of this form of question is that it conveys to the respondent acceptance by the interviewer of behavior that is usually seen as deviant. The form of the question demonstrates that the interviewer expects that such behavior has taken place and does not condemn the respondent for it.

There are many instances when a lawyer must talk with a client about a situation involving socially aberrant behavior. In these instances, the lawyer may well wish to use leading questions as a means of obtaining reliable information. Thus, to the extent it is pertinent to get into the subject of a past criminal record with a client whom the lawyer strongly suspects has such a record, the lawyer might try a phrase such as: "I guess you've had trouble with the police before?" Stated with an accepting tone of voice, this question may make the client more willing to talk about the record than a question such as: "Have you ever been arrested before?"

---

5. Gorden, supra note 2, at 215. 6. Gorden, supra note 2, at 214.

A CLIENT'S ABILITY TO PROVIDE ACCURATE INFORMATION

Implicit in the foregoing analysis of the advantages and disadvantages of various forms of questions is an assumption that bears examination. To some substantial degree, the discussion assumed that clients are capable of observing, remembering, and reporting the specific details of complex social events which occurred in the past. Thus, the discussion has assumed that, with the appropriate use of questions, lawyers can elicit the details or "actual facts" of complex past events such as business transactions, accidents, robberies, etc. Though we have emphasized that developing client motivation is often essential for gathering full information, we have not called into question the idea that people have an innate capacity to precisely perceive, recall, and report everything that has occurred.

Since there is growing evidence to suggest that people may not have this capacity, we believe we should discuss some current thoughts concerning the limits of an individual to perceive, recall, and report all that was presented to his/her senses. Knowledge of the factors which may influence an individual's potential ability to provide a full and accurate report may be useful to the lawyer for at least two reasons.

First of all, during the course of a law suit the lawyer will frequently confront a situation where what the client says conflicts with some other person's report of the same event. Knowledge of factors which tend to influence perception and recollection may be useful in determining which person is correct. Understanding what factors may influence accurate perception and recall may also aid the lawyer in assessing whether or not the client is fabricating or simply honestly mistaken.

Second, knowledge of the factors which may influence recall and reporting may aid the lawyer in deciding how the client should be questioned in order to stimulate accurate recall and reporting. In this regard, the knowledge may serve as a basis for deciding what form of question to use and what sequence of questioning to adopt.

Currently, there are two basic theories of social memory which attempt to explain how people perceive, store, and report information about past events—associationist and reconstructive.[7] Supporters of both theories would agree that clients are unable to perceive everything that transpires. They would agree, therefore, that perception is a selective process. Thus, when a client observes an event, some but not all of the details will be observed and stored. The theorists would disagree substantially on the extent to which clients have the

---

7. M. Peterson, Witness Memory of Social Events 1 (1976) (unpublished dissertation in the Education/Psychology Library, University of California, Los Angeles [hereinafter Peterson].

capacity to store, recall, and report the specific details of what they have observed and experienced.[8] However, despite their substantial disagreement, both schools of thought seem to agree that certain factors play a significant role in a person's ability to accurately perceive, recall, and report events.

The factors which commonly seem to influence an individual's ability to perceive, recall, and report events can be grouped into three broad categories:

1. Factors within the observer at the time the event occurred.
2. Factors within the environment at the time the event occurred.
3. Factors related to the manner in which the observer's perceptions are elicited.

Factors Within the Observer

The factors operative within the observer (client, witness) at the time the event occurred include the following:

1. Amount of Attention to Significant Event:

    Insignificant events generally do not motivate a person to pay close attention. Often the event which is significant to the lawyer was insignificant to the observer. At the time of the event, the observer's attention was focused on matters other than the event which the lawyer finds significant. For example, an accident or crime occurring on a busy street may have been embedded in a variety of other activities (children playing, cars moving, etc.) to which the observer was paying at least as much attention when the significant event of the crime or accident occurred.

2. Amount of Stress:

    A person in a stressful situation is likely to be more preoccupied with his/her physical and emotional well-being than with the details of the external environment.

3. Variations in Sensory Acuity:

    People vary enormously in the degree of acuity of their sensory facilities, such as vision, hearing, etc.

4. Biophysical Factors:

    Age, mental or physical illness, intoxication, and fatigue can impair a person's ability to perceive, store, and/or retrieve information.

5. The Observer's Set or Expectancy:

    We have already mentioned how lawyers can have a preconceived notion about what facts are involved in an event. Recall our discussion of "filling" as it related to rear-end

---

8. Peterson, supra note 7, at 8–50.

collisions and thirty-five-year-old divorcees. Just as lawyers' perceptions may be distorted by their preconceptions,
so will the perceptions of clients be distorted by their expectancies. Perhaps the most common form of set or expectancy
involves biases or prejudices. Every observer possesses a
variety of culturally conditioned attitudes and beliefs about
racial and ethnic minorities—"Jews," "Niggers," "Mexs,"
etc.; about members of "deviant" subcultures—homosexuals,
addicts, delinquents, etc.; and about men, women, and children in general. Biases and prejudices can distort perceptual
judgments without any conscious awareness or intent to distort information

Factors Within the Environment

Factors associated with the environment, at the time the event
occurred, include:

1. The degree of illumination, e. g., light vs. dark.

2. The speed with which the events took place.

3. General noise level.

4. Proximity to events.

5. Simultaneous occurrences.

Whenever a lawyer confronts the situation where there are two
or more disparate reports of the same event, the lawyer may be able
to obtain clarification by carefully questioning about factors associated with the observers or the situation at the time the event occurred.
By inquiring into these two groups of factors, the lawyer may be able
to ascertain which of the conflicting reports is more accurate.

Consider the following hypothetical in which a client and two
witnesses present contradictory observations of the same event. Giv-
en the statements of the client and the two witnesses, what factors
influencing perception and/or memory might account for the vari-
ances in the three stories?

The client, Karen Morgan, is an uninsured motorist who, at 8:15
a. m. on August 14 of last year, was involved in an automobile accident at the intersection of 6th Avenue and Oak Street. According to
Ms. Morgan, she was traveling westbound in her 1969 MGB on Oak
and had come to a stop at the 6th Avenue intersection. She intended
to cross 6th Avenue and then turn right on 8th Avenue to reach the
university. As she looked to her right, she saw a light blue Oldsmobile in the process of turning left off 6th Avenue to go eastbound on
Oak Street. The Oldsmobile was cutting the corner; the driver tried
to veer to the right and still complete the turn, but the left front
struck the left front of the client's car. After the collision, the Oldsmobile came to a stop on Oak, headed in a southeast direction, with
Ms. Morgan's vehicle remaining in its stopped position. On impact,
Ms. Morgan was thrown forward, struck the steering wheel, and

touched off the horn. The parties then exited their respective vehicles and exchanged names and addresses. The police were not called. Before the exchange of data, Ms. Morgan was approached by a Dorothy Miles, who left her name and address and said she would be a witness.

The insurance company of the driver of the Oldsmobile is suing your client, contending that the accident was caused when Ms. Morgan rolled through the boulevard stop sign for westbound traffic on Oak Street.

You have interviewed Ms. Miles and learned that she either did not see or cannot recall seeing the collision. Her story is as follows: On the morning in question, she was walking to the university with her boyfriend, Thomas Hansen. She and Hansen had been living together for about six months. The evening before the accident, she had told Hansen that she had decided to move out. Hansen, who had no knowledge of her intentions, registered great surprise and kept her up until 3:00 a. m. discussing the situation. At the time of the collision, she and Hansen were walking westbound on the north side of Oak Street. She was closest to the curb and they were about 50 feet east of the intersection. At the moment of impact, Hansen was in the process of inquiring why she wanted to leave and suggesting that they first try to work things out. The only thing she can remember is hearing Ms. Morgan honking her horn just before the collision; she does not even remember leaving her name as a witness.

From Answers to Interrogatories submitted to the plaintiff, you have ascertained that one of the plaintiff's witnesses is Tom Hansen. You are now in the process of interviewing Hansen in his apartment. Thus far he has told you the following: At the time of the impact, he was walking with his girlfriend, Dorothy Miles. They were about 30 to 50 feet east of 6th Avenue, on the north side of the street, when the impact occurred. He was closest to the curb. Just before the collision, he saw the MGB moving westbound into 6th Avenue at a very slow rate of speed and heard the driver of the Oldsmobile honk the horn. The Oldsmobile, which was in the process of turning, did not veer at any time, but rather was making a smooth turn when the MGB struck it.

Factors Related to the Form and Sequence of Questions

Factors related to the manner in which the observer's perceptions are elicited concern the form and sequence of questions. There are many ways in which lawyers' questioning may influence the accuracy with which clients recall and report information. We will briefly describe four common ways in which the questioning creates this kind of influence.

　1.　Too Many Narrow Questions:

　　As noted earlier, unless the client is given an opportunity to describe his/her observations in response to open-ended questions, certain facts and details will often not emerge. As a consequence, the story reported to the lawyer is often a limited one.

2. Improper Use of Leading Questions:

Particularly where the client is unsure of the answer, the use of leading questions will often cause distortion. Assuming the lawyer knows best, the client will often go along with the lawyer's suggestion rather than indicating that the client does not know or is unsure of the answer. By an unconscious use of leading questions, the lawyer can unwittingly lead a client into adopting a favorable but inaccurate view of the situation.

3. Pressuring the Client for Too Much Detail:

As indicated above, people do not perceive all of the details of any given event; therefore, they cannot usually report precisely everything that occurred. If lawyers press clients for too much detail, clients often "fill in" the details they can't remember. Clients "fill in" the details by taking what they can recall of the event and then using logic to reconstruct the event by imagining details that would be consistent with the facts they do remember. This reconstructive process is typically an unconscious one.

4. Obtaining Conclusions Which Distort:

In some instances, asking a client for a conclusion before obtaining the details on which the conclusion is based, can lead to distortion. For example, assume one issue in the case involves the client's sobriety. If the client is first asked for the conclusion, "Were you drunk?", the client's "yes" or "no" answer may shape the client's subsequent reporting of specific matters such as the number of drinks, the amount of food previously eaten, etc.[9]

During the ensuing chapters, we will discuss in more detail the manner in which questioning practices can bias information. However, at this point we will turn attention to the matters of how the lawyer might approach the tasks of ascertaining the client's problem and legal position.

---

9. For a more detailed discussion of this problem, see Chapter Seven at p. 133 infra.

Chapter Five

ASCERTAINING THE CLIENT'S PROBLEM
AND LEGAL POSITION

This chapter will discuss how an interview might be organized and conducted in order to gather complete information about the nature of the client's problem and legal position.

The lawyer-client dialogue typically begins with the lawyer attempting to gain a preliminary understanding of the client's problem. The lawyer's goal is to determine in a general way what relief the client seeks and what concerns the client faces. When the client's problem has been preliminarily identified, the lawyer usually proceeds to gather information about the client's legal position. Before there can be any meaningful discussion of what alternatives are available to solve the client's problem, there must usually be at least a tentative determination of the client's legal position.

A THREE–STAGED INTERVIEW

There are undoubtedly several ways of approaching the task of ascertaining the client's problem and legal position. What we will describe is a general approach we have found to be useful. Under this approach, the process of ascertaining the client's problem and legal position is divided into three stages: (1) Preliminary Problem Identification, (2) Chronological Overview, and (3) Theory Development and Verification.[1]

Preliminary Problem Identification Stage

In the Preliminary Problem Identification stage, the lawyer asks the client to provide a *general* description of at least the following: (1) the underlying transaction which caused the problem, and (2) the relief the client desires. During this stage, the lawyer encourages the client to describe the foregoing matters in whatever way seems comfortable. The lawyer refrains from imposing any particular order on the client's presentation and allows the client to proceed in a free-flowing narrative. The lawyer asks only for a general description and refrains from asking for any details.

Chronological Overview Stage

During the Chronological Overview stage, the client is encouraged to provide a step-by-step chronological narrative of the past transaction which underlies the client's problem. The client is asked

---

1. A case may require one or more interviews for the lawyer to complete these three stages.

to proceed from the point where the client believes the problem began, and follow through, step-by-step, up to the present. During the Overview, the lawyer does *not* attempt to obtain a detailed elaboration of the various points mentioned by the client during the chronological narration.

Theory Development and Verification Stage

At the conclusion of the Overview stage, the lawyer mentally reviews the entire story to determine what potential causes of action and potential defenses are possibly applicable. *Using his/her knowledge of the substantive law, the lawyer consciously asks himself/herself, "What are all of the possible legal theories that are potentially applicable given this factual situation?"*

When this tentative diagnosis has been made, the lawyer commences the Theory Development and Verification stage. Here the lawyer conducts a detailed examination to determine how many of the potentially applicable causes of action and defenses actually seem viable. The examination, as it relates to any particular theory, attempts to determine whether or not there are facts which will establish the existence of each of the substantive elements needed to invoke the causes of action and defenses which the lawyer has seen as potentially applicable. Thus, if one cause of action seen as potentially applicable is that of breach of contract, the lawyer's inquiry will be devoted to determining in detail whether or not there are facts to establish: (1) the making of an agreement, (2) performance by the plaintiff, (3) breach by the defendant, and (4) damages.

The Theory Development and Verification stage is a phase devoted to *exploring consciously, in a systematic manner,* whether or not the specific legal theories suggested by the Overview are indeed viable. It is a stage which is begun with several tentative diagnoses, and carried out with a goal of verifying, refining, and perhaps rejecting and replacing these diagnoses.

The Purpose of the Three-Staged Interview: The Problem of Premature Diagnosis

Why divide the process of ascertaining the client's problem and legal position into three stages? The purpose of the division is to increase the thoroughness with which cases are analyzed by encouraging lawyers not to prematurely decide what the client's problem is, and what should be done to solve it.

In legal interviewing, it is very common for lawyers to analyze cases on the basis of inadequate information. One common omission involves the lawyer's failure to make an initial inquiry about what relief the client desires to obtain. On hearing the client's initial description of his/her problem, the lawyer fails to inquire about what the client wants done. Rather, the lawyer *assumes* he/she knows what relief the client desires. Armed with this assumption, the lawyer proceeds to ask the client for information that would be needed in order to bring about the assumed desired result. The questioning, however, often turns out to be largely a waste of time since the information obtained is irrelevant in terms of the relief the client actually desires.

The following example is illustrative. When the client begins by talking about money that is due him/her on a loan, the lawyer assumes that what the client desires is a lawsuit to recover the amount due. Thereafter, the lawyer's questioning is geared to making sure the client has a viable cause of action for the recovery of the money. The client, however, was interested in learning what kind of a security agreement would be advisable, since what the client desired was to extend the loan. Accordingly, the lawyer's questions regarding the making of the original agreement and the nature of the borrower's default were largely irrelevant. The questions were also probably frustrating and annoying for the client, who wanted to talk about making a new agreement.

In obtaining an initial description of the client's problem, lawyers also commonly fail to realize that the client's description may be incomplete or inaccurate. As a consequence, lawyers often start out asking a lot of questions about, and sometimes fashioning solutions for, the wrong problem.

In the beginning of an interview, many clients will be reluctant to express all their concerns. Consider the following example: The client has lost her job, and there is a genuine question of whether or not the termination was lawful. With the loss of her job, the client fell behind in her rent. She has now been served with an unlawful detainer complaint. When asked to describe her problem, the client makes no mention of her loss of job. The incident seems unrelated to her present problem. In addition, the client is reluctant to discuss the situation because it involves revealing some personal matters concerning her relationship with her former employer.

Furthermore, many clients will have little understanding of what their problem actually involves. When asked to give an initial description of their situation, they often unknowingly omit reference to the facts constituting the real problem. For example, a man who is suffering from injuries received at work may not understand that the true source of his difficulty is "medical malpractice." As a consequence, when asked to state his problem, the client limits his description to something like the following: "I was injured on the job; I've been off work for three months. I don't seem to be getting any better. I can't work and the company has stopped paying my medical bills."

In sum, lawyers often fail to take into account that what the client has described at the beginning of the interview is only the tip of the iceberg, or perhaps even the wrong iceberg.

Moreover, lawyers often fail to develop all the relevant legal theories. After hearing a few facts, the lawyer quickly decides not only what the case is about, but also what legal doctrines can be used to solve the problem. Thereafter, the lawyer inquires about facts related to these theories and never bothers to ask about information which might suggest the applicability of still further legal doctrines. The situation is analogous to the doctor who makes a single diagnosis of the patient's problem after hearing only a few of the patient's symptoms, and thereafter conducts the rest of the examination as though this single diagnosis was the only one that needed investigation. Such a doctor, like the lawyer, never allows the patient (client) the opportunity to set forth all that is known because the doctor prematurely decides what the problem involves.

The following hypothetical is useful to illustrate this kind of premature and incomplete diagnosis. Assume the client, Ms. Jones, has been served with an unlawful detainer complaint. At the beginning of the interview she has shown the lawyer the complaint; it alleges breach of a written covenant to pay rent and seeks damages and restitution of the property. Ms. Jones has indicated to the lawyer that she wishes to remain in her apartment because she believes she cannot find other comparable housing.

If, when the lawyer looks at the complaint, the lawyer assumes that the only theories needing investigation are those regarding the existence of an unlawful detainer cause of action together with standard defenses such as habitability of the premises, the lawyer will be engaging in premature diagnosis. Perhaps if the lawyer allows the client the opportunity to narrate her story from beginning to end, the lawyer will learn of the possible existence of counterclaims, such as intentional infliction of emotional distress in connection with the landlord's unlawful attempts to evict the client. Perhaps the lawyer will learn of some facts which suggest there was a defect in the service of the complaint.

Moreover, even if the lawyer had sought to learn about proper service of the complaint as a part of the tentative diagnosis of possible defenses, it is quite likely the lawyer would not think to examine every possible defect. There is so much doctrine potentially applicable to any given case that it is unrealistic to expect the lawyer to inquire into each potentially relevant subject area. Although the competent lawyer can be expected to inquire into standard matters even if they are not brought up by the client—e. g., habitability defenses in unlawful detainer cases—one cannot expect lawyers to inquire into more obscure matters without the presence of some clue from the client which suggests the need for further investigation. Think about the situation involving Ms. Jones. What areas would you investigate with regard to a motion to quash on the grounds of improper service? Does your list include the ground that the process server was below the statutory age? Probably without some clue from the client—

e. g., "The complaint was served on me by a very young boy,"—you would not think to inquire about the age of the process server.

The Advantages of a Three-Staged Interview

Most any approach to legal interviewing will advocate that the lawyer begin by obtaining a statement of the client's problem. To know how to proceed with the interview, the lawyer must have a basic understanding of what the client's situation involves. Obtaining Preliminary Problem Identification in the manner we have suggested has several potential advantages. First, the approach increases the likelihood that the lawyer will quickly be perceived by the client as someone who is empathetic and therefore someone to be trusted with troublesome information. In our approach, the lawyer is to begin by having the client describe in narrative form what he/she sees as the problem. The lawyer's initial role is *to listen,* and to refrain from asking for details. The client, therefore, has an opportunity at the beginning of the interview to relate whatever the client sees as important.

Furthermore, since the lawyer is to get the description without interrupting the client for details, the client may be able to recall information that might be forgotten if the client were constantly being interrupted.

Finally, the lawyer is encouraged to avoid premature diagnosis. Although the lawyer is to ask what relief the client desires, the title of the stage, *Preliminary* Problem Identification, serves to remind the lawyer that much more information will be needed.

The Overview stage has some of the same advantages as the Preliminary Problem Identification stage. The Overview stage is also designed to counteract tendencies toward premature diagnosis. If the lawyer obtains a chronological Overview of the entire underlying transaction before attempting to develop specific detail, the lawyer is more likely to discover whether or not the client's initial description of the problem is incomplete or inaccurate. Moreover, having this broad description of the facts may cause the lawyer to see a wider range of potentially applicable legal theories. Having in mind the concept that one should obtain an Overview in order to seek out the true nature of the problem and the widest range of clues regarding potentially applicable legal theories may cause the lawyer to think in terms of avoiding premature diagnosis.

Furthermore, the Overview provides the client with the opportunity to tell his/her story unfettered by interruption concerned with specific details. The client is encouraged to relate his/her story step-by-step, in a chronological fashion. For many people, a chronological order may keep normal paths of association intact and, as such, stimulate them to remember matters that would be lost if their stories were constantly interrupted for further detail.

A separate Overview stage has another value. The value is one which relates to increasing client willingness to provide full information. Since this stage is designed to permit the client to tell the story in his/her own words, without the lawyer probing for detail, the lawyer will use mostly open-ended questions. As a consequence, the lawyer will be able to bring into play the rapport-building advantages of open-ended questions. The client will be allowed to set forth those facts which the client sees as important, and will be able to do so with the freedom to play down subjects which the client feels initially reluctant to discuss. This opportunity, particularly if buttressed by non-judgmental listening, is quite likely to result in increased client willingness to discuss more threatening subjects later in the more probing Theory Development and Verification stage.

There are some lawyers who decline to follow our suggested approach on the ground that it is too time consuming. "It makes a federal case out of even the most routine matter." We would concede that thoroughly going through the process we are advocating sometimes lengthens the task of ascertaining the client's problem and legal position. On the other hand, it seems to us that far too many complex cases are treated as though they were "routine." Furthermore, in far too many instances, lawyers require third and fourth interviews because they fail to adequately develop the facts in the first place.

To generally follow the three-staged model does not mean that every case must be made into a "federal case." In making inquiry during the Overview and Theory Development and Verification stages, the lawyer can use discretion in limiting the scope of the investigation. Lawyers can rely on their good judgment to determine when they have enough information to decide that a case can be treated as "routine." In our experience, however, a lawyer usually cannot adequately determine whether or not a case is "routine" unless the lawyer has at least obtained a somewhat detailed Chronological Overview of the underlying transaction.

Not every interview will lend itself to the three-stage approach we have suggested. In some instances, the lawyer will need to inquire into an auxiliary matter before endeavoring to fully ascertain the client's problem and legal position. The following situations are illustrative: (1) The client is incarcerated on a criminal charge and desires to be released pending the trial; (2) the client's child has been removed from the home pending a dependency hearing and the client wants the child placed with a relative instead, and (3) the client has been denied unemployment benefits but needs money immediately in order to feed the family.

In these emergency situations, it makes no sense for the lawyer to follow the Preliminary Problem Identification stage with a Chronological Overview. The client's immediate problem should, of course, be given attention before the lawyer proceeds with the overall approach we are suggesting.

Before turning to the subject of how the lawyer conducts the three-staged process, one further point should be made. The discussion in this chapter will take place against a background of assumed client cooperation. That is, there will be an assumption throughout the discussion that the client has a general willingness and capability to respond to the questions and structural guides set forth by the lawyer. In making this assumption, we do not mean to solely limit the discussion to clients who have no reluctance to converse. Rather, we also intend to include those clients who have some degree of reluctance to speak, especially about topics they initially find threatening. Persons we intend to exclude from our description include: Clients who consciously withhold information; clients who are extremely reticent to discuss specific topics, and clients who won't stay on the relevant topic. Techniques for handling these more difficult clients will be discussed in Chapter Six.

This chapter focuses on how a lawyer might proceed with a willing client for the following reason: It is generally easier to learn how to be effective with difficult clients if one has already learned basic skills for effectively dealing with cooperative clients.

TECHNIQUES FOR CONDUCTING THE THREE–STAGED INTERVIEW

The Preliminary Problem Identification Stage

The process of Preliminary Problem Identification is usually begun with open-ended questions calling for a narrative description of the client's situation. Questions such as the following are typical:

"How can I help you?"

"What brings you here today?"

"What can I do for you?"

These open-ended questions leave the client free to set forth his/her dilemma in any manner which feels comfortable, and in as much detail as seems appropriate. The questions do not, however, explicitly suggest that the lawyer is interested in obtaining a general description of the past transaction which underlies the problem, and the relief which the client desires. To encourage the client to include each of these factors in the description, it is sometimes useful to provide a structural guide which outlines the information the lawyer desires. A structural guide can be worded somewhat as follows:

"Give me a brief description of your problem, how it arose, and what solutions you hope to find."

"Tell me what your problem is, how it came about, and what you think you'd like to have done about it."

Such guides can be inserted into the dialogue either immediately after the initial open-ended question, or after receiving the client's initial reply.

If the client seems to have some difficulty providing a brief description of the problem, the lawyer can encourage further narration through the use of additional open-ended questions and active and passive listening responses. Brief instructions such as "Tell me a little bit more," can also be quite facilitative. If the client's description does not include information about desired relief, open-ended questions can be used to get this information.

"What would you like to see happen now?"

"What would you like to do about this situation?"

In describing what relief they seek, clients may express desires which go beyond the lawyer's concept of ordinary and extraordinary relief. They may express a desire for release from a host of feelings, such as anger, frustration, etc., associated with the controversy. The lawyer should not expect to be able to directly alleviate these feelings. Rather, the lawyer should simply provide empathetic understanding and avoid statements such as, "Don't worry, you'll get over that." Such statements, of course, treat the client's feelings as irrelevant.

Not all clients will have an idea of what relief they desire. Some clients will respond with comments, such as: "I don't know what to do; that's why I'm coming to you." Where clients make this kind of response, the lawyer can empathize with the client's concern and point out that the matter of relief will be discussed when more information has been developed. "I can understand your desire to know what to do, and we will definitely talk about that in detail in a little while. However, first I'll need to get some more information."

In general, the client should be encouraged to continue with the presentation until it appears the client has completed the general description. During this stage, the lawyer should not ask the client to provide details about the transaction. The lawyer's primary goal at this initial stage is to gain a general picture and at the same time provide the client with empathetic understanding. Secondarily, the lawyer is trying to stimulate the client's ability to recall by allowing the client to describe the situation in any order which seems appropriate.

Preliminary Problem Identification can be concluded with the lawyer providing an active listening response which summarizes the situation—i. e., explains that the lawyer understands what transaction has caused the problem, what relief the client desires, and what concerns the client feels. "So the situation is that your landlord wants you out, you'd like to remain, and you're concerned that the sheriff will take everything you have if you don't leave right away." This kind of summary is designed to take early and maximum advantage of the facilitator of empathetic understanding. The summary, if effectively put, lets the client know almost at the outset that the lawyer has heard and understood what the client sees as the principal difficulties. Hopefully, the conveying of this understanding will establish the kind of rapport that will make the client feel willing to respond fully to the subsequent inquiries.

Using our general approach as a guideline, we will illustrate some effective and some less effective attempts at problem identification. Consider these examples:

Case No. 1:

No. 1–L   Hello, Mr. Cabello; my name is Diane Richards. Why don't you start by simply telling me what is on your mind.

No. 2–C   My mother died about four months ago. When she passed away she and my stepfather owed me some money, and now my stepfather won't pay me.

No. 3–L   How much money does he owe you?

No. 4–C   Oh, I guess about $5,500.

No. 5–L   Has he signed a promissory note or anything in writing?

No. 6–C   No.

No. 7–L   How recently have you asked him for the money?

No. 8–C   About a month ago.

No. 9–L   What did he say?

No. 10–C   He said he'd pay me when he could.

No. 11–L   So you want to know if you're entitled to sue him to get the money back?

No. 12–C   I guess so.

No. 13–L   Beside the question of your right to get the money, are there other matters that are of concern to you?

No. 14–C   Not really.

No. 15–L   Are you sure?

No. 16–C   Yes.

No. 17–L   Are you worried about the possibility of a family squabble?

Analysis of Case No. 1:

Although in No. 1 the lawyer encourages the client to talk generally, the lawyer perhaps could have employed a structural guide by requesting a general description of the underlying transaction and desired solutions.

In No.'s 3, 5, 7, and 9, the lawyer probes for specific details about the underlying transaction. Given that these specific details will be gone into later in a systematic manner, these questions seem unnecesary at this preliminary stage. If the lawyer felt the need for more general description, perhaps a directive probe such as "Tell me a little bit more about the situation," would have been adequate.

In No. 11, the lawyer switches to the issue of relief. However, instead of inquiring about what relief the client desires, the lawyer, through a leading question, suggests a lawsuit. Perhaps the client was thinking about another solution, such as obtaining a security agreement. Not every potential plaintiff wants a lawsuit. No. 13, however, represents the kind of open-ended question we have recommended. It attempts to obtain a general description of the relief the client desires. No. 17, on the other hand, seems less appropriate. Remember, at the beginning of an interview, clients may feel hesitant to disclose all their concerns.

Case No. 2:

No. 1–L   Mr. Montgomery, I'm Maria Vasquez. How might I help you?

No. 2–C   Well, I've been arrested, and I don't know what to do. Nothing like this has ever happened to me before.

No. 3–L   I can tell you're quite concerned about the situation. I'd really like to help. Perhaps it would be best if you told me a little bit more about the situation, you know, how the arrest came about.

No. 4–C   Well, they say I'm guilty of shoplifting over at Sears on 48th Street.

No. 5–L   Can you tell me a little bit more about that?

No. 6–C   Well, as I was leaving the store they stopped me and searched my jacket. They took out the calculator I was going to buy, and then they arrested me. I was going to pay for the calculator.

No. 7–L   Okay, that gives me a general idea of what happened. In addition to knowing what you can do to avoid the shoplifting conviction, are there other matters which are concerning you at this time?

No. 8–C   Well, sort of; I'm worried about what will happen to my job.

No. 9–L   Okay, any other concerns?

No. 10–C   Not really.

No. 11–L   So the situation is you've been arrested for shoplifting at Sears, and you want to know what can be done to avoid a conviction. In addition, you're concerned about how all of this may affect your job.

Analysis of Case No. 2:

In No. 1, the lawyer begins appropriately with an open-ended question. This open-ended question elicits only minimal information from the client, so the lawyer goes on in No. 3 to attempt to elicit further information. In No. 3, the lawyer, through an active listening response, first demonstrates she understands the client's feelings. Additionally, the lawyer attempts to reasure the client by expressing a willingness to help. She then provides a structural guide which asks for elaboration. "Perhaps it would be best if you told me a little more about the situation. You know, how the arrest came about." The request for elaboration seems appropriate; as of this point, the lawyer knows little, if anything, about the underlying transaction. The request for elaboration does not press for details. Instead, it gives the client leeway to describe what, in all probability, is an ego-threatening event, in terms which are comfortable to the client. No. 5 seems to be another appropriately open probe. When the basic transaction is identified (No. 6), the lawyer goes on through generally open-ended questions (No. 7 and No. 9) to learn of other concerns the client is willing to discuss. Though the client's response, "Not really" (No. 10), gives some indication there may be still further concerns, the lawyer does not press. The lawyer recognizes that the client may feel reluctant to disclose all of his concerns at the beginning. The lawyer then concludes the process of problem identification with an active listening type response (No. 11) which summarizes the situation and the client's feelings.

Case No. 3:

No. 1–L   Hello, Mr. Rose, I'm Ronald Frement. I think it would be easiest if you started by telling me what's on your mind.

No. 2–C   Well, they took my car back and sold it, and now they say I owe them another $1400. I want to know if I have to pay them.

No. 3–L   You want to know if you're legally liable; I can tell by what you're saying that you're quite angry about the situation.

No. 4–C   That's right.

No. 5–L   Who wants the money?

No. 6–C   The car company, Briggs Motors.

No. 7–L   Have they sued you?

No. 8–C   Yes, I guess so; here are some damn papers they brought by my house about a week ago. They came at six o'clock in the morning.

No. 9–L   Okay, let's see. Yes, these papers are a complaint; it means Briggs is suing you. We'll talk about the papers in just a moment. When you got these papers, did the process server say anything to you?

No. 10–C   No, not really.

No. 11–L   Okay, tell me when you bought the car.

No. 12–C   Last March; I paid $650 down.

No. 13–L   Do you have a copy of the contract of purchase?

Analysis of Case No. 3:

Rather than providing an analysis of this case, we ask that you provide your own analysis by considering the following:

1. Is inquiry No. 1 appropriately open, or is it perhaps too vague? Why?

2. Assuming response No. 2 was delivered in a tone of voice that indicated frustration and anger, in what way, if any would you alter lawyer reponse No. 3? Why?

3. Inquiries No. 5 and No. 7 are narrow questions. They ask for specific information rather than calling for general elaboration. Are these inquiries, therefore, inappropriate at this point? Why or why not?

4. Assuming that inquiries No.'s 9, 11, and 13 represent the beginning of an attempt to gather the facts concerning the underlying transaction, what additional inquiries or statements, if any, would you have made before starting the factual investigation? Why?

Preparatory Explanation

Before moving into the Overview stage, it is sometimes useful to provide the client with an explanation of what will take place in the remainder of the interview. The explanation can give the client a preview of what to expect in terms of length and content, and also the activities in which the lawyer and client will engage.[2] We have labeled this explanation a "Preparatory Explanation."

A Preparatory Explanation may help avoid a number of problems which interfere with communication between the client and lawyer. The problems involve certain aspects of the inhibitor of "role expectations."

First, there is the matter of the client's perception of how active or passive a client should be in providing information. Does the cli-

---

2. Research indicates that patients who are given an explanation of what to expect from psychotherapy—"taught the rules of the game"—benefit more from psychotherapy than patients who are not given any prior explanation of what psychotherapy entails. M. Orne & P. Wender, *Anticipatory Socialization for Psychotherapy: Method and Rationale*, 124 Amer. J. Psychiat. 1202 (1968). Similarly, we believe that in legal interviewing many clients will be able to participate more fully in the interview if the lawyer provides an explanation of what will be required of them in the interview process.

ent believe his/her role is to tell the lawyer what the client believes is important? Or does the client feel the only information to be given to the lawyer is that which is specifically asked for? In addition to the active-passive expectancy, there is the related matter of the client's beliefs with regard to how quickly the lawyer will respond to the client's inquiries. Does the client assume the interview will be quite straightforward and short, with the lawyer asking a few questions and then moving quickly to a definitive analysis of the client's rights?

If the client has a set of expectations which conflict with the lawyer's questioning pattern, the client may feel frustrated or annoyed. As a consequence, rapport may suffer. Thus, if the client believes it is up to the lawyer to ask specifically about matters which the lawyer believes to be important, while the lawyer's questioning pattern employs a number of very broad open-ended questions, the client may feel annoyed and perhaps even perceive the lawyer as incompetent. Similar consequences may result if the client believes the lawyer will quickly reach the point of discussing the client's rights, and the process of ascertaining the client's legal position turns out to be lengthy.

Also, even if the client has no specific expectations, there may be difficulties. If the client is uncertain as to how far he/she is expected to go in providing information, the client may feel apprehensive. Under these circumstances, if the client is subjected to an open-ended questioning pattern and hence is continually confronted with his/her uncertainty, the uncertainty may turn to frustration and serve to damage rapport.

To help reduce the potential frustrations just described, we believe it is helpful to include a Preparatory Explanation between the Preliminary Problem Identification stage and the Overview stage. However, before one leaps to the use of a Preparatory Explanation, there are potential difficulties that bear consideration. How does one decide when it is appropriate to use the statement? For the client who has a fair degree of sophistication about what to expect during the course of the interview, an explanation of what to expect may create a negative reaction. To such a client, an explanation about process may be viewed as quite unnecessary and unduly patronizing. Similarly, for the person who feels confronted with an emergency, a Preparatory Explanation, particularly if at all lengthy, may be counterproductive in terms of establishing rapport. The explanation may be seen as unnecessarily delaying a resolution which the client feels must be found immediately.

Related to the question of when to use a Preparatory Explanation is the question of the statement's content. The degree of the client's sophistication and the client's sense of emergency are probably the two most important variables in determining the scope of information to be included. There is no standard content. The content should probably be varied, depending upon the client's degree of sophistication.

We will outline what might be included in a Preparatory Explanation when it appears the client has little idea of what to expect. When this outline is concluded, there will be a discussion of how the lawyer might go about appraising the degree of client sophistication and what modifications can be adopted if the lawyer concludes the client is relatively sophisticated or under great pressure to relate his/her story.

With the client who has little or no idea of what to expect, the Preparatory Explanation might include at least the following:

1. A brief description of what will take place during the Overview and Theory Development and Verification stages, together with some indication of the approximate length of the interview. Included in the description should be a brief explanation of the respective roles of the lawyer and client.

2. An explanation that at the conclusion of the Theory Development and Verification stage there will be a discussion of the client's legal rights as well as possible solutions.

The description of what will take place in the Overview and Theory Development and Verification stages can include a description of the kinds of questions that will be asked, and the kinds of responses that will be expected. Thus, the client might be told something along the following lines:

"Okay, Mr. Aronow, what I have found most helpful in this kind of situation is this: I'll start out by asking you to go over your story from the beginning, and to go in chronological order, step-by-step in some detail, telling me in your own words everything that has happened right up to today. In telling me the story, it will be important that you proceed step-by-step and give me some details. Tell me everything you can recall; don't worry about whether or not you believe it is legally important. When you finish going over the story, I'll go back and ask you some specific questions which, from a legal point of view, may be important. At that point, I'll probably be pressing you for some detail so that we can get at everything you can recall while your memory is still fresh. As you can guess, it may take us a little while to get out all these facts, but we'll have at least an hour today."

This explanation gears the client to expect the interview will contain two stages. Likewise, it explains generally what kind of questioning the client can expect, and what kind of activity the client will be expected to engage in during each of the stages. In the Overview stage, the client will be expected to give his/her own description in a somewhat detailed step-by-step, chronological narrative. During the Theory Development and Verification stage, the client will be expected to come up with rather specific detail. Finally, the explanation clarifies the issue of time by informing the client that the two stages may "take a little while to get these facts." Further, the lawyer lets the client know that the interview will last about one hour.

The description of what will take place at the conclusion of the Theory Development and Verification stage requires very little elaboration. Something akin to the following would seem sufficient: "When I've gotten the full picture, unless the matter turns out to be a somewhat complicated one, I'll be in a position to talk with you about your rights and we can begin to discuss what can be done." From the information obtained in the Preliminary Problem Identification stage, the lawyer may or may not have some idea of whether further legal research is likely to be called for before the lawyer can assess the client's legal position. If the lawyer believes further factual or legal research will probably be called for, then some mention of the possibility seems appropriate as part of the Preparatory Explanation. Mentioning the potential need for further research in the beginning may reduce the client's subsequent disappointment if, at the conclusion of the initial interview, the lawyer can provide only a tentative analysis of the client's position.

There is one additional instruction that is sometimes included in a full Preparatory Explanation. This instruction concerns what the client may expect with regard to note-taking. A lawyer cannot convey the impression that he/she understands and is concerned about what the client is saying if the lawyer is continually focusing on a piece of paper. On the other hand, if the lawyer takes no notes, it is very likely that important information may get lost. Hence, note-taking will be a necessity throughout the interview. To prepare the client for this reality, the explanation might include the following:

> "As we go through the story, I'll be jotting down some notes on some of what you tell me so that I can go back to the point if it becomes important. The notes are simply to make sure I don't forget. If you have any questions about what I'm writing down, feel free to ask me about it."

We will now turn to the question of how the lawyer might determine whether or not a full Preparatory Explanation is likely to be helpful or harmful. Ultimately, the decision with regard to how much of a Preparatory Explanation to use requires rather intuitive judgment. The questions to be answered are the following:

1. Is this client quite sophisticated, or anxious to relate his/her story immediately?

2. Is this client somewhat uneasy and perhaps unsure of what is going to happen or whether or not to be fully open?

3. Does the client appear to have a misconception of what will take place?

In attempting to answer the foregoing questions, the lawyer can appraise information presented during the Preliminary Problem Identification stage. In the first instance, the lawyer can look at the client's non-verbal behavior. How did the client speak? How did the client sit and move? What facial reactions did the client make? If the client spoke quite softly and with considerable hesitancy there is some indication the client may feel unsure or uneasy, and have little idea of how to proceed or what to expect. If the client sat forward on the edge of his/her chair, spoke calmly but deliberately, and looked directly into the lawyer's eyes, there is fair evidence the client felt at least somewhat comfortable, and perhaps confident, about how to proceed. If the client spoke loudly and rapidly in a rather exasperated tone of voice, this may indicate the client was quite anxious to relate his/her story. This may also be an indication the client believes the lawyer's role is to sit back and listen, and not ask too many questions.

Further, there can be an appraisal of the client's statements regarding his/her concerns and desired relief. If the client has stated a need for an immediate resolution of the situation, it is likely the client is quite anxious to relate the story and learn what to do. On the other hand, if in expressing concerns the client has stated he/she is uncertain about whether anything should be done, there is an indication that the client does not feel pressed to relate the story. In fact, the client may feel uncertain about proceeding at all.

In addition to appraising the foregoing factors, the lawyer can also look for clues about the client's previous experience with the legal profession. Has the client said anything to indicate that contact with lawyers is a common occurrence? If so, this may be taken as some evidence that a very detailed Preparatory Explanation may be perceived as condescending. If the client gives no indication about prior lawyer contact, the client can be asked about it. "Have you ever been to a lawyer before?" The answer, be it yes or no, need not bind the lawyer with respect to utilizing a Preparatory Explanation. If the answer is yes, but other factors indicate the client may be helped by a Preparatory Explanation, one can still be delivered. "Then you already know what will happen today is that first I'll ask you to tell me, step-by-step . . . ."

The final judgment about whether or not to employ a Preparatory Explanation need not boil down to an all-or-nothing decision. A review of the information received during the Preliminary Problem Identification stage can be used to tailor a Preparatory Explanation that meets the client's individual characteristics.

Finally, it should be noted that it can be useful to give even the most sophisticated and regular client some minimal explanation. The explanation can be limited to a brief description of what is expected of the client during the Overview stage. "George, let's get started by your going over everything that has happened, giving me a chronological, step-by-step outline from the beginning right up to the present."

Before closing the discussion of Preparatory Explanations, there is one further matter that bears mention. Instructions given in a Preparatory Explanation often have to be repeated during the course of the interview. Either the instructions were not heard or understood, or they were forgotten. Hence, repetition may be required to maintain rapport and to keep the client on the track. For example, if in the Overview stage the client suddenly asks, "Do you think I'll have to pay?", the client will have to be reminded that analysis of legal rights comes later: "Mr. Bryan, I can see you are quite concerned about whether you'll be liable; I understand that concern. (Pause) However, as we discussed, I'm not going to be able to tell you where you stand until we have all the facts. Remember, that's going to take a little time."

We will now review and analyze three hypothetical cases.

Case No. 1:

In this case, based upon an appraisal of the information received during the Preliminary Problem Identification stage, the lawyer has concluded the client does not feel pressed to reveal his story, and may be somewhat uncertain about what will take place during the interview.

Concluding the Preliminary Problem Identification stage:

No. 1–L   So, Mr. Hamlin, the situation is that you've suffered a whiplash as the result of the automobile collision and you want to know whether, under these circumstances, it makes sense to make a claim against the other driver.

No. 2–C   Right, can I recover anything?

No. 3–L   Okay, Mr. Hamlin, what I'm going to have to do first is get your story, including a description of your injuries, and then we can get into the question of how much you might expect to recover. Start in, why don't you, by telling me everything that has happened; just use your own words.

Analysis of Case No. 1 :

Given that in the lawyer's judgment the client was uncertain about what to expect, detailed instructions seemed called for, particularly since the client did not seem to feel an immediate necessity to relate his story. The instructions given, however, are quite shallow.

The client is given no sense that the interview will consist of stages. Nor is he given any idea that after he has provided an Overview, he probably will be subjected to a more probing inquiry before there is any discussion of his rights. Do these omissions perhaps set up false impressions of what will occur? Do these omissions create the potential for breaches in rapport associated with conflicts of expectancies? Moreover, the lawyer's statement omits any explanation of how the client should go about telling his own story. There is no indication the client should proceed chronologically with a step-by-step narration. Doesn't the lawyer's statement leave the client with a fair amount of uncertainty about how he should relate his story?

Case No. 2:

In this case, the lawyer has made an appraisal identical to that in Case No. 1 with one exception. The lawyer believes further legal research may be required at the end of the initial interview because the lawyer is not too familiar with the law which probably covers the client's situation.

Concluding the Preliminary Problem Identification stage:

No. 1–L   So what has happened is that your husband has mortgaged the house to AA Credit Company, and now they are trying to foreclose. What you want to know is whether there is anything that can be done to stop the foreclosure, and you are also quite concerned about what may happen to your relationship with your husband if you try to stop the foreclosure proceedings.

No. 2–C   That's it exactly.

No. 3–L   What I've found to be most helpful in these cases, Ms. Franklin, is that we start out by having you tell me in your own words exactly what has happened. I want you to start at the beginning and go step-by-step telling me in chronological order everything that has happened. Take your time and give me as much detail as you can. When you have finished, I'll go over the notes I'll be taking and ask you some more specific questions to bring out more detail. Hopefully, if I don't interrupt too much, that will help your memory. Of course, you probably won't remember everything, and that's why I'll come back and ask you for some more specific detail. Do you have a fairly good idea of what we'll do?

No. 4–C   Yes, I think I understand.

No. 5–L   Okay, just a couple of other points. When we finish going over the facts, unless the matter turns out to be fairly complicated, and it sounds as though it may, I'll then review with you what your rights probably

Finally, it should be noted the open-ended questioning pattern is in accord with the rapport-building goals of the Overview stage. Since the client is encouraged to speak about what is important to him/her, rapport may well be increased because the lawyer is cast primarily in the role of a listener. Hopefully, adopting this role will produce the reaction that the lawyer is an empathetic person—someone who is willing to sit back and listen to what the client believes to be important. Additionally, since the client is not asked about specific facts, the client is given the freedom to ignore, at least temporarily, matters which for one reason or another the client feels reluctant to discuss. Hopefully, these rapport-building advantages will result in increased client confidence so that later on these threatening topics can be confronted more comfortably.

It usually will not be possible to get an adequately detailed Overview by simply repeating the question, "What happened next?" Everything the client says will not necessarily be clear or comprehensible. From time to time there may be a need to seek clarification. Somewhat narrow questions can be used to obtain necessary clarification. The case of Mr. Kafka is illustrative:

No. 1–L   Okay, Mr. Kafka, what happened next?

No. 2–C   Well, he told me that either he or she would tell my employer about the rent if I didn't stop having those people over.

No. 3–L   When you say "he or she", who is the "she"?

No. 4–C   That's his wife.

No. 5–L   I see. All right, after he told you about possibly calling your employer, what occurred then?

Inquiry No. 3 is a simple demonstration of how narrow questions can be used to clarify what the lawyer does not understand. In examining No. 3, it is important to note the inquiry is limited to clarifying what the client has said; there is no attempt to discuss topics not mentioned by the client.

Clarification, as we use that term, is limited to clarifying vague or ambiguous language, or clarifying the sequence of events which the client has mentioned. "When did that occur, before or after . . .?" We do not mean by the term clarification to suggest it is necessary or appropriate to inquire into reasons or motives for particular actions. Thus, ordinarily it would be inadvisable at the Overview stage to ask questions such as, "Why did you do that?" This kind of interrogation would, of course, do violence to the concept that the client should be left free to set forth only those matters which the client feels comfortable in relating.

In reviewing the previous example, note should also be made of inquiry No. 5. This inquiry is intended to show how, after receiving clarification, the lawyer can attempt to put the client back on the chronological track. Instead of simply asking, "What occurred next?", the lawyer can first attempt to summarize where the client was before the break for clarification. "After he told you about possibly calling your employer, what occurred then?"

In addition to the need for clarification, there will be a need for elaboration. Without the latter, the lawyer may end up with only a very sketchy Overview. The request for elaboration should be confined to the subject currently under discussion; it should not take the client from the chronological track. The request can be made in the form of a relatively open probe. "Tell me a little bit more about that," is the most common form of interrogatory used to elicit elaboration. The question keeps the client focused on the specific incident under discussion and also leaves the client free to decide what details should be added. Consider the following example, again taken from the case involving Mr. Kafka:

No. 6–C   Well, nothing that day, but the next day my boss called me in and said how come I wasn't paying the rent?

No. 7–L   By boss, whom do you mean?

No. 8–C   The personnel manager, not the lady I report to normally.

No. 9–L   Okay, tell me a little bit more about what happened when the personnel manager called you in.

No. 10–C   Well, she said that Mr. Arnold had called and said he was my landlord and that I was two weeks behind in my rent and he hoped something could be done. The manager started asking me a bunch of questions. Finally, I got across my point about why I wasn't paying, and she said OK, not to worry about it. In fact, she said come back if I thought she could help.

No. 11–L   After your conversation with the personnel manager, what happened next?

This example shows both clarification (No. 7) and elaboration (No. 9). No. 9 seems to be an appropriate request for elaboration; there is the use of an open-ended probe calling for the client to expand upon a subject which the client has introduced. As in the previous example, the lawyer then (No. 11) returns the client to the chronological track with a summarizing statement followed by the basic interrogatory of, "What happened next?"

In evaluating the appropriateness of the request for elaboration (No. 9), it should be noted the lawyer refrains from asking narrow questions about subjects not mentioned by the client. Such questions might run the risk of harming rapport. Inappropriate questions would be ones such as: "Did she say what the landlord said about how far you were behind?"; "Did she say whether the landlord mentioned if there had been other incidents of a failure to pay rent?" Moreover, such questions, if continually asked throughout the Overview stage, run the risk of subtracting from the goal of keeping the client's paths of association intact. Pressing for specific detail can cause the client to lose the general chronological train of thought. Also, and quite significantly, pressing for specific detail at this early stage can, and frequently does, cause the lawyer to lose track of where he/she is heading. Such specific probing can cause the lawyer to forget the Overview and start in on specific, and perhaps premature, diagnosis.

Additionally, the lawyer refrains from using further open-ended questions to probe for still more elaboration. Thus, after receiving elaboration in response No. 10, the lawyer does not go on to ask questions such as, "What else was said?" Assume, for example, the facts in No. 10 suggest the possibility of a cross claim on the basis of a debt collection tort such as defamation or invasion of privacy. Is the lawyer's restraint in not obtaining more explanation appropriate? Probably, but there is no easy answer to this question. Continually asking for more and more elaboration, even in the form of fairly open-ended questions, will at some point start to undercut the informational and rapport goals of the Overview stage. The undercutting, when it begins, will usually not be noticeable. For example, it will not be easy to determine when the client begins to feel less free to provide the information the client believes to be important. Given that it will not be easy to determine when undercutting begins, and given our experience that it is very easy for the lawyer to lose the chronological tract, we recommend that probes for elaboration be used sparingly. Remember, the purpose of the Theory Development and Verification stage is to come back and gather the necessary detail.

Using Active Listening

During the Overview stage, it usually will be necessary to employ techniques in addition to questioning. The use of active listening, geared toward reflecting the client's past and present feelings, will usually be *essential*. Without the effective use of this technique, it is quite likely that the lawyer will be perceived as rather cold and unfeeling.

There are no rules for when or how often active listening should be integrated into the interview. The important point is that reflection of feelings should be an integral part of the lawyer-client dialogue; active listening cannot be viewed as a response which is somehow tacked on at the beginning or the end. Active listening responses should punctuate the questioning pattern as the client's feelings come to the surface. The responses should be delivered as a natural part of the dialogue and the questioning then resumed. Think about the previous example drawn from the Kafka case, (see p. 74 infra). Are there instances where an active listening response might have been useful? Contrast the lawyer's responses in the previous example with the following:

No. 11–L   After your conversation with the personnel manager, what happened next?

No. 12–C   That night when I got home, I went over to Arnold's to give him a piece of my mind.

No. 13–L   I can imagine you were quite angry.

No. 14–C   I was fuming; I told him if he ever called my employer again, I'd fix him good. He kept saying he was only trying to help. Bullshit.

No. 15–L   I can see you're still angry; tell me, what happened then?

After reviewing these responses (No. 13, past feelings, and No. 15, present feelings), go back and look at the client's response No. 10 in the previous example. What feelings might the client have been experiencing at that point? How could an active listening response have been integrated into the questioning pattern?

In closing these comments on active listening, we should point out that the lawyer need not, and indeed should not, reflect feelings every time they arise. Reflecting every feeling would unduly prolong the interview. Feelings must be recognized, however, with sufficient frequency to build rapport. How much reflection of feelings will be required will vary from client to client. The appropriate use of this skill ultimately comes down to a matter of judgment. The development of this judgment can come only through using this skill in actual interviews.

Providing "Recognition"

In addition to using the active listening technique to build rapport, there is a further technique which can be brought into play. This technique, which can be used throughout the interview, attempts to utilize the facilitator of "recognition." By telling the client that he/she is doing a good job in providing information, the lawyer gives the client recognition. Again, the Kafka case provides an illustration.

No. 16–C   Arnold started to yell, saying I couldn't stay another day. He told me to get out. He was screaming.

No. 17–L   What happened then?

No. 18–C   I went to my apartment and forgot about it. About 9:30 p.m., the phone rang. I answered and there was no response.

No. 19–L   Go on, Mr. Kafka, you're doing just fine; tell me what occurred next.

No. 19 illustrates how the facilitator of recognition is integrated into the fluid process of the interview. The appropriate frequency of use of recognition again rests with the lawyer's discretion. Other phrases that can be used to provide recognition include the following:

"You're giving me helpful information."

"The way you are going step-by-step is very helpful."

"You're being very thorough; that's most helpful."

Taking Notes

As indicated earlier, some note-taking is essential; without it, there is a substantial likelihood that important information will be forgotten. The most difficult part of note-taking is deciding what to write down. If nearly everything the client said were written down, it would be virtually impossible to keep the interview moving at a reasonable pace, or to maintain adequate eye contact. On the other hand, if only that which immediately strikes the lawyer as important is written down, there is a real danger of omission. Matters which initially seem irrelevant, and which become meaningful only in the light of subsequent information, may become lost.

The method of note-taking we suggest is the following: During the Overview stage, as each new topic along the chronological spectrum is introduced, jot down a key word(s) which will serve as a reminder of the topic's existence. Do the same for specific facts which seem important. If the words jotted down can be the same as those used by the client, so much the better. During the Theory Development and Verification stage, these words can be used to reintroduce the subjects which need a more detailed investigation. The use of the client's own words will demonstrate the lawyer was listening, and also may help stimulate the client's memory. During the Theory Development and Verification stage, try to use the same procedure of writing down key words or phrases that will serve as a reminder of the significant facts. Recognize, moreover, that at the Theory Development and Verification stage the note-taking will often have to be more copious since more detail is being elicited, and since the lawyer is more certain that salient information is being obtained. In jotting down notes, get in the habit of leaving a fair amount of space between the entries; this procedure tends to provide more freedom to write without looking at or concentrating on the page.

After the client has left the office, while the meaning of the key words is still fresh, prepare a detailed memorandum of the facts. This follow-up procedure is *essential* if one is going to take notes in the abbreviated form suggested here. The failure to prepare such a memorandum will, after a very short passage of time, leave the lawyer without a detailed description of the facts.

We will illustrate the suggested form of note-taking for the Overview stage through an example. The example involves a client accused of being an accomplice in a liquor store robbery. The other defendants are Bill Jones, Charlie Fingers, and Ralph Dill.

Interview	Notes
Lawyer: Tell me, from the beginning, what happened that night.	
Client: We were sitting around at Charlie's. I guess I got there about 6:00 p. m. Bill was already there. We had some beer and Charlie's wife made some dinner. It was real good. After dinner we had some more beer.	Charlie's, 6:00 p. m. Charlie's wife. Beer
Lawyer: I see.	
Client: Bill kept asking Charlie whether Ralph had called. Charlie kept saying no, it probably wouldn't be today. I didn't pay much attention. I hardly know Ralph.	Had Ralph called?
Lawyer: You're doing fine. Tell me more.	
Client: We had the TV on, watching the fights. We were talking about playing poker. Charlie's wife came in and said the phone was for Bill. Bill came back and told Charlie that Ralph wanted to talk with him. Charlie answered. He came back and said he and Bill were going to pick up Ralph, buy some booze, and come back. He said I should set up for poker.	TV Ralph called Pick up Ralph.

The note-taking in this example is fairly sparse; however, it is probably adequate for the Overview stage. The notes preserve the basic chronological Overview and story. In so doing, the notes provide a basis for a subsequent memorandum on the general facts, and also a reference point for any detailed topic exploration which the lawyer might desire to undertake in the Theory Development and Verification stage. Additionally, the notes pick up potentially significant facts, such as possible witnesses—Charlie's wife—and a possible defense regarding intoxication—beer.

In concluding this discussion of note-taking, mention should be made of the practice of electronically recording the interview. Assuming the client's consent is obtained,[3] the procedure of recording the interview can be a useful supplement to note-taking. Recording, however, usually cannot serve as a substitute for written notes. As indicated above, written notes are useful in serving as a reminder of additional topics to be explored during the course of the interview.

If a tape recording is used to supplement note-taking, the recording can be very useful in preparing a comprehensive memorandum of the facts at the conclusion of the interview. By reviewing the recording and the written notes, the lawyer can usually prepare a very complete outline of all relevant information. The practice of using a recording in this fashion is, of course, time-consuming since it usually requires the lawyer to re-listen to much of the interview. Some lawyers attempt to cut down on the time required for this kind of review by obtaining a verbatim transcript of the interview. Though this practice will often save a lawyer's time, the practice is usually very expensive, since it commonly requires from three to twelve hours to transcribe each hour of recorded dialogue.[4] Moreover, it usually will not be sufficient to merely have a transcript of the entire interview. If the facts gathered during the interview are to be readily accessible, it will generally be necessary to review the transcript and prepare an organized outline of the facts. Such an outline will permit the facts to be subsequently reviewed without the necessity of taking the time to pour through various parts of a lengthy transcript to find a specific fact.

Problem Areas

Before concluding this discussion, we will briefly mention some common difficulties which arise during the Overview stage.

1. The Phrase "At the Beginning:"

One difficulty which some clients experience is determining where to begin. The phrase, "at the beginning," is fairly vague. Where does a transaction really start? Does an automobile accident case commence when the client starts on the trip or when the client nears the collision point? Perhaps the case starts the night before, or even earlier, with the onset of some medical problem.

How can the lawyer deal with the client who recognizes the ambiguity in the term "beginning" and says, "What do you mean, beginning; where do I start?" Additionally, what can the lawyer do when the lawyer suspects the client has not commenced at the "true" beginning? Finally, in general, how can the lawyer be assured that the true beginning point has been identified?

3. Recording an interview without the client's permission could constitute a crime. See West's Ann.Cal.Pen.Code § 632; People v. Belkota, 50 A.D.2d 118, 377 N.Y.S.2d 321 (1973); People v. Patrick, 46 Mich.App. 678, 208 N.W.2d 604 (1973).

4. R. L. Gorden, Interviewing Strategy, Techniques and Tactics 175–176 (1969).

When the client says words to the effect of "Where shall I start?", the simplest approach may be to tell the client to commence where the client believes the problem begins. "Start wherever you feel the story begins." This kind of instruction permits the client to begin where the client feels comfortable.

With respect to the situation where the lawyer senses the client has begun in the middle, the same freedom must be permitted. Perhaps the client has misunderstood the instructions, or perhaps the client is consciously trying to avoid some threatening subjects. Criminal defendants, for example, often start by discussing their arrest rather than with the facts leading up to the arrest. The latter may be quite case-threatening. When the client has finished going from the middle up to the present, the lawyer has several options. Among these are: (1) taking the client back to the beginning and finishing the Overview; (2) conducting a Theory Development and Verification interview on that part of the story which has been obtained, and then going back for the remainder of the Overview, and (3) adjourning the interview and scheduling another appointment. Which option the lawyer chooses should be guided primarily by the lawyer's judgment of which tack will best promote client rapport.

With respect to being satisfied the client has started at the beginning, even though there is no suspicion that the client has not, it is almost always important to ask about the possibility of an earlier beginning. The inquiry can be conducted by reminding the client where he/she began and then asking the client through a very open-ended question to think carefully about whether or not there were any other incidents of significance which preceded the identified beginning. Consider this example:

> "Ms. Keely, you've really given me a great deal of helpful information. Before we go back and get some more detail, let me ask you this. You started out by describing what had happened to you on the evening preceding the accident. Think carefully for a moment; is there anything else at all that occurred before that evening which in any way relates to the accident?"

2.   A Quick Overview:

Sometimes, the client will fail to hear, or understand, the instructions to proceed with a step-by-step chronological Overview. As a consequence, the client will provide an Overview which describes the basic transaction from the beginning to the present in a very few sentences. When the client provides this kind of quick Overview, it can be helpful for the lawyer to repeat the instructions about what is expected of the client, and then start again. Consider this example:

> No. 1–L   Okay, Mr. Thomas, start from the beginning and tell me in your own words, step-by-step, everything that happened.

No. 2–C   Well, we were headed East on 43rd, when all of a sudden this car came out of a driveway. I tried to swerve, but he hit us. I was in the hospital about a week and off work for four. Now he is suing me.

No. 3–L   You're quite angry and I understand that. (Pause) What would help me, Mr. Thomas, is if you could start again and tell me, one step at a time, each and everything that has happened. Try not to leave out anything. I need details like what else happened before the collision, and everything that happened afterwards Remember, you were there and I wasn't. I need you to give me the picture. Take your time and go ahead slowly, one step at a time. . . .

Conclusion

We will conclude this discussion of the Overview stage by reviewing three hypothetical cases. In each instance, it will be assumed that the process of Preliminary Problem Identification and the Preparatory Explanation have been completed.

Case No. 1:

No. 1–L   Tell me now, step-by-step, everything that has occurred. Start at the beginning.

No. 2–C   Well, about four months ago, I lost my job. At first I wasn't worried, but pretty soon my savings started to disappear. I tried to find another job, but I couldn't. Two months ago, in June, I missed the payment on my second mortgage.

No. 3–L   Okay. What happened next?

No. 4–C   Well, I got this letter from the mortgage company. They talked about foreclosing.

No. 5–L   Do you have the letter?

No. 6–C   Yes.

No. 7–L   Can I see it?

No. 8–C   Sure, here it is.

No. 9–L   Did you contact them about this letter?

No. 10–C   Yes, later I did.

No. 11–L   Go ahead, tell me about that.

No. 12–C   I called up and said I'd lost my job, and asked if I could have more time.

No. 13–L   Whom did you speak to?

No. 14–C   I talked with a couple of people, a Mr. Casper and a Ms. Howl. They said under the law I had time and not to worry.

No. 15–L   That must have made you feel better.

No. 16–C   It did. But a few days ago I got this notice; it says they are foreclosing.

No. 17–L   When exactly did you get this notice?

No. 18–C   Last week.

No. 19–L   What happened when you received it?

Analysis of Case No. 1 :

This hypothetical is intended primarily to illustrate the principal ways in which chronological gaps creep into the Overview. Examine first response No. 4 and question No. 9; doesn't No. 9 potentially start to pull the client away from the chronological track by diverting the client's attention from the point of the receipt of the letter to the point of contact? Isn't it quite possible that other significant events, such as the arrival of further letters, occurred between these two points? Assuming the lawyer could not resist the temptation to look at the letter, shouldn't inquiry No. 9 have been something to the effect of, "After you received this letter, what occurred then?"

Examine next No. 14 through No. 16. Isn't it possible the client has skipped events that occurred between the point in time in No. 14, the telephone call, and the point in time in No. 16, the receipt of the notice? Shouldn't the lawyer, therefore, have gone back in either No. 17 or No. 19 and asked a question similar to the following: "Let's go back for a moment to your conversation with the mortgage people. What is the very next thing that occurred after this conversation?"

In the Overview stage, chronological gaps can occur either as the result of the lawyer drawing the client "off side," or as a result of the lawyer's failure to note the client may have followed a path of association which skipped some territory. Enormous concentration is required if the lawyer is to be effective in preventing chronological gaps. The lawyer must constantly keep in mind the goal of obtaining a step-by-step narrative; the lawyer's instructions to the client must be consciously in the front of the lawyer's mind. This goal of concentration on the step-by-step narrative is easily broken if the lawyer lets himself/herself become drawn into the search for detail. Question No.'s 5, 7, 13, and 17 are intended to show this kind of unnecessary search for detail. These questions, while not calling for undue elaboration or clarification, take the lawyer's mind unnecessarily from the goal of a step-by-step narrative. The questions are unnecessary in that they ask for specific detail which could easily be gotten during the Theory Development and Verification stage. They call for information which is not needed for a general understanding of the story, and they are unlikely to produce the kind of additional client clues that can be obtained from questions or directive probes such as, "Tell me a little bit more about that."

Finally, note should also be made of No. 15, which illustrates the integration of an active listening response geared to reflect past feelings. Although the response may have triggered a chronological gap, the response nonetheless seems appropriate. The gap, if it exists, could easily have been covered by an inquiry that put the client back on the chronological track.

Case No. 2:

No. 1–L   Start at the beginning now and tell me, step-by-step, everything that has happened.

No. 2–C   About six months before I got fired, this friend of mine came to me and said she was being fired for insubordination.

No. 3–L   Tell me a little more about that.

No. 4–C   She said she had gotten into an argument with the shift boss who called her a "Mex," and that she was really being fired for reporting him. She was angry and asked me to help her.

No. 5–L   I see.

No. 6–C   Anyhow, I went to the shift boss and asked what was happening.

No. 7–L   Between her request and your going to the shift boss, did anything else occur?

No. 8–C   Yes, we formed a committee to help Monica, and I was elected as the representative to see the shift boss.

No. 9–L   Okay, what you're telling me is very helpful. After you were elected, what happened then?

No. 10–C   I went to see him. He told me Monica was always demanding too much and not following orders. He said he was sorry for calling her a "Mex," and that he really had nothing against Mexicans. I told him we had a committee, and we intended to protect Monica. He said there was nothing he could do; so, I went to see the personnel manager.

No. 11–L   After you saw the shift boss and before you saw the personnel manager, did you do anything else?

No. 12–C   No.

No. 13–L   What happened when you saw the personnel manager?

No. 14–C   Not much. We just discussed the situation.

No. 15–L   Tell me what you can remember of the conversation.

No. 16–C   Not really very much, except that she said she would check with the shift boss and get back to me.

No. 17–L I take it your conversation with the personnel manager left you somewhat frustrated.

No. 18–C It really did.

No. 19–L What occurred next?

No. 20–C Well, a meeting was set up to discuss the whole thing.

No. 21–L Who was to be at the meeting?

No. 22–C Monica, myself, the shift boss, Ms. Dawson from personnel, and Donald Furnish, an Anglo on our committee.

No. 23–L Did everyone come to the meeting?

No. 24–C Yes.

No. 25–L What happened?

No. 26–C We just discussed how Monica was doing and how her complaints were proper. The shift boss said he called her a "Mex" because she often used that term in referring to Chicanos. I got real angry and called him a liar.

No. 27–L I can understand how you would be angry. Has he ever used the term "Mex" in talking to you?

Analysis of Case No. 2 :

No.'s 1 through 20 illustrate, with one exception (No. 11), the approach we believe should be followed in conducting the Overview. No. 7 illustrates a tack that can be employed when the lawyer senses there may be a chronological gap. No. 11, however, illustrates how one must be careful to use open-ended questions when seeking information about possible chronological gaps. The question merely asks, did "you do" anything else during that time period; it does not use the more open-ended form of "Did anything else occur during that time period?"

No. 3 and No. 15 illustrate open-ended requests for elaboration. As framed, they ask for further client clues. Contrast these requests with the specific elaboration attempts in No. 21 and No. 23.

The beginning of No. 9 illustrates the use of "recognition" and No. 17 illustrates the integration of active listening skills.

Finally, there is No. 27. The first sentence illustrates once again the proper use of the active listening technique. However, what about the question in the second sentence; isn't this the kind of inquiry that really takes the client, and potentially the lawyer, away from the chronological track?

Case No. 3:

No. 1–L Go step-by-step from the beginning, Ms. Jong, and tell me everything that has happened.

No. 2–C   Two police came to the door and asked if they could come in. I asked why, and they said they had a report of child neglect. I said I had done nothing wrong, and they were welcome to come in and look around.

No. 3–L   Go ahead.

No. 4–C   Well, they looked in all the rooms and asked if they could check the kitchen. I said sure. They went into the kitchen and came back and asked why there was so little food. I said I had been ill, but that I was going to the market soon. Then they said they would have to take the baby and that my daughter Sylvia had already been detained at school.

No. 5–L   You must have been stunned.

No. 6–C   I was. I began crying and saying "You can't do that." I was almost hysterical.

No. 7–L   I can understand how you would be. Tell me, what else happened when the police were there?

No. 8–C   Not much. They told me I'd hear about a court date in a couple of days.

No. 9–L   Okay, what happened then?

No. 10–C   I ran over to my sister's. We tried to find a lawyer but we couldn't. She finally took me home, and that's when I found this telegram from the Welfare department.

No. 11–L   Do you have the telegram?

No. 12–C   Yes, but not with me.

No. 13–L   What did the telegram say?

No. 14–C   Just whom to call about my children.

No. 15–L   Did you call?

No. 16–C   Sure, and they said court would be tomorrow.

No. 17–L   What happened after the call?

Analysis of Case No. 3 :

Of No.'s 3, 7, 9, 13, and 17, which serve the function of asking the client to continue the narration, and which serve the function of elaboration or clarification? Are No. 5 and No. 7 geared toward reflecting past or present feelings? At what point toward the end of the dialogue does the lawyer perhaps cause a chronological gap?

Theory Development and Verification Stage

We will begin this section with a discussion of the planning considerations to be undertaken at the conclusion of the Overview stage prior to actually commencing the Theory Development and Verification stage. Then we will examine the specific interviewing techniques to be employed in conducting this stage.

Determining What Theories are Possibly Applicable

The objective of the Theory Development and Verification Stage is to conduct an investigation which will reveal what legal theories can reasonably be relied upon to provide the client with legal relief. To accomplish this objective, the lawyer should undertake at least two tasks. There should be an endeavor to determine (1) what legal theories are possibly applicable, and (2) which of the possibly applicable theories are potentially viable.

Why the distinction between possibly applicable and potentially viable? As noted earlier, one of the major defects that occur in legal interviewing is premature diagnosis. The lawyer recognizes facts which suggest the possible applicability of one or two theories, investigates these, and concludes the inquiry. The lawyer fails to look into theories other than those that immediately "leap to mind." If the lawyer can learn to think of Theory Development and Verification as requiring, first of all, an effort to see how many theories might be applicable before trying to determine which are viable, then the likelihood of premature diagnosis may be reduced.

Determining what theories may possibly be applicable requires a very specific focus. At the conclusion of the Overview stage, the lawyer must consciously ask, "Given these facts and what I know of the client's desires and concerns, what legal theories, *regardless of how weak or strong they may now appear,* might entitle my client to the relief he/she seeks?" Certain causes of action or defenses will perhaps be obvious, but the lawyer's mental effort must be geared toward the development of the maximum number of possibilities. Critical to the success of this endeavor will be the lawyer's knowledge of the substantive law; the more substantive knowledge the lawyer has in his/her head, the more successful the lawyer will be in executing this task.

What about the situation where the lawyer, for one reason or another, has little or no substantive knowledge of the legal theories that are potentially relevant? [5] Where the lawyer lacks adequate substantive knowledge the available choices seem to be: (1) adjourn the meeting and research the law; (2) go back through the Overview to learn more detail about the story in general since the additional detail might aid subsequent research; (3) refer the client to another lawyer or associate counsel who is familiar with the area. Which option the lawyer should choose is dependent upon many factors, but time will not permit an analysis of these factors here. What must be

---

5. By our definition, a lawyer has substantive knowledge of a legal theory when the lawyer has general familiarity with the basic substantive elements of the cause of action or defense involved.

noted, however, is that if the client appears to need immediate help, the latter choice will probably be called for.[6]

If the lawyer has knowledge of some, but only a limited number of, causes of action or defenses, an additional option is available. The choice is: (4) investigate the theories with which the lawyer has familiarity, deferring until later, investigation of those theories which require legal research. Indeed, this choice might be combined with option number 2, a general review for more facts. Again, time will not permit an analysis of what factors should be considered in reaching a decision. What is important to remember is that the decision should be made in the client's best interest. At the conclusion of this chapter, we will discuss how the lawyer can adjourn the interview when time is needed for more research.

Finally, it must be remembered that any diagnosis of which theories are possibly applicable must be considered tentative. During the Theory Development and Verification stage, the lawyer may come upon information suggesting that the initial theories are invalid, but additional legal theories are possibly applicable.

We will conclude this section by presenting an abridged Overview. As you read the Overview, try to determine what legal theories are possibly applicable. The interview picks up at the conclusion of the Preliminary Problem Identification stage.

L. So, the situation is that you're being sued by a collection agency to collect a medical bill that you don't feel you owe. In addition to not wanting to pay the bill, you want to stop the collection agency from harassing you.

C. That's right.

(The lawyer makes a Preparatory Explanation and then goes on with the interview.)

L. Okay, Mr. Little, why don't you start at the beginning and in your own words tell me, step-by-step, everything that has happened.

C. Well, about 14 months ago, I was playing in a company softball game and I broke the little finger of my right hand. Actually, it was a lot more complicated than that, but the only real problem was with my right hand.

L. Tell me what happened.

C. I was playing second base, and this guy didn't try to slide. He just rammed into me and I was knocked out. I was taken to a nearby hospital where I stayed overnight. But the only lasting injury was to my little finger.

---

6. A lawyer should not undertake to represent a client where the lawyer's effort to become familiar with the substantive law may cause unreasonable delay or expense. ABA Code of Professional Responsibility EC 6–3. See also DR 6–101(A)(1).

L. Tell me what happened at the hospital.

C. They checked me out for a concussion and broken bones. There was no concussion, and the only broken bone was in the little finger of my right hand. I don't remember too much about it; I remember them putting a splint on my finger.

L. You're giving me just the kind of information I need. Go ahead, what happened then?

C. Well, the next morning I left the hospital, and in a couple of weeks everything was back to normal, except for the finger. I decided to go to my own doctor. She X-rayed me and said the finger needed to be reset. She gave me a local and put a cast on my right hand.

L. I imagine having to have your finger reset was pretty frustrating.

C. It really made me angry.

L. What is your doctor's name?

C. Sharon Wexler.

L. After your finger was reset, what occurred?

C. Eight weeks later, the cast came off and I thought that pretty soon I'd get the full use of my finger, but I haven't.

L. That must make you pretty angry.

C. It does, and that's why I don't think I should have to pay the hospital.

L. I can understand your feelings. Tell me, between the time the cast was put on and the time it was taken off, did anything else occur that is related to the present situation?

C. No.

L. What happened after the cast came off?

C. Nothing much. Doctor Wexler said that within six weeks everything should be back to normal, but I've still got a problem bending the finger.

L. Well, after the cast came off, what occurred next?

C. About that time, I got a call from the hospital asking why I wasn't paying. I told them why.

L. When was that call?

C. About four weeks after the cast came off.

L. What happened after that call?

C. Nothing until recently; then this collection agency started to hassle me.

L. Think carefully now, after you talked with the hospital, what is the next thing that occurred?

C. Well, about a month or two later, around September, I went back to Doctor Wexler. She examined my finger, and said she was afraid that I may have some permanent loss of movement. She said it might take another year to tell for sure.

L. I guess that must have been frustrating news. (Pause) What happened after you saw Doctor Wexler?

C. Nothing, until I got this letter from the collection agency saying they wanted $450.00.

L. When did you get that letter?

C. About a month ago.

L. What happened then?

C. I called them up and told them I wasn't going to pay. They said if I didn't pay, they would sue me. I told them to sue, because I wasn't paying.

L. What occurred next?

C. The collection people called the controller where I work and asked about me. They said I wasn't paying my bills and wanted to know if the company could talk with me. They said I owed money to people other than the hospital. I don't owe anybody money.

L. How do you know about the call?

C. The controller called me in and told me about it. We discussed the situation and she understands why I'm not paying.

L. When did this conversation take place?

C. About three or four days after I talked with the collection agency.

L. After your conversation with the controller, what happened?

C. The controller called the collection agency and told them there was nothing the company could do, but yesterday I got those papers saying I'm being sued.

Assume the Overview is now complete. What basic causes of action and defenses are possibly applicable in this case? List them; you should be able to see at least five potential causes of action and one potential defense.[7] If you commenced Theory Verification with only two or three causes of action in mind, you would have been guilty of premature diagnosis.

7. The basic causes of action we see as possibly applicable are: (1) workman's compensation, (2) battery against the base runner, (3) malpractice against the hospital and doctor who initially set the finger, (4) invasion of privacy against the caller and the collection agency, and (5) slander against the caller and the collection agency. On the defense side, isn't there a potential problem with the statute of limitations?

Determining What Subjects to Investigate and in What Order to Proceed

To investigate the potential viability of particular legal theories the lawyer should, before commencing the Theory Development and Verification stage, consider a number of matters in addition to what substantive elements must be investigated. Among the matters bearing consideration are the following: (1) what specific topics should be investigated in order to explore each of the relevant substantive elements?; (2) to what extent should the questioning delve into the existence of credible proof to establish the necessary elements—e. g., witnesses, documents, etc.?; and (3) in what order should potential causes of action and defenses be examined?

In an initial interview, there is not going to be a great deal of time to consider these questions; yet their consideration can be quite important. If the lawyer does not proceed to conduct the examination in a systematic manner, there are likely to be omissions. Additionally, the issue of the order of the inquiry may be important with respect to the continued development of client rapport. If the lawyer takes up legal theories in an order which is convenient to the lawyer —e. g., more familiar with the law; ease of proof, etc.—the choice may be at odds with the client's comfort. The Theory Development and Verification stage may be a great deal more comfortable for the client if it begins with subjects that are familiar to the client, or subjects which, from a lay point of view, seem to put the whole investigation in the most logical order. If the lawyer's order of investigation conflicts with what makes the client comfortable, rapport may suffer.

To deal with the problem of possible omissions, many lawyers employ legal checklists. The types of checklists, even as they relate to the same substantive area, vary greatly and so far as we know have never been systematically studied to determine their effectiveness. The lists are undoubtedly an aid, but should be used judiciously. Relying solely on checklists and slavishly following their already determined outlines can cause problems.

The use of checklists often unintentionally sets the order of the inquiry. The lawyer starts at the top of the list and works to the bottom. In light of the specific facts of the case, the order may be illogical, or may not coincide with the client's sense of what is important. Further, although the lists typically enumerate the standard causes of action or defenses to be investigated, the lists are sometimes incomplete. They fail to include such matters as the unusual cause of action or defense, or in respect to any given cause of action or defense, they fail to list exceptions to substantive standard elements. When such lists are relied upon as an exclusive checklist, without independent research of the law, important substantive areas may not be investigated.

Moreover, and most significantly, when the checklists go beyond the enumeration of standard elements, as they usually do, they often set forth specific facts or topics to look for in investigating particular substantive elements. When this kind of listing occurs, these facts are often the only ones that are gone into. The case tends to be investigated in a routine manner, and important complexities are often overlooked. As a consequence, the investigation may be too shallow.

At present, we have no definitive ideas about how detailed an effective checklist should be; we hope that in the near future research will emerge on this point. To the extent lawyers do use formal checklists, we hope they will keep in mind the problems we have delineated here. We hope, in particular, lawyers will develop the kind of flexibility which will permit them to adopt an order of examination that seems tailored to the needs of the individual client, and a questioning pattern which allows them to reach for facts other than those delineated in the checklist.

In closing this discussion of planning for the Theory Development and Verification stage, we wish to emphasize two points. If a lawyer attempts an inquiry without a formal checklist, the lawyer probably should not commence the actual examination without at least making a list of the causes of action and basic substantive elements to be investigated. Secondly, we wish to emphasize that whether or not the lawyer uses a formal or an informal checklist, the lawyer should consider, if only for a brief moment, the question of what order the investigation should follow to best serve the client's needs for rapport as well as the lawyer's needs for substantive information.

When a lawyer commences the Theory Development and Verification stage with only a minimal knowledge of the law and an informal checklist, an additional interview will almost always be necessary. *At a minimum*, the lawyer should, after concluding the interview, research the applicable law and review the interview notes and informal checklist to make sure that all substantive points have been completely covered. Additionally, consideration should be given to the question of whether there has been a complete investigation of the issue of credible proof. Where any deficiencies are noted, a new interview should be arranged.

To conclude this section, consider the following questions with respect to the previous hypothetical involving Mr. Little, the client with the collection agency problem. Assume that under local law a defendant has thirty days to file an answer.

(1) Which of the possibly applicable legal theories would you investigate now and which, if any, would you defer for investigation at another time? Why?

(2) In regard to each legal theory to be investigated now, what would your checklist include in addition to the legal elements?

(3) In what order would you investigate the legal theories? Why?

There are no simple answers to these questions, but their consideration is very important.

Questioning: The T-Funnel Sequence

To conduct a thorough inquiry, we suggest that lawyers learn to examine topics through the use of a questioning pattern we have labeled the *T-Funnel*. With respect to many subjects such as the substance of a conversation, the lawyer may have some idea of what was said. On the other hand, the lawyer often will not have thought of all the possible areas of discussion. The T-Funnel pattern explores a topic by employing a series of open-ended questions at the beginning. These questions are used to get at the facts the client recalls. When these questions are no longer productive, the lawyer employs a series of narrow questions. The latter are used to ask about those possibilities the lawyer has thought of but which were not mentioned in response to the open-ended questions. In using the T-Funnel, the lawyer should make more than one attempt to determine what the client can remember before narrowing down and attempting to get a picture of the subject by asking about specific items.

In discussing the advantages and disadvantages of open-ended and narrow questions, we pointed out that people will sometimes remember more if left to narrate their story. Unstructured narration leaves paths of association intact and by so doing may stimulate memory. Narrow questions may be harmful because they adopt a narrow focus and usually jump from subject to subject, thereby interrupting paths of association. On the other hand, we noted that there are some cases where narrow questions will prove advantageous. Some facts will be remembered only if specifically brought to a client's attention. This specific focus is usually achieved through narrow questions. When the open-ended question is unsuccessful in stimulating memory, the narrow question will often produce a response similar to the following: "Now that you mention prior ownership, I guess that he did say something about the previous owner." In sum, the T-Funnel sequence has two major advantages. First, it allows both the client and the lawyer to exhaust their respective senses of relevancy. Second, it provides for wide memory stimulation by exhausting both recall and recognition.

We will illustrate the T-Funnel questioning pattern through an example. Assume that a lawyer is investigating the possibility that the client may have a cause of action to recover damages for fraud in the sale of a used car. Assume further that the lawyer now wishes to determine what *representations were made* by the salesperson about the car.

No. 1–L   Tell me everything he said about the car.

No. 2–C   He said it was in good condition, had new tires, and that it had always been serviced regularly at their shop.

No. 3–L   What else did he say?

No. 4–C   That's about it; he said there had been just one previous owner.

No. 5–L   Okay, he mentioned the condition, the tires, the one owner, the regular service; what else did he tell you?

No. 6–C   That's all.

No. 7–L   I know it's difficult to remember, but it's really important to your case that you try. Go back in your mind's eye. Try to picture yourself there with the salesman. Think very carefully, what else did he say?

No. 8–C   He said the car had new tires, not because of a lot of mileage, but because the prior owner had just let it sit around a lot; I think he said it had only 23,000 miles.

No. 9–L   Okay, that's helpful. What else did he say?

No. 10–C   That's all, really.

No. 11–L   Did he say anything about the engine?

No. 12–C   Sure, when he was talking about the car being in good condition. He said the engine has just been tuned up and there were new spark plugs and something else.

No. 13–L   New points?

No. 14–C   Yes, that's it.

No. 15–L   Did he say anything about the transmission?

No. 16–C   No.

No. 17–L   Did he say anything about the heating or radiator?

No. 18–C   No.

No. 19–L   Did he say anything about gas mileage?

No. 20–C   He said it got good mileage, but he didn't say how much.

No. 21–L   Did he say anything about prior accidents?

No. 22–C   No.

Inquiries No. 1 through No. 9 illustrate the open questions used at the beginning; in terms of the T-concept, they constitute the horizontal crossbar of the T. The balance of the inquiries illustrate questioning on specific possibilities thought of by the lawyer. In terms of the T-concept, these questions illustrate the more specific focus which is adopted when the questioning drops into the vertical and hence narrower stem of the T.

The example also illustrates several other matters of technique in addition to the combined use of open-ended and narrow questions. Only when one understands these additional techniques can one really comprehend the potential efficacy of the T-Funnel sequence. Of all the inquiries, No. 7 is perhaps the most significant.

> "I know it's difficult to remember, but it's really important to your case that you try. Go back in your mind's eye. Try to picture yourself there with the salesman. Think very carefully, what else did he say?"

In No. 6, the client implies he cannot remember anything else; open-ended questions appear to be no longer productive. The lawyer, however, does not simply accept the implicit assertion that the client can remember nothing else. Moreover, in rejecting the implicit assertion, the lawyer does not immediately move to his/her own list of possibilities. No. 7, like its predecessors, is an open-ended question. To keep the questioning going in an open form, the lawyer does several things. First, the lawyer empathizes with the client's difficulty —"I know it's difficult to remember." However, after so doing, the lawyer goes on to hold out potential reward for the client if he tries once again to remember—"but it's really important to your case that you try." In short, after using the facilitator of "empathetic understanding," the lawyer brings in the facilitator of "reward." Next, the lawyer instructs the client on how to go about trying to remember—"Go back in your mind's eye. Try to picture yourself there with the salesman." The lawyer realizes that some people may recall more if they can actually picture themselves at the scene. The lawyer then instructs the client to think carefully about the matter and then asks, "What else did he say?" Note the lawyer does not ask, "Did he say anything else?" The latter would imply that the lawyer would be satisfied with an answer which concluded that nothing else was said. The form "What else was said?", however, implies the lawyer believes that other things must have been said and, hopefully as a consequence, causes the client to adopt an attitude that it is incumbent upon the client to try to recall these additional matters.

The last instruction, "think carefully," and the question "what else?", represent an attempt to bring into play the facilitator of "expectancy." Presumably, the lawyer is in a dominant role position in relation to the client; therefore, when the lawyer instructs the client on how to proceed and uses a question form which suggests that other things might have been said, the lawyer hopefully motivates the client to devote additional energy toward searching his/her memory. It has been our experience that using this technique of pressing the client to think harder is frequently successful in motivating the client to go back and put still greater effort into searching his/her memory. The technique is, therefore, one which we believe should be regularly employed when attempting to develop complete information about topics of substantial importance.

As a note of caution, however, we would add that the lawyer should be willing, after pressing the client once or twice, to accept the client's response, "Nothing else happened." If the lawyer continues to press, the client may be motivated to simply "fill in" what he/she thinks the lawyer expects. Further, the lawyer should be careful to state the narrow questions in a neutral, rather than a leading, manner. A question such as, "Did he say anything about the transmission?", can be stated with the kind of voice inflection which suggests a "yes" answer is appropriate.

Inquiry No. 5 also bears individual examination.

"Okay, he mentioned the condition, the tires, the one owner, the regular service; what else did he tell you?"

Here the lawyer does not merely ask "What else?" Rather, the lawyer summarizes the information that has been revealed thus far before making further inquiry. The summary is an active listening response geared to reflect content. It not only lets the client know the lawyer has heard and understood what has been said, but it also helps the client keep track of what has been mentioned thus far. Hopefully, the conveying of this information will free the client to think about additional data.

Finally, it is extremely important to note that throughout the entire questioning pattern the lawyer stays with the original topic— what did the salesperson say about the car. Though the client at various times mentions specific things that were said about the car (No.'s 2, 4, 8, 12, 14), the lawyer never becomes sidetracked into further exploration of exactly what was said about these specific items. Thus, though in No. 4 the client mentions a representation about a previous owner, the lawyer does not move from the initial topic of "everything said about the car" into the narrower topic of "everything said about the previous owner." Rather, the lawyer simply jots down the specific details such as "one previous owner," and reserves examination of this subject for a later time.

In our judgment, the ability to have the presence of mind to exhaust the original topic before turning to the more specific topic is frequently essential for a thorough examination. If this ability is not developed, the lawyer will soon become so sidetracked that he/she may forget to return to the original topic. Of course, some sidetracking will inevitably occur; lawyers cannot function like machines. However, we believe that for lawyers to become thorough, they should train themselves to conduct much of their inquiry through the T-Funnel sequence shown here. We will illustrate the process of being sidetracked through a couple of examples.

Case No. 1:

No. 1–L   Tell me all the problems you had with the car after you bought it.

No. 2–C   The first problem was with the transmission.

No. 3–L   What was wrong with the transmission?

No. 4–C   When I stopped on a hill, the transmission would slip out of drive.

No. 5–L   Beside the transmission, what else?

No. 6–C   It burned oil.

No. 7–L   How much oil?

No. 8–C   A quart every 300 miles.

No. 9–L   Was this at first?

No. 10–C   No. At first, it was a quart every 500 miles.

No. 11–L   Then what happened?

Analysis of Case No. 1:

The lawyer started with the general topic of "all problems with the car." In No. 2, the client describes one problem, the transmission. In No. 3, the lawyer does not proceed with the initial topic, "all problems," but rather seeks elaboration of a specific problem, the transmission. This very small request for elaboration does not, by our definition, constitute a major deviation from the ideal T-Funnel sequence. Indeed, in No. 5, the lawyer returns to the initial topic. However, when the client responds with the second problem, the oil, the lawyer becomes sidetracked. In No.'s 7, 9, and 11, the lawyer attempts to obtain detailed elaboration on the oil problem. The lawyer is leaving the initial topic of "all problems" to develop facts about one specific problem. Perhaps the lawyer will remember to return to the original topic. However, our experience suggests the likelihood of the lawyer's doing so, particularly when the lawyer becomes sidetracked more than once, is not great. Under the T-Funnel sequence, the lawyer would stay with the initial topic of "all problems" until that topic had been exhausted. As the client mentioned specific problems, such as the transmission, the oil, etc., the lawyer would note these down, and return to those meriting further inquiry after finishing the initial topic. Of course, some elaboration along the way, such as that found in No. 3 , "What was wrong with the transmission?", is going to be required. What experience shows, however, is that if the requests for elaboration start to develop, as they did in No.'s 7, 9, and 11, the lawyer will soon become permanently sidetracked.

Case No. 2:

No. 1–L Tell me what difficulties or inconveniences you and your family suffered the first time the car was in the shop.

No. 2–C Well, first of all, I missed a day of work.

No. 3–L Okay, what else?

No. 4–C That's about it, that time.

No. 5–L I understand it's difficult to remember, but think back to the first time the car was in the shop. Try to picture the situation in your mind as it happened. Beside missing a day's work, what other difficulties were there? Think hard.

No. 6–C We had to get a neighbor to take the kids to school.

No. 7–L Fine, that's helpful. What else?

No. 8–C I had to constantly arrange rides to work; it was a real pain because no one in my section lives near me.

No. 9–L It must have been annoying to always have to ask others for a ride; what else?

No. 10–C That's all I can remember.

No. 11–L Think hard now. Beside the day off work, the school for the kids, and arranging rides for work, what else?

No. 12–C That's it.

No. 13–L How about shopping, any problem there?

No. 14–C No.

No. 15–L How about having to cancel plans?

No. 16–C Oh, yes, we had a weekend at Lake Arrowhead planned, but we had to give it up.

No. 17–L Any other plans?

No. 18–C Well, I don't know if you would call it plans; I had to drop some night school courses.

No. 19–L Tell me about that.

No. 20–C Well, I'm taking some advanced math courses at Daleview Junior College. After I have finished six more courses, I'll be eligible for a raise at work.

No. 21–L What kind of a raise will you get?

No. 22–C $50.00 per month.

No. 23–L How many classes did you have to drop?

No. 24–C Two.

No. 25–L Have you picked them up again?

Analysis of Case No. 2:

No.'s 1 through 17 illustrate the ideal use of the T-Funnel. No.'s 1 through 11 represent the open-ended questions forming the crossbar of the T. In this series, note should particularly be made of No. 11— "Think hard now. Beside the day off work, the school for kids, and arranging rides for work, what else?" This inquiry demonstrates that in pressing the client during the open-ended question portion of the T-Funnel sequence, the lawyer may on more than one occasion wish to urge the client to think deeply about the topic under investigation.

No.'s 13 through 17 represent narrow questions in the stem of the T-Funnel. At No. 19, however, the lawyer becomes sidetracked and begins an investigation, not of the initial topic of "all difficulties," but of the specific difficulty of dropping classes. Maximum use of the T-Funnel sequence would defer examination of this subject until the lawyer had first exhausted the initial topic.

Reality dictates that each topic which might profitably be examined through the T-Funnel sequence usually will not be known in advance. How, therefore, does the lawyer use the T-Funnel sequence when, in the middle of the interview, he/she comes upon a totally new topic? By way of example, assume the interview develops to a point where the lawyer wishes to know "everything the police officer said to the client after the accident." How would the T-Funnel sequence be used? How would the lawyer go about developing the specific subject to be gone into when the open-ended questions were no longer productive? There is no formula by which such questions can be developed. What is important, however, is that the lawyer try in some conscious and systematic way to develop a list. Without this kind of an effort, there is a fair likelihood that the examination during the narrow phase of the T-Funnel sequence will be less than thorough.

The usual approach to the development of an on-the-spot list is the following: Just before commencing the open-ended questioning, the lawyer takes a moment or two and consciously thinks, "What are all the possible things that might have occurred in this type of situation?" Using the lawyer's own experience, actual and vicarious, the lawyer tries to quickly develop a list of possibilities. When the list has been developed, the open-ended questioning is commenced. When this questioning is concluded, the lawyer narrows down to the subjects on the list which have not been mentioned by the client. The questioning is concluded when the lawyer can no longer think of additional possible specifies. By way of illustration, if the client, in responding to open-ended questions about the conversation with the police officer, could only recall a discussion of the speed and direction of the cars, the lawyer might then ask questions, such as:

"Did he ask about the signal?"

"Did he ask about witnesses?"

"Did he ask about injuries?"

"Did he ask about drinking?"

Consider next the question of how extensively the T-Funnel sequence can be used during the Theory Development and Verification stage. There is no way to describe precisely when the sequence should be employed. Experience in interviewing, accompanied by constructive feedback from supervisors, will hopefully develop a good sense of judgment about when the technique can be used effectively. Assuming, however, the lawyer has decided to employ the technique, how thoroughly should the lawyer pursue any given topic? How many times during the open-ended question phase is the client to be pressed to think harder? During the more narrow phase, how many specific possibilities need the lawyer inquire into in order that the examination can be considered thorough? Again the answer, to the extent there is one, lies in the realm of good judgment which, hopefully, experience will develop.

One principal criteria in judging how extensively to use the T-Funnel sequence concerns legal significance. Another factor will be the lawyer's assessment of the degree of rapport with the client. At some point, the client may feel that the repeated pressing represents cross-examination by a lawyer who disbelieves the client. Finally, as noted earlier, too much pressing may be leading or may cause "filling."

Before closing this discussion of the Theory Development and Verification stage, we wish to make one suggestion. Often it is useful to conclude the interview with a question such as the following: "Is there anything at all you think might be relevant which we have not discussed so far?" In our experience, even in the most seemingly thorough interviews, such a question often elicits new information.

In closing this section, we wish to stress the importance of using the T-Funnel sequence. In our judgment, the failure to competently utilize this technique is, perhaps more than any other omission, responsible for the most infamous of all post-trial lawyer-client colloquies:

L.   Why didn't you tell me that before you got on the stand?

C.   Because you never asked me.

Adjourning Without Assessing the Client's Legal Position

Frequently, an initial interview will have to be adjourned under circumstances where the lawyer does not have enough information to ascertain the client's legal position. In some cases, the lawyer will simply not have enough time to fully develop the facts. In other cases, the lawyer will need to do legal research, or seek factual information from third persons. In such circumstances, how can the lawyer communicate his/her lack of knowledge and adjourn the interview without undermining the client's confidence in the lawyer's professional ability?

A client will typically expect an immediate explanation of his/her legal rights. For most clients, the law is not fraught with uncertainty. On the contrary, most clients think of the law as clear, definite, and straightforward. Given these kinds of assumptions and the expectation of an immediate answer, how can the lawyer proceed? If the lawyer says in effect, "I can't tell you yet where you stand until I do some more research," the client may perceive the lawyer as less than competent. Another reaction might be something like, "Well, if you can't tell me, who can?"

On the other hand, if the lawyer says something to the effect, "I think you have a good case, but I'll have to do some more research," the client may feel reassured, but there are problems. The reason the lawyer is delaying a diagnosis of the client's legal position is that in the lawyer's professional judgment the lawyer lacks the data on which to competently base such a diagnosis. Therefore, a statement to the effect, "Your chances look good," even if modified by, "but I'll have to check," is less than honest. Moreover, if subsequent investigation reveals the lawyer was probably incorrect, the client's confidence may be substantially shaken when the lawyer changes his/her assessment. Similarly, an unduly pessimistic appraisal seems inappropriate. Not only is the statement dishonest, but it may well cause the client undue worry.[8]

The question of what the lawyer can say to reassure the client, while appearing competent and remaining honest, is one on which research is needed. Our experience does, however, give us some idea of what may be said to a client. Primarily, it seems useful to center on a statement which provides a basic legal analysis of the situation without turning the analysis into an overall evaluation. An example is illustrative.

Assume the client has purchased a house and subsequently has sustained substantial damages when the roof developed several major leaks. According to the client, throughout the negotiations the seller said nothing about the condition of the house, and especially nothing about the roof. The nature of the leaks, however, provide, in the lawyer's judgment, strong circumstantial evidence that the seller must have known of the leaks. Since the lawyer believes there is no way to resolve the situation through the law of contracts, the lawyer feels the client's case, if one exists, rests on the law of misrepresentation. In this regard the principal issue, as the lawyer sees the situation, is one of whether or not the law imposes an affirmative duty on the seller to disclose the condition of the roof. To answer this question, the lawyer feels a need to research the applicable law.

---

8. For a discussion of the propriety of presenting medical patients with unnecessarily pessimistic prognoses, see M. Siegler, *Pascal's Wager and the Hanging of Crepe*, 293 New Eng.J. of Med. 853 (1975).

In these circumstances, the lawyer might center an explanation about why the interview must be adjourned on a statement similar to the following:

> "Cases of this type are governed by the law of misrepresentation. Usually the law requires that for someone in your position to recover money for damages sustained there must be proof the seller actually represented that the property was in good condition. That is, usually the buyer must be able to prove the seller actually said something that wasn't true.[9] In this case, the seller apparently never said anything about the roof. However, in some situations, sellers will still be liable under the law of misrepresentation even where they have said nothing about the condition of the property. In some cases, the law imposes a duty on sellers to disclose defective conditions of which they are aware. In your case, I think from what you have told me so far that you have a fairly decent chance of proving the seller knew about the problems with the roof. However, before I can really say what your rights probably are, I'm going to have to research the latest court decisions in this area carefully and see if your situation is one where the seller must disclose the defects. I want to make sure I'm absolutely up-to-date on the law before we discuss what you might do."

The foregoing statement provides a description of what, in general, the law requires; it does not, however, provide the client with any overall evaluation of the case. The language used is not overly technical, but the explanation is specific in terms of legal elements which a plaintiff must establish. We believe the lawyer's use of language indicating in some specific way what the law does require, and tying those requirements to the facts of the case, gives the client a sense the lawyer is competent. It seems that specific analysis in terms of the legal requirements results in the client feeling that the lawyer is knowledgeable.

The statement may contain seeds of other factors which perhaps reassure the client of the lawyer's competency. The lawyer seems to know just what must be done to get the needed additional information—legal research on a specific issue. Additionally, the lawyer is going to be thorough; there is going to be a careful checking before any definitive analysis is made. Finally, the statement probably contains a fairly strong implication of integrity. Implicitly, there seems to be the message of "I know certain things, but I'm willing to be up front about what I don't know."

---

9. For a discussion of the potential ethical problems involved in telling the client what needs to be proved to establish a case, see F. Chilar, *Client* *Self-Determination: Intervention or Interference*, 14 St. Louis Univ.L.J. 604, 621–623 (1970).

There is an additional point which is probably useful to add to the statement about why the meeting must be adjourned without a definitive analysis of the client's legal position. It seems likely that the client's anxiety will be reduced if the lawyer explicitly states how long the additional work will take and when the parties will meet again for a further analysis of the situation. Thus, rather than saying such things as "I'll do the research and get back to you," it probably is preferable to say something like, "I'll have this additional point researched in three days, so let's plan to meet again on Thursday. By then, I'll be able to give you a clearer idea of where you stand." Hopefully, such a statement will not only reduce anxiety, but also imply competence. The lawyer knows what to do and is going to act quickly.

Undoubtedly there are other points which could be mentioned when the lawyer wishes to adjourn the conference without making a commitment on the question of the probable legal outcome. Hopefully, the factors discussed here provide at least a useful starting place from which to begin an explanation of why there must be an adjournment.

In concluding this discussion of adjournment of the interview, it may be useful to consider one further example. Assume the client is a defendant in an unlawful detainer action. Thus far, the interview has revealed the following: The plaintiff is correct in asserting the client has failed to pay rent for the last two months. For the past three months, there has been no heat in the client's bedroom. Two and a half months ago, the client orally complained to the landlord about the lack of heat. Though the landlord promised to remedy the situation, she failed to do so. The client has continued to make some use of the bedroom, though her use of it has been substantially diminished. It's frequently too cold to use a desk in the room, and reading in bed is no longer possible. The client's failure to pay the rent is, at best, only partially motivated by the lack of heat in the bedroom. Slightly over two months ago, the client lost her job.

Assume that at this point further research is necessary to determine whether a defense based upon lack of habitability of the premises can be asserted. Is the following statement regarding adjournment adequate?

> "Ms. Rohr, at this point it seems as though we might be able to do something for you. I don't want to say for sure until I've checked the latest court decisions. The point I'll be checking is one regarding what offsets in rent a tenant such as yourself can make when the landlord fails to adequately maintain an apartment. I should be able to look that up over the noon hour; so I'd like to meet with you again about 1:30. I realize you are anxious to know what can be done, and I want to let you know just as soon as I can."

What additions, subtractions, or modifications, if any, might be made to the foregoing statement?

At this point, we will conclude the discussion of how the lawyer might organize and conduct the interview of a "willing client" in order to assess the client's legal position. In Chapters Eight, Nine, and Ten, there will be an examination of how the lawyer might speak with the client once the lawyer has made this assessment. Before turning to that examination, however, we will focus on the subjects of gaining information about the client's legal position from unwilling clients (Chapter Six) and from witnesses (Chapter Seven).

Chapter Six

DEALING WITH CLIENT RELUCTANCE

In this chapter, we will discuss techniques that may be useful for motivating clients who indicate an unwillingness to provide full information. There are undoubtedly an endless variety of situations in which a reluctance to provide complete information can arise. The discussion in this chapter will be confined to techniques potentially useful in four circumstances that commonly arise in interviewing.

RELUCTANCE TO DISCUSS SPECIFIC TOPICS

Frequently during the course of an interview, the lawyer-client dialogue will touch upon topics which even an otherwise willing client is reluctant to discuss. Although most topics discussed posed no difficulty for the client, the topic now under consideration is to some degree unpleasant or threatening. The client feels the topic should either be avoided altogether, or not fully discussed. In terms of the motivational model developed in Chapter Two, the topic raises an inhibitor such as ego threat, case threat, trauma, etc.

Indications of Reluctance

The lawyer's awareness of the client's reluctance usually comes about in one of two ways. The topic, by its very nature, suggests to the lawyer that it may be a discomforting topic for the client. Or alternatively, observations of the client's demeanor may indicate the client's discomfort. Consider first the nature of the topic itself. Assume a case involves a potential action for wrongful death as the result of medical malpractice. The apparent malpractice occurred when the deceased was in the hospital for routine surgery. The surgery was apparently successful, but five days after the operation the decedent suddenly became radically ill. Ten days later, after becoming progressively worse, he died. To develop full information about potential liability, the lawyer wishes to ask the client, the surviving spouse, about the communications between the principal doctor and the decedent during the fifteen days following the operation. In such circumstances, a reasonably empathetic lawyer may intuit the potential presence of the "trauma" inhibitor. Asking the spouse to recall the communication may well cause her to relive all the emotional pain of seeing her husband on his deathbed. To avoid this painful experience, the client may well want to avoid thinking carefully about what the doctor said to her husband.

Consider next reluctance indicated by the client's demeanor. Often, even the most sensitive lawyer will not realize in advance that a topic may involve an inhibitor. Assume the client is a twenty-year-old man who contends he was defrauded in the purchase of a used automobile. During the Theory Verification stage of the interview, the lawyer begins questioning the client to learn precisely what was said in his conversation with the salesperson. In this situation, it seems fairly unlikely that even a very sensitive lawyer would intuit the topic *per se* was a threatening one. However, assume the client felt that somehow the whole problem was his fault since he did not question the salesperson carefully enough. For this client, because of this feeling, the topic is to some degree ego-threatening. He feels he will look like a real "dummy" if he reveals how careless he was. In this circumstance, it is unlikely that the lawyer will be aware of any potential inhibitors until the lawyer actually starts to question the client about the subject. Once the questioning commences, the client's non-verbal behavior will probably indicate his discomfort.

As noted in Chapter Three, non-verbal signs of reluctance may be manifested in various ways. Body movements, such as a sudden shift in position, may indicate uneasiness; a change in the facial expression may show the client's concern; or changes in the client's tone of voice may provide some clues. Perhaps a change in the speech pattern, such as a sudden and marked degree of hesitancy, may highlight the reluctance. In all events, regardless of what the sign may be, the sign will usually *not tell the lawyer why* the topic is unpleasant or painful. Generally, all the lawyer will realize is that the topic has made the client feel uncomfortable.

Techniques For Handling Client Reluctance

When the lawyer senses a topic may be threatening, what specific techniques might be employed to perhaps overcome the inhibitors? As soon as the lawyer suspects client unwillingness, he/she must make the following decision: Should the problem be ignored until more rapport can be established, or should there be an attempt to deal with it now? There is no formula by which this question can be answered. Resolution of the problem requires good judgment on the part of the lawyer. "Can I get further with this client by waiting, or should I attempt to pursue the topic now?" Experience will become the key in making this decision. For now, all we can do is draw attention to the fact that a *conscious* decision should be made.

Motivational Statements

Once the lawyer has made a decision to explore the potentially discomforting topic, the lawyer may be able to help the client overcome the reluctance by employing a technique we have labeled a "motivational statement." As will be discussed in more detail later, this statement may or may not be followed by a change in the questioning pattern the lawyer was using at the time a conscious decision to deal with the reluctance was made.

A motivational statement has two aspects. First, the lawyer expresses empathetic understanding of the discomfort the client is feeling. An active listening response is used to let the client know the lawyer recognizes the client's anxiety or discomfort about making the disclosure. Second, there is a statement utilizing a facilitator, usually that of "reward," to point out the benefit the client will receive by overcoming the inhibitor. This second portion of the statement generally includes an explanation of why it will be beneficial to the client to provide the sought data. Typically, the second aspect of the motivational statement is phrased somewhat along the following lines: "The way you can best help yourself is by letting me know what happened. Only if I have all the information can I adequately protect your interests."

Assume the empathetic portion of the motivational statement is based upon the lawyer's intuitive sense that the topic may be unpleasant or threatening. In this circumstance, the active listening response will generally reflect the feelings which the lawyer believes the client is experiencing. The lawyer's statement may or may not, however, attempt to reflect the precise source or cause for the client's feelings. Thus, in the potential malpractice case, the lawyer's reflective response may be something like either of the following:

1. "Ms. Bridges, I imagine that having to talk about things that were happening when your husband was so ill, is not easy."

2. "Ms. Bridges, I imagine having to think about what was happening at the time your husband was so ill must be difficult since it brings back unpleasant memories."

The second statement goes further than the first. The second statement attempts to identify the source or cause of the client's current discomfort. We cannot assert with any certainty which of these two approaches might be preferable. However, if the lawyer is going to attempt to include the source or cause of the client's discomfort, the lawyer will usually want to have a fairly good sense that he/she is correct, and not simply playing amateur psychologist. In the case just discussed, we assume most people would agree that thinking about a recent death would likely bring back unpleasant and painful feelings. Thus, response number two would not, in our judgment, constitute "playing psychologist."

Assume, on the other hand, the empathetic portion of the statement is based upon the lawyer's observation of the client's demeanor. In these situations, the lawyer often will have little idea what constitutes the source or cause of the client's discomfort. The only information the lawyer will have is the client's non-verbal behavior indicating uneasiness. In this kind of situation, it is important that the lawyer avoid putting the client on the defensive. Assume that in the case of the 20-year-old man who purchased the used car, the lawyer wanted the empathetic portion of the motivational statement to empathize with the client's hesitancy. To accomplish this objective, the lawyer says: "You look uncomfortable. I guess something is bothering you." To some degree, this reflective response provides empathetic understanding. The lawyer recognizes how the client is feeling. However, frequently this kind of a statement can cause a client to feel that an explanation is due. When this kind of feeling arises in the client, the client will often reply with a vague or defensive response. A defensive reply might be something like, "I don't feel uncomfortable. What makes you think that?" A vague response would be something like, "Oh, I guess I feel uncomfortable talking with a lawyer."

To avoid eliciting these vague or defensive responses, we would suggest a lawyer might try either of the following approaches: (1) a normalizing response or (2) a request for corrective feedback.

In a "normalizing" empathetic response, a lawyer alludes to the client's discomfort by speaking about how clients as a group often hesitate to tell lawyers all the facts.

> "You know, many people feel there are some things they would rather not tell their lawyers. This is understandable; after all, the lawyer is a relative stranger. I can understand how there can be aspects of this situation that you might feel reluctant to discuss."

In this approach, the lawyer lets the client know the lawyer is aware the client may be feeling reluctant, but also communicates the information that this kind of reluctance is common—many clients feel reluctant to tell everything. Our experience indicates that this kind of information often puts the client at ease.

In a response which seeks corrective feedback, the lawyer takes responsibility for the client's discomfort. Instead of saying something like, "You look uncomfortable," which puts the focus on the client, the lawyer says something like:

> "I get the sense there is some difficulty here; I wonder if I have said something that has made you feel uncomfortable; or perhaps there is something I've failed to say that would put you more at ease."

With this kind of statement, the lawyer identifies some discomfort. In addition, the lawyer opens the door for some corrective feedback from the client. Thus, in the used-car case, the client may respond with something like, "No, it's just that I think maybe there is something that I should have done that I didn't." This kind of feedback sometimes will help the lawyer identify that a particular inhibitor, say ego threat, is influencing the lawyer-client dialogue.

We cannot say precisely why the foregoing two approaches tend to make clients feel less defensive than a response which simply identifies the client's feelings. All we can say is that in our experience these responses do seem to be effective. The responses are certainly not the only ones that can be applied, and they will not prove effective in every case. We have described them, however, because we find they often are useful.

Confidentiality

In utilizing motivational statements, consideration can also be given to stressing the confidentiality of the communication.

> "Remember, whatever you tell me is strictly confidential. I cannot and will not divulge anything you say to anyone else without your express permission."

Changing the Questioning Pattern

In addition to employing a motivational statement, the lawyer should consider whether or not a change in the questioning pattern will help the client overcome the reluctance. As noted earlier, open-ended questions have the motivational advantage of allowing clients to avoid, or ease into, troublesome areas. Perhaps if an open-ended question were used to get at the troubling information, the client could ease into the sensitive material "one step at a time." On the other hand, narrow questions might be more fruitful. Narrow questions are sometimes more easily answered since they do not raise a dilemma about how much to tell. The client need only provide the precise information called for by the narrow question. If the lawyer has some idea about what the troublesome data consists of, then perhaps the lawyer can help the client ease into the disclosure by using a number of narrow questions which allow the client to proceed "one step at a time." There is no way to formulate in the abstract which approach is preferable.

What must be remembered is that, given the difficulty of disclosing troublesome information, it is important that the lawyer try to *consciously judge* which approach might be better.

Summary

To summarize the basic techniques which might be employed to assist a client in overcoming reluctance to discuss specific topics, we will provide an example. Assume a lawyer is interviewing a client who, as a result of an automobile accident, has a potential personal injury claim. The interview is well into the Theory Verification stage. In general, the client has been very responsive to the questions. However, during the Overview stage, the client omitted any reference to why she was at the scene of the accident. She merely stated the accident occurred while she was parking her car. Additionally, earlier in the Theory Verification stage, when the lawyer had asked her through an open-ended question, to detail how she had gone about starting to park her car she stated, "There was a truck stopped in front of me in my lane. I pulled up behind the truck; I was parallel to a car at the curb. I started to look for—I mean I—I looked in the rear view mirror as I started to back into the parking space. All of a sudden the truck backed into me." Based on the client's omission to state why she was at the scene in the first place and her hesitancy and apparent change of statement, the lawyer has surmised perhaps the client is reluctant to mention why she was at the scene. The lawyer has also decided that he now has a reasonable degree of rapport with the client, and that it would be best to try to ease into the troubling subject through narrow questions.

No. 1–L   You have been quite open with me and I appreciate that; it's been very helpful. I know it's not easy to talk with a stranger. However, I have the feeling that probably there is a little more you could tell me but somehow you're not sure you should. I can understand that; really, lots of people are concerned about whether they should tell their lawyer everything. Many clients are afraid that if something not so good comes out, the lawyer will think badly of the person or not take the case. What I want to do, Ms. Smith, is help you; that's my job. However, if I don't have all the information, then I'm not going to be able to do the best kind of a job for you. I must know the full situation in the beginning; it's often very detrimental when the lawyer gets surprised in the middle of the case. I'm sure you can see how telling me everything is important. Remember, anything you tell me is strictly confidential; nothing goes beyond me unless you authorize me to speak about it. So let me ask you this, were you parking because you had some place specific to go?

No. 2–C   Yes.

No. 3–L   Were you there to see a specific person?

No. 4–C   Yes, John Hooper.

No. 5–L   Were you going to see him for a particular reason?

No. 6–C   Yes.

No. 7–L   Would you prefer that your going to see him remain confidential?

No. 8–C   That's right.

In evaluating the foregoing attempt to assist the client in overcoming her reluctance, consider the following:

1.   What additions, subtractions or modifications, if any, seem called for in the motivational statement?

2. In the empathetic portion of the motivational statement, has the lawyer attempted to analyze the cause of the reluctance? Does the lawyer's decision seem appropriate?

3. In No. 1, does the lawyer bring into play facilitators in addition to that of reward?

4. Assuming it made sense to adopt a narrow questioning pattern, do No.'s 1, 3, 5, and 7 seem to be adequate in terms of a step-by-step approach?

RELUCTANCE TO COMMENCE THE INTERVIEW

Although clients are generally quite anxious to get their story before the lawyer, this is not always the case. Sometimes after the initial introductions, the client says virtually nothing in response to the lawyer's request for Preliminary Problem Identification. The following example is illustrative:

No. 1–L Mr. Collins, how can I help you?

No. 2–C I'm not sure.

No. 3–L Well, why don't you tell me just a little bit about what's troubling you.

No. 4–C I was in this car accident.

No. 5–L I see; go ahead.

No. 6–C Well, my daughter was hurt and now my wife is all upset. I really don't know. . . .

No. 7–L Could you tell me a little more?

No. 8–C My wife thinks we should sue, but frankly I'm really . . . ah . . . not sure, I guess, I guess I want, well, humm. . . .

In situations such as these, moving into a typical Overview stage will often be an exercise in futility. The client's general reluctance is likely to cause the client to provide very little information in response to open-ended questions. As just discussed, the usual method for dealing with reluctance is to employ a motivational statement and perhaps a shift in the questioning pattern. In the case of an initial general reluctance it is often helpful to provide a motivational statement, and then shift to an extremely narrow line of questioning. The questioning usually should not attempt to meaningfully or deeply probe into the facts comprising the underlying transaction. Instead, the narrow questions usually should be limited to topics which hopefully are non-threatening. Thus, in a dissolution case, the client might be asked for statistical data such as the place and length of the marriage, etc. In an automobile accident case, the questions might concern such statistical matters as the date, time, and place of the accident. Though one cannot know what questions will be non-threatening, questions calling for statistical data are usually relatively safe.

The theory behind this very specific and yet non-probing line of inquiry is this: Narrow questions are generally easier to answer than are open-ended questions, especially if they concern non-threatening topics. Perhaps if the client can feel comfortable in answering narrow questions, the client's general reluctance will decrease, and then the lawyer can move on more successfully to the Overview stage.

We will conclude this discussion of initial client reluctance by illustrating how the lawyer might have proceeded with Mr. Collins before turning to the Overview stage.

No.   9–L   You know, Mr. Collins, people often feel somewhat uncomfortable discussing problems with lawyers. After all, the lawyer is a relative stranger. People don't know how much they should tell a stranger; I can understand that. I've seen many people who feel that way at first. What I would like to do, however, is to try and help you decide what you want to do. But the only way I can help is if I first have some basic information. I want you to know that everything you tell me is strictly confidential, and that because you tell me something about your problem you are not obligating yourself to go any further with the case. Okay?

No. 10–C   I guess so.

No. 11–L   Tell me first, where did the accident occur?

No. 12–C   Holmby and Le Conte Avenues.

No. 13–L   When was that?

No. 14–C   About three weeks ago.

No. 15–L   What time of day was it?

No. 16–C   About 5:30 in the afternoon.

No. 17–L   Was there anyone else with you beside your daughter?

No. 18–C   No; just the two of us.

No. 9 is a standard motivational statement. Through a discussion of reluctance of clients in general, the lawyer implicitly indicates understanding and acceptance of the client's reluctance. Additionally, the lawyer articulates the idea that the only way the client can receive help is by providing information. In short, No. 9 utilizes the facilitators of empathetic understanding and reward.

No.'s 11 through 17 illustrate a narrow line of questioning devoted to obtaining statistical data. When the lawyer believes the client feels more comfortable, the lawyer can then switch, through a Preparatory Explanation, to the Overview stage.

"Mr. Collins, at this point it would perhaps be easiest if I got the whole story in your own words from beginning to end. What I'd like you to do is start at the beginning and go step-by-step in chronological order and tell me everything that has happened right up to today. .   . .''

FABRICATION

In some instances, clients are more than merely reluctant to discuss a particular topic. We will now explore the subject of overcoming conscious fabrication. Fabrication includes both the giving of false information and the withholding of information. With respect to withheld data, it is difficult to draw a line separating general reluctance from falsification. The matter is probably one of degree—the degree having to do with certainty of the client's conscious intent to withhold the data. We have drawn this line, however, between reluctance and outright fabrication for a specific reason. We believe the techniques to be used to overcome suspected falsification require procedures in addition to, and in some ways different from, those used to overcome general reluctance.

Indications of Fabrication

The principal causes of falsification are usually the inhibitors of ego threat and case threat. To avoid revealing information believed to be detrimental to the case and/or information which might cause the client to experience feelings such as shame, guilt, or remorse—the client lies. The clues indicating the existence of fabrication are much the same as those signifying general reluctance, except that there are often additional signs. In the case of simple reluctance, the lawyer must generally deal with what is not said; in the case of fabrication, it is often what is said that provides the clue. The client's story contains internal inconsistencies. The client says one thing at one point, and a contradictory thing at another point. Or, the client's story may be internally consistent but quite inconsistent with everyday experience. In terms of the manner in which events of the kind described ordinarily happen, the story makes very little sense. Assume, for example, the client is charged with prostitution. She was arrested at 3:00 a. m. "on her way back from the library." She tells her lawyer, "I had just returned my friend's book to the library. If I didn't get it back, she would be fined." Though there are people who would go out alone at 3:00 a. m. to avoid a fine, most people do not behave in this fashion. The client's story would strike most people as inherently incredible.

In addition to the foregoing kinds of inconsistencies, there are situations where the client's story is inconsistent with what the lawyer knows, or at least is fairly certain, is true. For example, the client in a child abuse case says his little girl (age 6 months) broke her leg when she rolled off the living room couch. The medical records indicate the girl sustained a spiral fracture. According to medical theory, spiral fractures can only be caused by an enormous amount of rotating force, and such force cannot occur in a fall of the type described by the client.

Techniques for Handling Fabrication

Suggesting, even in the most indirect way, the client may be fabricating can often cause enormous ruptures in lawyer-client rapport. Therefore, it is essential that the lawyer not attempt to overcome suspected falsification until there is a reasonable certainty that strong client rapport exists.   Furthermore, where the lawyer's suspicion arises on the basis of what a third person has said, the lawyer must proceed very cautiously.   As noted in Chapter Four, people often perceive and recall events differently.   The lawyer, therefore, must consider the possibility that the outside source, rather than the client, is in error.   For example, were the contradicting witnesses really in a position to observe all they claim they saw?   In the child abuse case, did the diagnosing doctor look at the correct set of X-rays?   Furthermore, what of the possibility that the client is honestly mistaken.   Did the client perhaps have his/her attention diverted at the critical moment?   If so, is the client guilty of nothing more than "filling," i. e., reporting what he/she honestly imagines happened?   It is one thing to suggest that perhaps the client is mistaken; it is quite another to suggest that the client is lying.

With these cautionary remarks in mind, we will turn to a discussion of the techniques which can be used to deal with potential or suspected fabrication.   The techniques will be broken down into two categories, prevention and confrontation.

Prevention

Apart from using techniques which build general rapport, e. g., active listening, providing recognition, etc., there are two preventive techniques which may be helpful.   The first is "topic avoidance."   If the topic to be discussed is one which the lawyer intuits to be particularly ego-threatening or case-threatening, the topic can be skipped if there is a prospect of further development of overall rapport.   The subject can be returned to at a later time.   Some criminal lawyers utilize this technique by not engaging in a detailed examination of the facts until one or two interviews have been completed.

Secondly, there is "disclosure."   Frequently, the lawyer will, in advance, come into possession of information which suggests a particular topic may be threatening to the client's ego or case.   If, as the topic is approached, the information is revealed to the client, the matter can be explored without running the risk that the client will deny the existence of the data.   However, to disclose the information directly to the client may damage the relationship between the parties.   The client may form the impression the lawyer has been "checking up on me."   When the data is revealed, the client may conclude, "I guess my lawyer doesn't trust me."   To avoid the risks inherent in outright disclosure, the lawyer may be able to explore the topic by using leading questions. Let us illustrate the techniques of direct disclosure and disclosure through leading questions by way of an example.

Assume in a criminal case the lawyer has read the client's "rap sheet." The rap sheet discloses a prior conviction which, if valid, would increase sentence upon conviction. The lawyer wishes to determine if the "prior" is valid, but suspects the client may, for reasons of ego or case threat, not wish to disclose its existence. If the lawyer believes that telling the client what the lawyer knows will not seriously disrupt overall rapport, the lawyer can proceed as follows:

> "The District Attorney indicates that you have a previous conviction for armed robbery. What I would like to know about is whether you had a lawyer in that case."

If, in the lawyer's judgment, it is best not to employ the direct disclosure technique, the leading question form of disclosure can be used, e. g., "I guess this is not the first time you've been brought to court?"

Regardless of which technique is employed, the lawyer should give strong consideration to initiating the discussion through the use of a motivational statement. The statement should empathize with the client's fear of disclosure, and indicate how the client will probably be helped by providing the information. The following statement is illustrative:

> "I've handled many cases like this and one matter which usually comes up is whether or not the defendant has ever previously been convicted of a crime. When there has been a previous conviction, sometimes a defendant may be questioned about it when he/she testifies. Whether or not the defendant can be questioned is frequently a highly technical matter which depends upon precisely what the prior conviction involved.

> "Sometimes clients won't level with me and won't tell me about prior convictions; they are afraid if the prior comes out, the case will be over with or I'll no longer believe them. Clients don't realize that if I have time to prepare, I may be able to keep the prior conviction out of evidence. They also don't realize that even if I can't, they can often be made to look like a liar when they deny the prior and then, on cross-examination, the district attorney introduces a record of the prior conviction. Once the jury finds someone lying about one thing, the jury often concludes they are lying about the rest of the case as well. I want to help you and I don't want to see you in the position that some other clients have been in. In your case, I guess there probably has been some trouble with the law before, right?"

In delivering the motivational statement, it is essential the lawyer's demeanor be congruent with the idea the lawyer is concerned and wants to help. Thus, an accepting and non-accusatory tone of voice will be critical.

Confrontation

When the lawyer decides the client is fabricating and wants to get at the actual facts, there must be a confrontation.[1] Several confrontation techniques are available. They range from indirect to direct. Direct confrontation involves an express statement of the lawyer's disbelief, e. g., "I don't believe that." We will consider four basic techniques, taking them in the order of most indirect to most direct.

In using each of these techniques, the lawyer will want to strongly consider employing a motivational statement before attempting the confrontation. The statement should contain the factors included in the illustrative statement just presented, i. e., empathy for the fear of disclosure and an explanation of why telling the truth will probably be of benefit to the client. In each instance, the specific wording will have to be modified to fit the particular case. In all cases, it is very important that the reward facilitator be stated very strongly. To the extent possible, the client should be made to understand that he/she will probably benefit from telling the truth. For example, a criminal defendant who insists he is innocent and tells a wholly implausible story should be made to understand that if he tells that story at trial, he will (1) probably be convicted and (2) perhaps be treated more harshly when sentenced.[2] Since the lawyer is in a position to predict these negative outcomes, the lawyer will want to clearly point out how it is to the client's benefit to tell the lawyer what actually happened.

1. Lawyer Request for Clarification:

This technique involves articulating the clues that suggest fabrication exists, and asking the client to help unravel the lawyer's confusion. For example, inconsistent statements or hesitancy to talk about a particular subject might be handled in the following ways:

Lawyer: "I'm a little confused. One time you indicated this happened at 9:00 a. m.; another time you said it happened at 6:30. Can you clarify this difference for me?"

Lawyer: "There is something I don't think I fully understand. Every time the topic of who was there comes up, you sort of hesitate. Have I brought up something that makes you feel uncomfortable?"

1. For a brief discussion of whether or not a lawyer will always want to obtain all the facts, see M. H. Freedman, *Professional Responsibility of the Criminal Defense Lawyer: The Three Hardest Questions*, 64 Mich.L. R. 1469, 1471–1472 (1966) [hereinafter Freedman].

2. See Specter, Book Review, 76 Yale L.J. 604, 608 (1967).

2. Confrontation Through the Medium of a Third Person:

This technique involves putting before the client a version of the incident which contradicts the client's version, and then asking the client to explain. In using this technique, the lawyer structures the dialogue so that it appears that a witness or an adversary lawyer is contesting the client's version. The technique can be executed in a number of different ways. The least confrontive approach, although the most difficult to execute, is one where the lawyer asks the client to help the lawyer figure out what version of the incident the adversary will present and how to refute it. The first step is to have the client set forth the client's perception of the adversary's position. The second step involves having the client refute the adversary version. If the client has difficulty in refuting, the client is asked to explain why. If the version the client presents is too easily refuted, the lawyer points out that the constructed version is not likely to be the one to come up because the version is too easily overcome. At this point, the process is started again by the lawyer asking, "What else might they say?" The dialogue is continued until the point of conflict is apparent. The client is then asked to explain.

A second form of the third-person confrontation technique involves putting the adversary version before the client and asking the client how it can be overcome. For example, when a client claims an injury occurred in a particular manner but expert medical opinion is to the contrary, the expert opinion is put before the client, who is asked to explain. Again, the form is always, "This is what *they* are going to say."

> "Mr. Jones, the doctor's report says the type of fracture your son has could not come from a fall like you have described. The doctor will testify in court as an expert; he has seen hundreds of cases like your son's. He is going to testify that, in his opinion, the fracture could have resulted only from a tremendous amount of twisting force and that most likely that twisting force was applied by a human being. No one else but you has been taking care of the baby and you can see how bad it is going to look for you. As I just mentioned, I really want to help; how can we explain the situation?"

A third form of the technique is to tell the client that he/she is going to be prepared for cross-examination. To this end, the lawyer will assume the role of the adversary lawyer.

> "Okay, Mr. Williams, we are going to prepare you for cross-examination. I'm going to play the district attorney and you play yourself. I'm going to ask you questions just the way the district attorney would."

At this juncture, the lawyer would cross-examine with a view toward getting the client to see the unbelievable aspects of his/her story.

Role-playing can have a very strong impact on the client. It can directly confront the client with the unpleasant reality which he/she is trying so hard to avoid. The client is likely to be quite threatened by this technique, especially if the lawyer adopts a hostile tone of voice during the examination. Therefore, when the defects in the story become "painfully obvious," the lawyer must interject and reiterate the basic messages of: "I'm trying to help you. I must know everything so I can prepare the best defense for you. It's hard to face these things, but you must face them. It's better to face them now while there is still time to prepare as best we can."

3. Silence:

The technique described here can be used as a follow-up procedure to the techniques already described, or as a separate technique. The clues forming the basis for the lawyer's suspicion are put before the client with the kind of voice inflection and facial expression which suggest disbelief and call for an explanation. Direct eye-contact is most important in executing this technique. Apart from these non-verbal expressions of disbelief, the lawyer does nothing but wait in silence. There is no direct request that the client explain. If the explanations which are made are unsatisfactory, the lawyer simply shakes his/her head to indicate disbelief and then waits.

This technique is extremely difficult to learn. Most of us are too uncomfortable with silence to wait out a fellow human being. We are particularly uncomfortable if, while waiting, we must stare directly at the other person. However, with practice, the technique can be developed. Practice is worthwhile as the technique can be a very powerful one.

4. Direct Confrontation:

Direct confrontation involves articulating the clues which have raised the suspicion of fabrication and telling the client his/her story is not believable. "Ms. Smith, you say you were out at 3:00 a. m. to return your friend's library book. You wanted to avoid having to pay a fine. Ms. Smith, I find that hard to believe. People don't go out alone at 3:00 a. m. to avoid paying a 10¢ fine. I want the truth."

Indirect confrontation techniques are usually more appealing to lawyers. There is something quite discomforting about looking a client in the eye and suggesting, even if somewhat euphemistically, that he/she is lying. There is a fear and a recognition that the client may be so affronted that the relationship will be ended. There is the further fear and recognition that the client may react by trying to put the lawyer on the defensive by accusing the lawyer of all sorts of misdeeds. Obviously, indirect approaches are less likely to be destructive of lawyer-client rapport since they will be less likely to be perceived as accusations. However, they also put less pressure on the client to tell the truth. If the indirect approach fails, the client may become more "entrenched" in his/her lie. The more "entrenched" the client becomes, the more difficult it becomes to break through the fabrication, no matter how direct the approach. The prospect of having to admit both an initial falsification and a further falsification when specifically asked about a subject, is very ego-threatening. Strong motivational forces will be required once an indirect approach fails.

As to which of the four approaches one should attempt in any given situation, we again have no pat answer. Judgment is the key, and experience in developing that judgment is most helpful. We do believe that in most cases the confrontation, regardless of its form, should be preceded by a motivational statement. Moreover, the statement, especially when direct confrontation is involved, must be delivered with a demeanor which is congruent with the idea the lawyer is concerned, wants to help, and can understand the client's fear of the truth.

Finally, we should note that people do not readily admit to having fabricated. Not only must there be strong motivational statements, there must be several of them. The lawyer who wishes to "break the client down" is going to have to persuade the client that (1) it is in the client's interest, and (2) the lawyer will still accept the client even if he/she has been lying. To convince a client of these notions is going to require time. Often the client must be given time to think over what the lawyer has said. Second and third interviews are often necessary. These should be used to demonstrate the lawyer's continued interest in the case despite his/her suspicions, as well as for the purpose of trying to motivate the client to "come clean."

In many cases, confrontation will prove ineffective. The lawyer will remain suspicious while the client sticks with his/her story. In these circumstances, the lawyer should consider the possibility that conscious fabrication is *not* present. Perhaps, the client is actually unaware he/she is not telling the truth. If the client's statements are a product of the client's subconscious, referral to or consultation with a mental health specialist may be in order. Perhaps such specialist can help the client remove the psychological resistances which are causing the distortion. Or perhaps the specialist will be able to explain why the client cannot report accurately. We will discuss referral to a mental health professional in Chapter Eleven.

In all events, if the lawyer believes there is conscious fabrication, the lawyer must decide whether to continue or to withdraw from the case.[3]

3. The decision to withdraw is very complex; an examination of the issue is beyond the scope of these materials.   For an interesting perspective, see Freedman, supra Note 1, at 1475–1478.

RELUCTANCE TO STAY WITH THE SUBJECT: RAMBLING

At the polar extreme from the client with general reluctance to communicate is the client who says too much. The client who is unwilling to stay with the designated topic—who rambles—is for many lawyers the most difficult of all clients.

A variety of inhibitors may account for the tendency to ramble. The designated topic may be threatening, the topic may be perceived as irrelevant, or the client may have a "greater need" to talk about the subject to which he/she switches. Finally, it may be the client lacks the ability to stick to any topic and hence will ramble at all stages of the interview.

As with most unwillingness, the initial decision to be made is whether the problem should be ignored for the time being, or should be dealt with now. Again, there is no formula by which the judgment can be made; the decision calls for an overall judgment about which tack will best promote the informational and rapport goals of the interview. Allowing the client to talk about what is important to the client, instead of directly answering the lawyer's questions, may help the client devote full attention to the lawyer's subsequent inquiries. Permitting the client to ramble often allows the client to discuss what is important to him/her. When the client has had this opportunity, the client will often feel more comfortable and ready to focus on topics which are significant from the lawyer's perspective.

When the lawyer decides to overcome the rambling by attempting to have the client stay with the designated topic, the lawyer can often be successful by adopting one or both of the following two approaches. The first approach is to empathize with whatever concern the client raises in the rambling response, and then return to inquiring about the designated topic. The second approach, which is usually adopted only if the first fails, is to employ a motivational statement and then a rather narrow questioning pattern. The narrow questioning is used in order to keep the client's point of reference more sharply focused. Hopefully, this narrow focus will prevent extraneous thoughts from intruding into the client's responses.

Generally, it may be useful to add to the motivational statement an explanation which explicitly points out that the lawyer is asking about one subject and the client is replying about another. Finally, it is sometimes helpful to conclude the lawyer's statement with an attempt to obtain an explicit agreement from the client that he/she will stick with the lawyer's topic.

An example will illustrate how a lawyer might utilize the foregoing approaches. Assume the interview is in the Overview stage and involves a client with a potential personal injury claim.

> No. 1–L   Okay, after you slammed on your brakes, what happened next?

No. 2–C   My car started spinning and for me things have never really stopped. For days after the accident I had this dizzy feeling all the time and I still get dizzy. It's awful.

No. 3–L   Being constantly subjected to dizzy spells must be very disconcerting. After the car started to spin, what occurred next?

No. 4–C   For me there has been no next, just spinning. The doctor can't find out what is wrong.

No. 5–L   I guess you must be quite concerned.

No. 6–C   I really am. I'd at least like to know what is wrong.

No. 7–L   I can understand how it must be frustrating not to have any idea of what's wrong and when you might get better. Tell me, though, what did happen after the car started to spin?

No. 8–C   My car slammed into Mr. Schwartz's car, and then into a traffic light. I knew right away I'd been hurt badly. Right away I was spinning and the doctor can't tell me when I'm going to stop spinning. If the doctor could only tell me something. Sometimes I think I'm getting better, but then it starts in again. Always the dizziness.

No. 9–L   Mr. Plime, I can understand it must be very frustrating not to know what's wrong and how soon you'll be better. I really can understand that. I know you're probably anxious to tell me about all your injuries and in a little while I'll be asking you about them in detail. But for me to help you be compensated for all the suffering you've gone through, I must have the information about just how the accident occurred. Without that information, there is no way I can help you receive compensation for all your suffering. What I'm asking you to focus on now is how the accident happened, and what you're telling me about is your dizziness and how the doctor doesn't seem to be able to diagnose what is wrong. I can appreciate that not knowing is very worrisome, but if I'm going to be able to help you, I need facts about the accident itself. Can we agree that for now you'll tell me about the accident and later we will discuss your medical situation?

No. 10–C   Sure.

No. 11–L   Now you're just going to tell me about the accident, not your medical problems, right?

No. 12–C   Yes.

No. 13–L   When you hit the pole, what is the first thing that happened; just the very first thing?

No.'s 3 through 7 represent approach number one. In this series, there is an attempt to continue the Overview by acknowledging the client's feelings through active listening responses, and then returning to the topic under consideration. In No. 1 through No. 7, normal open-ended questions are used. After response No. 8, the lawyer realizes the client will continue to focus on the medical situation, rather than on how the accident occurred. At this juncture, the lawyer concludes it no longer makes sense to try to bring the client back to the designated topic through the standard techniques employed in No.'s 3, 5, and 7. Three attempts have failed to change the client's focus. The lawyer's choice at this juncture is, therefore, either to shift to the client's topic—medical problems—or to stay with the lawyer's topic—the Overview.

No. 9 demonstrates how the lawyer might use approach number two. It consists of a motivational statement and an explanation of the client's rambling. The motivational statement empathizes with the client's medical concerns. The statement also employs the reward facilitator by pointing out how the client can be compensated only if the lawyer has information about the accident. Added to the motivational statement is an explanation of the way in which the client is being non-responsive. "What I'm asking you to focus on now is how the accident happened and what you're telling me about is your dizziness and how the doctor doesn't seem to be able to diagnose what is wrong."

At the end of No. 9 and in No. 11, the lawyer attempts to secure the client's agreement to stay with the lawyer's topic. Finally, in No. 13, the lawyer moves to a much narrower line of inquiry than would normally be used in obtaining an Overview. Contrast the breadth of No. 13 with the breadth of No. 7.

Consider one further example. The client has been served with an unlawful detainer complaint; the lawyer is in the process of obtaining an Overview.

No. 1–L   After you paid the August rent late, what happened then?

No. 2–C   She started in on me; boy, is she some bitch. She is always trying to tell me what to do. She is always butting into other people's business.

No. 3–L   Okay, but what happened after you paid the August rent?

No. 4–C   She came over and started yelling just like she always does. Damn it; she really doesn't care about other people. Just her damn money, that's all she cares about.

No. 5–L   Look, Mrs. Hirsch, it really doesn't do you any good to get angry. Getting angry doesn't help your case. If you'll tell me facts, that is what will help.

No. 6–C   These are the facts; she started yelling and hasn't stopped.

No. 7–L   After she started yelling, what happened?

No. 8–C   She said if it happened again I'd have to leave. Leave, where would I go? I can't afford to move. All I have is my little pension. Now she wants me out just because of a lousy $20. She really is no good.

No. 9–L   Mrs. Hirsch, I can only help you if you tell me the facts. You keep telling me your landlord is no good. That's probably true, but that won't win the case. All you're doing is getting worked up and making things harder for yourself. Help yourself by telling me exactly what happened. Give me just the next thing that happened after she told you you would have to leave if you were ever again late with the rent.

In analyzing the foregoing example, consider the following:

1.   What kind of active listening responses might have been delivered in No.'s 3, 5, and 7? How would you characterize the way in which the lawyer treated the feelings articulated in No.'s 2, 4, and 6?

2.   In No. 9, how could the lawyer have pointed out more clearly the way in which the client was being non-responsive?

3.   In No. 9, what could the lawyer have said to have made stronger use of the facilitator of reward?

4.   In No. 9, what might have been the content of an active listening response? Would the content be substantially different from that which might have been used earlier in No.'s 3, 5, and 7?

5.   Could the lawyer have ended No. 9 with a still narrower question which allowed the lawyer to stay with the Overview?

6.   What else might the lawyer have done to help keep the client on the track?

CONCLUSION

In this chapter, we have attempted to provide some guidelines for handling four common problem areas: reluctance to discuss specific topics, reluctance to commence the interview, fabrication, and rambling. The techniques we have outlined are certainly not the only ones available. Further, the techniques we have discussed will not always prove to be effective. With experience and practice, each lawyer seems to learn which techniques seem to work best in which situations. Many lawyers will want to add their own modifications. Hopefully, the discussion in this chapter has provided the new lawyer with a general idea of how to deal with each of these four difficult problem areas.

Chapter Seven

WITNESS INTERVIEWING

Before witnesses are interviewed, the lawyer will often develop an overall plan for pretrial discovery. Typically, these pretrial discovery plans cover subjects such as: what facts are needed, what sources can most likely provide the needed facts, what facts should be developed by informal investigation, and what facts should be obtained by formal pretrial discovery. There is much that can be said about the development and execution of these plans. However, we shall not discuss overall pretrial fact gathering strategy.[1] Rather, since our primary focus is on interviewing theory and techniques, we shall limit our discussion to the subjects of the purposes and techniques of witness interviewing.

We mention the need to develop pretrial discovery plans for two reasons: first, to emphasize that usually witness interviews are conducted most effectively after the lawyer has consciously thought through what facts should be developed; second, because we must briefly examine one aspect of the pretrial planning process if our discussion of the purposes and execution of witness interviewing is to be meaningful. This aspect involves the process of deciding what facts should be gathered.

DECIDING WHAT FACTS SHOULD BE OBTAINED

Four Necessary Fact Sets

A pretrial fact gathering plan should be designed to develop at least four sets of facts: (1) facts establishing the existence or non-existence of the substantive elements entitling the plaintiff to relief; (2) facts corroborating the client's version of the case; (3) facts constituting the adversary's version of the case; and (4) facts contradicting the adversary's version of the case.

In dispute resolution cases, there will almost always be conflicting versions about what "in fact" occurred. Therefore, the lawyer's role as an advocate will *not* be confined merely to producing evidence which establishes the existence or non-existence of the necessary substantive elements. Assume, for example, the action is one to recover damages for the breach of an oral contract. Typically, it will not be sufficient for plaintiff's counsel to prove the making of the contract by merely having the plaintiff testify that the parties entered into

1. For a general discussion of planning a pretrial fact gathering strategy, see Legal Services Training Program, Training Legal Services Lawyers, a Manual for the Design of Local Training Programs and the Teaching of Basic Lawyer Skills, III 15–34 (1972).

the agreement. Usually, the lawyer must also present evidence which will make the client's version the *believable* one. To this end, the lawyer must be concerned both with producing evidence which corroborates the client's story and with producing evidence which contradicts the adversary's story. Thus, in the hypothetical regarding the oral contract, the plaintiff's lawyer would be concerned with presenting testimony that would corroborate the plaintiff's story that an agreement had been made, and with contradicting the defendant's story that no agreement had been entered into.

Given the goal of discovering and contradicting the adversary's version, and the goal of corroborating the client's version, how does the lawyer go about determining what facts should be sought out?

Discovery of the Adversary's Position

Before the lawyer can successfully be prepared to refute the adversary's version, the lawyer must attempt to learn what the adversary intends to say. In developing a plan to discover the adversary's position, the lawyer should take care to learn not only what the adversary intends to say on his/her own behalf, but also what the adversary intends to say in rebuttal to the client's version.

Facts in Corroboration and Contradiction: The Hypothesis Model

The planning process generally should include an effort by the lawyer to determine in advance the events which *might have occurred* that would corroborate or contradict the differing versions of the case. That is, the lawyer should attempt to start out by developing *a tentative theory* about what facts might exist that would tend to corroborate the client's version and contradict the adversary's version.

But how does a lawyer decide in advance what facts might corroborate or contradict? One suggested method of approach is to develop a hypothesis model.[2] This model is built in part on the following concept: Two events of the same type rarely occur in precisely the same manner. However, events of the same type do tend to occur in a somewhat similar manner. Therefore, experience dictates that with respect to most events, where a given fact is found to exist, one can expect to find certain related facts regarding people, activities, etc. On the basis of this concept, the lawyer can fashion a tentative hypothesis about what facts ought to exist which would corroborate the client's story or contradict the adversary's story.

With respect to a client's version of the case, not only should there be the facts described by the client, but in addition, if the events took place in a "normal fashion," there should be facts commonly associated with such events. For example, assume a client charged with rape provides the alibi that he was at his bank when

2. See supra, Note 1, at III 16–18.

the crime occurred. If what the client says is true, his lawyer can expect to find not only someone who saw him at the bank, but also bank records evidencing a transaction on that date.

In planning for the development of facts corroborating the client's version, the lawyer can go through the entire story continually pondering the question, "If this fact is true, what else would one expect to find?" By proceeding in this fashion, the lawyer can develop an elaborate outline of what facts to seek for purposes of corroboration. The identical process can be employed in developing a set of facts to contradict an adversary's story, "If this fact is not true, what can one expect to find?"

In thinking about what facts may tend to corroborate or contradict, it will often be useful to keep in mind the various factors mentioned in Chapter Four which tend to influence the accuracy of perception. These include: (1) factors associated with the observer at the time the events occurred, and (2) factors within the environment at the time the events occurred.[3] The foregoing factors will often provide the lawyer with valuable avenues of investigation. Assume, for example, that an adversary witness contradicts the client's version of how the automobile accident occurred. Perhaps it can be established the witness is mistaken because of one of the following circumstances: The witness's attention was focused on another event, the witness was under personal stress, the witness was not actually in a good position to observe the collision, etc.

MOTIVATING WITNESSES

Witnesses, like clients, will be fully responsive only if they are genuinely motivated to communicate. Therefore, as in client interviewing, one task the lawyer will have in conducting the interview will be that of developing rapport.

In general, witnesses and clients will be influenced by the same set of inhibitors and facilitators. However, it is often far more difficult to develop rapport with a witness than with a client. This greater difficulty often exists even when the witness is "on the client's side." Most people feel extremely threatened by lawyers. The source of this feeling is often not well thought through, but often involves at least these notions: "I'll end up in court where some lawyer will trick and embarrass me," or "I'll be giving up my time to go to court and get nothing in return." As a consequence of such beliefs, the typical witness reaction is, "I don't want to get involved." In many instances, the reaction emerges almost as soon as the lawyer introduces himself/herself and states a reason for being present. In short, lawyers often start with one strike against them.

The witness's fears of being tricked and embarrassed frequently involve the inhibitor of "ego threat." The witness's concerns about

---

3. See Chapter Four supra at pp. 48–50.

time better spent often involve the inhibitor of "greater need." From the witness's perspective, there is nothing to gain from being involved in the case; therefore, the witness's time can be better spent elsewhere.

Looking at witness motivation in terms of available facilitators, a major facilitator employed in client interviews is often not specifically available. In client interviews, the lawyer can frequently point directly to the "extrinsic rewards" the client can gain by communicating fully. With clients, the lawyer can employ phrases such as, "If I have that information, it will be very helpful in preparing your defense." However, in witness interviews, this kind of direct extrinsic reward is generally not available. Witnesses usually will not obtain any concrete benefit if one side or the other prevails.

In general, however, each of the facilitators utilized in an effort to overcome client reluctance can also be used to overcome witness reluctance. Two facilitators in particular are often used with witnesses, though rarely used with clients. These facilitators are "substitute rewards" and "altruistic appeals."

Substitute Rewards

Substitute rewards usually involve the time, energy, and expense the witness can avoid at a future time by being cooperative at the interview stage. Thus, substitute rewards potentially provide the witness with specific *external gains* and therefore can be seen as indirect extrinsic rewards. Typically, the lawyer attempts to point out that if the witness cooperates in the present interview, the witness may avoid the time and expense likely to be involved in subsequent court or deposition appearances. The explanation of how the witness may obtain a long-run gain from participating in the interview can be incorporated into a motivational statement. The statement can include empathetic recognition of the witness's reluctance to "get involved" and an explanation of the potential substitute reward—the potential saving of time and energy at a future date.

In explaining why the witness may ultimately save time and expense by being cooperative at the present time, the lawyer must be careful not to encourage a "know nothing" attitude. Trying to motivate participation in the interview by simply indicating that if the witness now tells what he/she knows, the witness may not have to testify in a formal setting, may encourage the witness to remember very little. The witness will reason: "If I say I don't know anything, the lawyer will have no reason to call me to court." To reduce the possibility of this kind of "know nothing" attitude, it is sometimes useful to employ the facilitator of "expectancy." The witness is informed the lawyer believes the witness has information about the case and the lawyer expects the information will be revealed, either now or in court. The idea behind using the expectancy facilitator in this manner is the following: If the witness believes the lawyer knows the witness has the information and expects one way or another to obtain the information, the witness may be motivated to provide the information during the interview, rather than in the more expensive process of testifying in court.

In conveying the possibility of a substitute reward along with the "expectancy of cooperation," the lawyer should exercise restraint. If the lawyer conveys the message in a manner that causes the witness to feel threatened, the witness's reluctance may turn into hostility. For many people, a threat produces resistance, not cooperation. Additionally, the lawyer must be careful not to promise that talking during the interview will obviate the necessity to testify in court. It cannot be known in advance that the witness's information will not be needed at trial; therefore, any promise about not testifying would be misleading. Furthermore, if the witness is subsequently called to testify, the witness often will be less than cooperative at trial. Having been promised that a court appearance would not be required, the witness may feel betrayed and "lash out" by being less than responsive on the witness stand.

The following example illustrates how a lawyer might attempt to motivate a reluctant witness through the use of the facilitator of substitute reward. Assume a witness has observed an automobile accident. Assume further that the witness's non-verbal behavior strongly evidences a desire not to be involved. Observing the witness's reluctance, the lawyer attempts to provide a motivational statement:

> "Mr. Billings, I can understand you would probably rather be doing something else than talking with me. Many people feel reluctant to talk with lawyers. They feel talking with a lawyer can't do them any good, and they'll end up getting involved in something that's not their concern. I can understand that feeling. On the other hand, I think you know something more about this situation. As Mr. Mato's lawyer, I have to find out what you know; my job is to get at all the facts. If I don't get the facts now, then for sure I'll have to get at them in court. I can't say for sure that if you talk with me now you won't have to testify in court. Perhaps what you know can be testified to by some other witness, or perhaps, once I have the full facts, this case can be settled and there won't even be a trial. So the situation is that if you talk with me now, you may well end up saving yourself some time and perhaps expense later on, because maybe I won't have to subpoena you to testify. So let me ask you this .   . ."

The empathetic portion of the motivational statement seems fairly thorough. The lawyer recognizes the client would like to avoid being involved in another person's problem and would rather spend time elsewhere. In utilizing "expectancy," perhaps the lawyer could have made a stronger appeal. For example, the lawyer might have said something like, "Mr. Billings, I know you were there when the accident occurred and you observed generally what happened. I think you know more about this situation. . . ." In providing an explanation of why participation now may save time later, the lawyer again seems to do a fairly good job. The lawyer indicates two ways in which participation now may result in time saving in the future. Can you see both of them? Can you think of other substitute rewards that could have been added? Moreover, what about the phrase, ". . . perhaps, once I have the full facts, this case can be settled"? Does this phrase tend to give the witness the idea he might be best off by somehow "coloring" his statement?

Though substitute rewards typically concern the time and expense that may ultimately be saved by not having to testify, these rewards sometimes concern other kinds of time and energy savings. Consider the following example. The plaintiff, Ms. King, has been injured in an automobile accident. A neighbor who has been helping to care for Ms. King is reluctant to talk with the plaintiff's lawyer. This neighbor, who has direct knowledge of the plaintiff's suffering, does not seem to want to get involved.

"Ms. Henderson, most people feel uneasy about being a witness. It's a common reaction, and I can understand how you feel. Thinking about testifying can make one nervous, especially if one has never been to court before. But you know, it's really not bad at all; nothing like on TV. A witness just tells what she knows, and that's it. You know a lot about this case, Ms. Henderson, because you have seen Ms. King almost every day since the accident. By telling what you know, you'll not only be helping Ms. King, but probably also helping yourself. If Ms. King can win the lawsuit, she will probably be able to afford the medical care she needs and won't require the care you've been so great about giving her. In other words, if Ms. King wins the case, it will probably free up some of your time."

In reviewing this example, consider the following:

What modifications, if any, might be made in the empathetic portion of the motivational statement?

In what manner, if any, could the facilitator of expectancy be more strongly worded?

Is the explanation about the witness's potential gain in any sense ethically improper?

Altruistic Appeals

The second facilitator primarily used for motivating witnesses is "altruistic appeals." These appeals are generally cast either in terms of assisting the client or in terms of performing a civic duty. Typically, the appeal is interjected into the interview through a motivational statement. The following example is illustrative:

> "Mr. Jenkins, I can understand your feeling that this whole thing is not your concern; it's somebody else's problem. You probably feel you haven't got enough time for your own problems and here is something that has absolutely nothing to do with you. But I'd really appreciate your taking just a few moments to talk with me. Not only may the information be helpful to my client, who is in a pretty bad way, but it will also help make sure the case is resolved on the basis of the real facts. People like you, who take the time to talk with lawyers, are really performing a civic duty because they are helping our judicial system function properly."

In reviewing this example, consider the following:

What modifications, if any, might be made in the empathetic portion of the statement?

To what extent, if any, does the statement incorporate the facilitator of recognition?

Is the statement limited solely to making an appeal in terms of performance of a civic duty?

To what extent, if any, does the previous example concerning Ms. King's case include an altruistic appeal? How might a stronger altruistic appeal be worded in that case?

We will conclude this discussion of witness motivation by providing and analyzing one further hypothetical.

Gail Clemon is the Deputy District Attorney assigned to prosecute the case of *People v. Pike.* Mr. Pike is accused of felony manslaughter as the result of a hit-and-run accident which killed a 16-year-old boy. Two witnesses took down the license number of the hit-and-run vehicle. The vehicle was registered to Mr. Pike. Mr. Pike, however, was not arrested until four months after the incident. At the time of the arrest, Mr. Pike's car showed no evidence of having been involved in an accident. A police expert who examined the car has told Ms. Clemon that he cannot say with certainty how recently the car's right front fender was repaired and repainted. In fact, the repair might well have taken place before the date of the accident. Acting on the assumption that the two witnesses to the incident correctly took down the license number, Ms. Clemon has, for purposes of obtaining corroboration, employed the hypothesis model. As a result, she has concluded that one factor she would expect to exist is a person who repaired Mr. Pike's car shortly after the accident, as well as some record of the repair. Ms. Clemon has decided to do some investigating on her own. Sensing that Mr. Pike may have stayed away from any major repair shop, she has decided to call upon the three smallest body shops in Mr. Pike's neighborhood. Her first stop is A–1 Repair, owned by Bob Wilson, age 55. Mr. Wilson's shop is crowded but has obviously seen better days.

No.   1–L   Mr. Wilson, I'm Gail Clemon. I'm a deputy district attorney. I'm trying to get a little information about a car that may have been repaired here. I just need a couple of facts. I'll be quick because I'm sure you're anxious to get to your work. The owner's name was Richard Pike. The repair would have been made last September.

No.   2–W   Look, I'd like to help, but people come and go. I don't remember who was in here five months ago.

No.   3–L   Right, I can understand that you're not going to be able to remember each of your customers; it's probably frustrating not to be able to remember more of them. But I'm sure there are some customers you'll never forget. Maybe the fellow I'm looking for is one of those. Perhaps you've got some records I could look over?

No.   4–W   No, anything that old would be back at my house, and to tell the truth, once they get back there, I don't keep them in very good order.

No.   5–L   Mr. Wilson, I can understand how you feel. My case has nothing to do with you; you don't want to get involved with a court case. I can really understand how you feel because people tell me that all the time. But some people choose to get involved. You know, this case is an important one. A 16-year-old boy is dead; he was cut down by a hit-and-run driver while he was in a crosswalk. I'm doing my job of trying to find out who did it. If this guy Pike isn't the one, then he shouldn't be convicted. On the other hand, if he is, well .   .   .   You know, Mr. Wilson, if you could just give me a little of your time, you would be doing your duty. You'd be helping out in your community.

No.   6–W   Like I say, I don't remember anyone named Pike.

No.   7–L   Well, maybe you'll remember the car. It was a dark green 4-door Chevy, 1972 or 1973. It must have had front-end damage, probably on the right side. Think hard, Mr. Wilson. It would have been last September.

No.   8–W   No, I don't think so; really, I don't remember.

No.   9–L   I can see by the expression on your face you're trying to go back and think it through. I appreciate that. I really do. Maybe we can try another line of attack.   If you could remember, we would both be saved time since I wouldn't have to come back and go through your records.   Do you remember a guy with very blond hair and a lisp?

No. 10–W   Is he about 6' 1"?

No. 11–L   Yes.   Did he have a Chevy?

No. 12–W   Can't say, but it was a dark color.

No. 13–L   Hey, you've got a pretty good memory.   I really appreciate your taking your time like this.   With this information perhaps the case won't even go to trial.   Can you tell me some details about the damage to the car?

No. 14–W   Yes, the front grill was damaged and the right headlight.   .   .   .

In No. 1, the lawyer employs an active listening response to empathize with the witness's time demands.   Again, in No. 3, there is an active listening response which empathizes with the witness's current situation—difficulty in remembering.   However, the lawyer goes on to indicate she "expects" more effort on the part of the witness, "But I'm sure there are some customers you'll never forget   .   .   .." No. 5 utilizes a motivational statement.   First, the lawyer provides empathetic understanding of the present feelings of not wanting to be involved.   The lawyer then goes on to make an altruistic appeal cast in terms of civic responsibility.   In No. 7, the lawyer again "expects" the witness to "think hard."   No. 9 also utilizes a substitute reward, "If you could remember, we would both be saved time   .   .   .." In addition, No. 9 uses "recognition," "You're trying to go back and think it through.   I appreciate that."   No. 13 also utilizes recognition and substitute reward.   In sum, in this example, the lawyer utilizes a wide range of facilitators to increase the witness's motivation to communicate.

QUESTIONING WITNESSES

Assume the lawyer knows what facts he/she desires to investigate and is ready to use the appropriate motivational techniques.   How should the lawyer proceed with the actual questioning?   Given the variety of purposes and situations in which witness interviews may be conducted, there does not appear to be any overall order of questioning which is generally preferable.   Thus, there does not appear to be any basis for suggesting that witness interviews should generally be broken down into stages, such as Overview and Theory Development and Verification.

Where the lawyer anticipates that certain topics may be threatening, discussions of these topics should usually be deferred until a fair degree of rapport has been established.   In terms of question sequencing patterns, the lawyer will usually have occasion to use the same patterns that are used in client interviewing. Thus, both the Overview sequence and the T-Funnel sequence will probably be utilized. Assume the lawyer represents a person accused of robbing a market. The lawyer is to interview a prosecution witness who allegedly saw the holdup. A major part of the interview is to be conducted to discover the prosecution's version of the case. One tack the lawyer might take to accomplish this goal would be to have the witness relate in his/her own words, from beginning to end, everything that was observed. Such an approach would probably be useful to get at facts the lawyer may not have anticipated. However, the approach would certainly not provide a complete review. There would be a number of specific areas where the lawyer would want to know in great detail everything that was observed. For example, what was observed about the robber's face, physical features, and dress? To investigate these areas, the lawyer could utilize the T-Funnel sequence.

There is one further question sequencing pattern which bears mention. The questioning pattern has been labeled the Inverted Funnel sequence.[4] There are many instances in which the lawyer seeks to obtain a conclusion or a generalization based upon the witness's observations of a number of specific facts. In a child neglect case, the defense lawyer may wish to learn from neighbors whether the defendant was a "good mother." In a will contest case, the lawyer may wish to learn from witnesses whether or not the deceased was sane. If the lawyer is to gain accurate information about these sorts of conclusions or generalizations, it will be best to stay away from a questioning pattern which first asks the witness to state his/her opinion. Assume the issue to be investigated is the sanity of the deceased, Mr. Mitchell. In this situation, the lawyer should not initiate an investigation of Mr. Mitchell's sanity by asking narrow or yes/no questions such as, "Was Mr. Mitchell sane?" An example may be helpful in illustrating why the questioning pattern should not commence with these kinds of questions when the lawyer seeks a conclusion based upon the witness's observations of a number of specific facts.

Assume Ms. Smith is charged with child neglect. Her lawyer is about to interview Ms. Smith's next-door neighbor to corroborate the fact that Ms. Smith is a "good mother." Assume the witness is first asked, "What kind of mother is Ms. Smith?" Thereafter, the witness is asked if Ms. Smith fed her children regularly, took them to recreational events, etc. If this order of questioning is used, it is quite likely the answer to the first question will bias the answers to subsequent questions. If, in answering the open-ended question, the witness reaches a general conclusion—e. g., the defendant was a "good mother"—the witness's subsequent responses to narrow questions—e. g.,

4. See Kahn & Cannell, The Dynamics
of Interviewing 160 (1957).

did she feed the children regularly—are likely to conform to the witness's initial characterization. In short, once having made a general conclusion, a witness is not likely to report individual facts inconsistent with that conclusion. To avoid this biasing effect, lawyers should use an Inverted Funnel sequence when inquiring about generalizations of the kind described here. This sequence calls for a questioning order in which the specific factors upon which the conclusion is to be based are inquired into before the witness is asked a question which prompts an ultimate judgment.

The Inverted Funnel sequence is usually not difficult to employ. However, it is often difficult to recognize when its use is called for. Assume a lawyer is interviewing a witness in a personal injury case. The plaintiff claims to have been "rear-ended" while stopped at a traffic signal. The defendant admits "rear-ending" the plaintiff's car. However, the defendant claims this happened only because, when the signal changed to green, the plaintiff started up and then literally slammed on his brakes for no apparent reason. As the interview progresses, the witness admits that she took her eyes off the traffic just before the signal changed to green. The lawyer wishes to know how long the witness's eyes were off the road. Is Inverted Funnel sequencing called for? Probably it is. If the witness is first asked to describe what she saw when her eyes were off the road, and then asked how long her eyes were off the road, the witness may give a series of answers quite different than if a reverse order of questioning was used. If the reverse order were used, the number of things seen while the witness's eyes were off the road would quite likely not exceed a number that reasonably could have been seen within the time frame given in response to the initial question.

In this chapter, we have tried to provide some basic guidelines for interviewing witnesses. Additionally, we have suggested that the basic techniques for interviewing clients and witnesses are similar. At this juncture, we will return to the principal focus of this book, the lawyer-client dialogue. Chapters Eight, Nine, and Ten will explore the subject of client counseling.

Chapter Eight

THE NATURE OF THE COUNSELING PROCESS

The first seven chapters have concerned the process of interviewing. At this point it will be assumed that through the interviewing process the lawyer has ascertained the client's legal position, or at least formulated a tentative hypothesis sufficient to proceed with the case. In Chapters Eight, Nine and Ten there will be a discussion of how, once the client's legal position has been ascertained, decisions are made regarding what solutions can best resolve the client's problem.

As noted in Chapter One:

"Counseling" as used in this book refers to the process in which lawyers help clients reach decisions. Specifically, "counseling" refers to a process in which potential solutions, with their probable positive and negative consequences, are identified and then weighed in order to decide which alternative is most appropriate.

In the dispute resolution context, the counseling process is applied to the basic decision of whether or not to proceed with, settle, or forego litigation. Additionally, the counseling process is brought to bear on a host of other dilemmas which concern the client during the course of litigation. Some of these dilemmas relate quite directly to the basic question of whether to proceed with or abandon litigation; others are at best only tangentially connected with this basic decision. A defendant's question of whether or not to attempt to raise money in order to make a settlement offer will probably have considerable bearing on the final decision to litigate. In contrast, a criminal defendant's dilemma about whether or not to tell his spouse he has been arrested may have less bearing on the basic decision. In this chapter, the discussion of the counseling process will focus primarily on the basic decision to litigate. However, unless otherwise noted, the discussion will apply both to the basic decision to litigate and to decisions involving auxiliary dilemmas.

ALTERNATIVES

We will begin our analysis of the counseling process by examining the concept of alternatives. Though it would be unduly time-consuming to discuss the entire range of alternatives available to solve client dilemmas, it may be useful to consider what alternatives are typically available to the client faced with the basic question of whether or not to litigate. First, consider civil litigation from the perspective of a potential plaintiff. In addition to the obvious alternatives of attempting settlement or abandoning the claim, there is often the possibility of having the dispute resolved through the intervention of some outside party or agency. For example, in the consumer area there may be a governmental agency, such as the consumer protection division of the district attorney's office, that could investigate the claim. Perhaps relief can be procured through a private entity such as the "Call for Action" department of a local radio or television station. If the dispute is with a professional person, perhaps referral to a regulatory body, such as a bar association, will be available as an avenue of approach.

Apart from the possibility of outside intervention, the potential plaintiff may be best able to resolve the situation through some form of self-help. Perhaps the matter can best be handled through the small claims court where the client serves as his/her own counsel. Or, if the client seeks to obtain some tangible item of property, the law may permit the client to simply take physical possession of the property.

Finally, it should be noted that the foregoing alternatives need not be mutually exclusive. Thus, a client who believes he/she has a claim against a former attorney may both proceed to litigation and report the situation to the bar association.

A potential defendant in a civil matter is probably more limited in terms of possible alternatives. There are the standard options of defending the action, asserting a counterclaim, effecting settlement, or foregoing litigation by allowing a default judgment to be entered. In some instances, the alternative of bankruptcy or some less formal arrangement with creditors may make sense.[1] However, the defendant usually has no recourse to intervention by an outside agency. Absent circumstances which make it apparent that the defendant is being unlawfully harrassed, there is usually no way in which the defendant can place the dispute in the hands of some non-judicial body.

Typically, a defendant in a criminal case is in a situation even more restrictive than that of the civil defendant. There is no option akin to bankruptcy, and no practical possibility of resort to intervention by an outside agency. The criminal defendant is therefore left with the standard options of proceeding with, settling (plea bargaining), or abandoning (pleading guilty) the litigation.

---

1. For a discussion of possible informal options, see Personal Bankruptcy and Wage Earner Plans, Ch. 1 Alternative Debtor Remedies §§ 1.4–1.12 (Cal. CEB 1971).

CLIENT		TYPICAL CLIENT ALTERNATIVES			
Civil Litigation					
Plaintiff	Settle	Proceed to trial	Abandon claim	Seek resolution through outside agency.	Self-Help
Defendant	Settle	Proceed to trial	Forego litigation by allowing a default judgment	Bankruptcy or some other informal arrangement.	
Criminal Litigation					
Defendant	Settle (Plea bargain)	Proceed to trial	Abandon litigation by pleading guilty.		

[B6277]

CONSEQUENCES

The consequences to be considered are, as the ABA Code of Professional Responsibility points out, both the legal and nonlegal results which will occur as a result of the basic decision.[2] We would add that generally legal and nonlegal consequences must also be considered when the decision involves an auxiliary dilemma. Thus, an auxiliary decision about whether or not to borrow money to sustain oneself until the time of trial, as well as a basic decision about whether or not to accept a settlement offer, would require consideration of both legal and nonlegal consequences.

Legal Consequences

The term legal consequences refers to the legal status in which the client will be placed should the client follow a particular course of action. For example, the legal consequences to a client who is a suc-

2. ABA Code of Professional Responsibility EC 7–8:
"A lawyer should exert his [her] best efforts to insure that decisions of his [her] client are made only after the client has been informed of relevant considerations. A lawyer ought to initiate this decision-making process if the client does not do so. Advice of a lawyer to his [her] client need not be confined to purely legal considerations."

cessful plaintiff in civil litigation will usually be a judgment legally entitling the client to obtain money from the adversary. The legal consequence to a client who is a defendant in a criminal case and chooses to plead guilty will usually be the legal obligation to serve time in a penal institution, or to pay a fine and serve time on probation. There may also be the consequence of suffering certain civil disabilities, such as the inability to hold public office.[3]

Nonlegal Consequences

What, however, about nonlegal consequences? What is involved here? Nonlegal consequences refer principally to the economic, social, and psychological results that will arise upon choosing a given course of action. Some examples will perhaps be useful in illustrating the existence of these consequences. Consider the following hypotheticals involving clients faced with the decision of whether or not to accept a settlement offer. For the sake of brevity, in each instance the example will be limited to exploring the consequences that may result if the offer is accepted.

Case No. 1:

Betty Burstein has instituted suit to recover damages for injuries sustained in an automobile collision. The complaint seeks recovery of $15,000; Ms. Burstein's lawyer has been retained on a contingency-fee basis. Since filing the suit, Ms. Burstein has told several of her friends about the case and has bragged repeatedly that she will recover at least enough money to pay her medical bills and purchase a new Volkswagen Rabbit. Her friends have told Ms. Burstein that she is way off; she wasn't hurt that badly and has no chance to get enough money for the car. The friends have indicated that if Ms. Burstein gets enough money for a new car, she is nothing but a faker who runs up insurance premiums. Ms. Burstein is hopeful that the case will settle because she is afraid of testifying in court. Ms. Burstein's lawyer has now contacted her about possibly settling the suit for an amount which will net her $3000 after attorney's fees and court costs. Ms. Burstein's unpaid medical costs stand at $650; she has only $150 in the bank. The lawyer indicates that Ms. Burstein has a fairly good chance of recovering an additional $1,000 if the case proceeds to trial.

Given the foregoing circumstances, what are some of the economic, social, and psychological consequences that may result if Ms. Burstein chooses to accept the settlement offer? The economic results seem fairly clear: Ms. Burstein will end up with a net of $2350, but unless she obtains a loan, there probably won't be a new "Rabbit" in the garage. Next, what about social consequences? Will settling

---

3. See   Goldstein,   Dershowitz   &
    Schwartz, Criminal Law Theory and
    Process 707 (1974).

the case have any effect on Ms. Burstein's stature among the friends to whom she bragged?   Finally, from a psychological point of view, will Ms. Burstein feel embarrassed and perhaps humiliated if she accepts the settlement offer?   Apart from these feelings, how will Ms. Burstein feel in the long run about not taking her chances and going to trial?   Ms. Burstein will avoid her immediate fears of going to trial, but will she criticize herself later for not going to trial?   After all, her lawyer said she had a fairly good chance to recover an additional $1000 if the case went to trial.

Case No. 2:

David Hanks is employed as a high school teacher.   Last month he was arrested and charged with the crime of assault on a police officer.   The assault allegedly occurred when the officer pulled Mr. Hanks over to give him a citation for having a defective muffler. The altercation between Mr. Hanks and the police officer was observed by two students at the school where Mr. Hanks teaches.   The incident is now common knowledge at the school.   Mr. Hanks considers himself innocent;   he may have sworn at the officer, but he never assaulted him.   He has already paid his lawyer $300, and if the case proceeds to trial there will be an additional $400 in fees.   Mr. Hanks' lawyer has now told him there is a 60% chance he will be convicted if he goes to trial and, in the event of conviction, there is a good chance he will be sentenced to a week in jail.   The lawyer has also indicated that if Mr. Hanks chooses to plead guilty the sole legal consequence will be a fine of $200 and informal probation for six months. Mr. Hanks cannot be fired from his job because of a criminal conviction, whether as a result of a guilty plea or a trial judgment.

Given Mr. Hanks' situation, what are some of the economic, social, and psychological considerations that may result if Mr. Hanks accepts the plea bargain?   The immediate economic consequences are fairly obvious, but what about the future consequences?   Mr. Hanks cannot be fired from his current job.   But will the conviction harm his chances of being promoted or changing jobs in the future?   How about the social consequences?   Are Mr. Hanks' relationships with students, fellow teachers, or school administrators likely to be affected by a conviction?   Furthermore, what about Mr. Hanks' own feelings?   Mr. Hanks believes he is innocent; how is he going to feel about himself, especially in the long run, if he pleads guilty?

As the foregoing examples illustrate, typical decisions about whether or not to litigate may carry with them a wide range of economic, social, and psychological ramifications.   Furthermore, as the examples also illustrate, these ramifications may not be self-evident from the nature of the decision itself.   For example, a plea of guilty will have quite different nonlegal consequences for different clients. The specific ramifications will depend, in most instances, upon the client's particular personality and the client's circumstances at the time when the decision is being made. Isn't it quite likely that Ms. Burstein's feelings about standing up to her friends will depend a great deal upon Ms. Burstein's own feelings of self-worth? Also, isn't it likely that the social consequences of Mr. Hanks' deciding to accept the plea bargain would be considerably different if no one at the school knew of his arrest?

The Process of Predicting Consequences

Given that the various consequences will not be fully self-evident from the nature of the decision itself, how are the consequences going to be brought to the fore so they can be considered? It is to this task of ferreting out and predicting consequences that we will now turn our attention.

Initially, it should be recognized that the process of determining the potential consequences usually involves the process of prediction. Generally, until the decision is actually translated into action, one cannot say with absolute certainty what the results will be. In some instances, the consequences will be relatively apparent and certain. If a defendant in a civil action fails to file an answer within the time required by law, one can be relatively certain a default judgment will be entered against the defendant. However, as a general matter this kind of advance certainty about the actual consequences of a decision will be rare. Some examples may be illustrative. Assume the previous example regarding the failure to file an answer involved a case based upon an unliquidated claim for damages arising from personal injuries. Typically, until the plaintiff has "proved up" the case and the judge has made a ruling, one cannot say with great certainty what amount of damages the plaintiff will recover against the defaulting defendant. Similarly, in Mr. Hanks' case, one cannot say in advance with great certainty what social ramifications will befall Mr. Hanks should he in fact be convicted.

In short, in many instances all that can be done by way of determining the potential consequences is to *predict* what consequences will result should a particular decision be made. Moreover, as the foregoing examples of Ms. Burstein and Mr. Hanks indicate, the predictions about what consequences will result usually involve predictions about human behavior. For instance, how Mr. Hanks will feel about a conviction, or how Ms. Burstein's friends will react should Ms. Burstein recover enough for a "Rabbit" involve predictions about how people will react. Similarly, the matter of what damages the judge or jury will award Ms. Burstein, should she decide to proceed to trial, involves the same kind of prediction.

Predictions are statements of probability. Precise mathematical probability is ascertained by observing the same phenomena over a period of time and measuring the percentage of times particular outcomes occur. For example, by observing the effects of a general anesthetic on a population of patients over a given period of time, doctors can ascertain that death will occur in a given percentage of cases. The percentage of time a particular outcome occurs (death) as the result of a particular interaction (use of anesthetic) becomes the basis for predictions of future occurrences of the same outcome. The data (experience) collected in arriving at an overall percentage can be called a *data base*.

Where the forecasts required are those of predicting human behavior, there are very few truly accurate data bases. Human behavior is so complex that it does not lend itself to precise mathematical or statistical analysis. Any data bases the lawyer and client have individually acquired for predicting future consequences have usually been arrived at by a highly selective and intuitive process. A lawyer may have been involved in dozens of similar cases. In each of these prior cases, despite the general similarity, there will have been important differences which introduce uncertainty into the data base.

Assume, for example, the lawyer is currently confronted with a case in which the client is defending an unlawful detainer action on the ground of lack of habitability of the premises. Assume further that the lawyer's past experience (data base) includes 20 cases where a client has asserted the same defense. In these cases, even though the points of law have been identical, there have been variations in the evidence and in the interpretation of the law. Thus, in each of the cases, the demeanor of the defense witnesses and the availability of photographic evidence, etc., has been somewhat different. Moreover, in each case, the judge's interpretation of the law has been slightly different. In some cases the defendant prevailed, and in other cases the defendant lost. Given these varying, though similar, prior cases as a data base on which to make predictions, there is no way the lawyer will be able to predict with mathematical or statistical certainty what legal consequences will result in the current case.

However, though lawyers and clients have only an imperfect data base on which to predict the consequences of basic and auxiliary decisions, these data bases are the ones which must be used. Reality dictates that as a practical matter only these imperfect data bases will be available for the purpose of making any necessary predictions.

For every decision made during the counseling process, it will usually be either the lawyer's or the client's personal data base which will be used to predict the likely consequences. When, however, will it be the lawyer's task to predict the consequences, and when should these predictions be left to the client?

Predicting the Legal Consequences

Consider first the category of legal consequences. When considering the alternatives of either settling or foregoing litigation, the legal consequences will usually be relatively certain. In the case of settlement, unless the agreement leaves some point unresolved, the lawyer generally will be able to say with some certainty what legal rights the client will have should the settlement be achieved. Similarly, should the client decide to forego litigation, the lawyer can often say with certainty what legal result will occur.

However, where the alternative being considered involves proceeding to trial, the prediction process is often quite complex. To make a prediction about the likely legal consequences of trial, the lawyer must predict *the likely outcome* of the trial. To make this prediction, it may be necessary to make at least three different kinds of specific sub-predictions.

In the first instance, if the case involves disputed questions of fact with regard to issues of liability or damages, there must be predictions about how the fact finder will resolve these questions. The typical personal injury action provides a useful example. In such a case, there must be a prediction about whether or not the jury will find the defendant negligent, what injuries the jury will believe the plaintiff suffered, and what amount of damages the jury will award.

The second kind of sub-prediction is one which relates to the state of the law. Assuming *arguendo* that the facts are clear, what result does the law dictate? In many situations, the law on a given point will be unsettled, either because the point has not been previously considered or because the law is in a state of flux. For example, under Federal law the following question is still unresolved: Absent "hot pursuit," may a peace officer make a warrantless entry into the home of a felony suspect for the purpose of arrest upon probable cause if he reasonably believes the suspect is inside?[4] If the law is in an unsettled state, prediction about the legal consequences of going to trial must include a prediction about how the open question of law will be resolved. Indeed, it may be necessary to predict not only how the trial court will resolve the question, but also what disposition is likely in the appellate courts.[5]

The last of the common sub-predictions related to the legal consequences of proceeding to trial concerns the trial judge's use of discretion. In many situations, the law provides that with respect to a given set of circumstances, the trial judge has wide latitude to decide what result shall obtain. The following are examples of situations in which the trial judge has considerable discretion to decide what the judgment shall be: The amount of monthly child support that shall be paid; the amount of wages which shall be exempt from garnishment; the amount of attorney fees that shall be awarded; the amount of time the defendant shall spend on probation or under incarceration.

4. Coolidge v. New Hampshire, 403 U. S. 443, 480–481, 91 S.Ct. 2022, 2045, 29 L.Ed.2d 564 (1970).

5. ABA Code of Professional Responsibility EC 7–7.

"A defense lawyer in a criminal case has the duty to advise his [her] client fully on whether a particular plea to a charge appears to be desirable and as to the prospects of success on appeal . . . ."

In sum, to predict the legal outcome and legal consequences of choosing the alternative of trial, it may be necessary to make sub-predictions about at least each of the following:

1. How the trier of fact will resolve disputed issues of fact;
2. How the trial judge and perhaps the appellate courts will resolve unsettled questions of law;
3. How the trial judge will rule on issues which the law places within the judge's discretion.

The Lawyer's Responsibility to Predict Legal Consequences

Given the nature of legal predictions, it seems clear that the responsibility for identifying the probable legal consequences of any particular alternative must rest with the lawyer. In theory, and usually in practice, the client has little or no experience with how the judicial system resolves questions of the type just described. Indeed, it is this lack of knowledge which constitutes one of the client's principal reasons for retaining the lawyer.

There may be exceptions to the conclusion that the lawyer has the superior data base for making predictions about the probable legal consequences. For example, the litigation-wise client may know better than the lawyer how a case will probably be resolved. Thus, a criminal defendant with five prior convictions may be quite capable of predicting the legal outcome of the current case. However, by and large, it will be the lawyer who has the *superior data base,* and therefore the lawyer who should make the necessary predictions with respect to the probable legal consequences.

It might be pointed out that the new lawyer often has inadequate training and experience (data base) to make the necessary predictions. In particular, with respect to issues of factual determination and the exercise of judicial discretion, the new lawyer often has very little knowledge of what can be expected. Clinical education is attempting to remedy lawyers' deplorable lack of knowledge and training in these areas. However, even when this training exists, the new lawyer may feel, and rightly so, that he/she is not sufficiently familiar with the legal system to competently predict what result is likely to occur. Nonetheless, professional responsibility demands that a lawyer should not permit a client to proceed to trial when the lawyer has *no idea* what legal outcome will result. When a lawyer is totally uncertain about what the outcome will be, the lawyer should gather the data necessary to predict the outcome, or withdraw from the case.[6] Permitting a lawyer to try a case with no idea of the likely

6. ABA Code of Professional Responsibility EC 6–3.

"While the licensing of a lawyer is evidence that he [she] has met the standards then prevailing for admission to the bar, a lawyer generally should not accept employment in any area of the law in which he [she] is not qualified. However, he [she] may accept such employment if in good faith he [she] expects to become qualified through study and

outcome would, in our judgment, be equivalent to permitting a doctor to conduct surgery with no idea of what consequences might befall the patient as the result of the operation.

Generally, a lawyer who has competently investigated, prepared, and analyzed a case will be able to predict the general degree of risk involved should the case proceed to trial. In some instances, the lawyer's pretrial investigation and analysis will indicate that the chances of the client prevailing are only fifty-fifty. Typically, however, the competently prepared lawyer will have some idea of the extent to which the client's case falls on one side or the other of the fifty-fifty line. Thus, the competently prepared lawyer will usually be able to assert that the client's chances of prevailing are eighty percent or forty percent, etc. Although these predictions will lack certainty, they will be different in kind from the uncertainty which comes from a lawyer who says, in effect, "I really know little or nothing about how the legal system handles cases of this type, and all I can tell you is that it is uncertain how this case will come out. If you go to trial, you will simply be taking your chances." Such statements fail to provide the client with any professional assessment of the risks involved.

When a lawyer recognizes that he/she lacks the basis to competently predict the legal outcome, the lawyer should undertake various kinds of research if he/she is to continue to represent the client. In many instances, the type of research required will be consultation with more experienced members of the bar rather than traditional legal research. Assume the lawyer has little experience with how the judge will exercise discretion in ordering child support. In such a situation, the lawyer should, before discussing a proposed settlement with the client, learn from other members of the bar what amounts of support the judge usually orders for persons in the client's general financial position. Perhaps consultation with the court clerk or bailiff will also be useful.

Predicting Nonlegal Consequences: Whose Responsibility?

Next, consider predictions about nonlegal consequences. Between the lawyer and the client, who should make predictions about the probable economic, social, and psychological ramifications of a particular decision? With respect to psychological consequences, unless the lawyer knows the client extremely well it usually will be the

investigation, as long as such preparation would not result in unreasonable delay or expense to his [her] client. Proper preparation and representation may require the association by the lawyer of professionals in other disciplines. A lawyer offered employment in a matter in which he [she] is not and does not expect to become so qualified, should either decline the employment or, with the consent of his [her] client, accept the employment and associate a lawyer who is competent in the matter."

See also DR 6–101(A)(1).

client who has the more enlightened data base for making needed predictions.   For example, in the case of Ms. Burstein, unless her lawyer knows her extremely well, it is unlikely the lawyer will have a basis for predicting how bad Ms. Burstein will feel in the long run about giving up the opportunity to gain an additional $1000.

When it comes to predicting social consequences, it is again the client who will usually have greater knowledge of his/her family, friends, and associates.   Therefore, the client will usually be in the best position to forecast the probable reactions of these people should a particular course of action be adopted.   For example, unless Mr. Hanks' lawyer knows Mr. Hanks' fellow teachers fairly well, it will be Mr. Hanks who will be in the best position to predict how the teachers will react to a conviction.

With regard to economic consequences, it may or may not be the client who has the more informed data base for making the prediction.   Often it will be the client who has the greatest knowledge of his/her financial position and needs.   Consequently, it may be the client who is in the best position to predict the actual financial consequences of adopting a particular course of action.   There are going to be many situations, however, in which the lawyer will be best able to predict the economic consequences.   For example, it may be the lawyer who will have the best data base for forecasting the probable effect on the client's future credit should the client allow a judgment to be entered against him/her or file bankruptcy.   Similarly, the lawyer's knowledge of tax law may place the lawyer in the best position to forecast the ultimate financial consequences of accepting a settlement.

There may be many potential economic and social consequences, and at times psychological consequences, for which neither the lawyer nor the client has an adequate data base for a prediction.   For example, perhaps neither Mr. Hanks nor his lawyer has sufficient knowledge to predict whether or not a conviction will hinder Mr. Hanks should he try to obtain a job in another school district.   When neither the client nor the lawyer has an adequate data base on which to base an important prediction, one of two things usually should occur: either a knowledgeable third person should be consulted, or it should be made clear that the consequence may exist, but that there is insufficient information upon which to base a reasonable prediction.   For example, in Mr. Hanks' case, there could be a check with a representative of the teachers' union to ascertain the job consequences that would result from a conviction.   If this check provides no meaningful information, Mr. Hanks should be made aware that if he pleads guilty there is an open-ended risk his future employment in other school districts may or may not be limited.

Summary of Process of Predicting Consequences

In summary, we have developed the following points with respect to the process of identifying and predicting probable consequences:

1. The consequences to be considered are both legal and nonlegal.

2. Nonlegal consequences include economic, social, and psychological ramifications.

3. Often the potential consequences of adopting any given decision cannot definitely be known in advance, but must be predicted.

4. Predictions must be made on the basis of a reasonably adequate data base.

5. It is the lawyer who should have the data base for predicting potential legal consequences.

6. If the lawyer lacks adequate information on which to base a prediction, the lawyer must gather the needed information in order to continue to represent the client.

7. It will generally be the client who has the most adequate data base for predicting psychological consequences.

8. It will also usually be the client who has the superior data base for predicting social consequences.

9. Insofar as economic consequences are concerned, it may be the lawyer or it may be the client who has the superior data base.

10. In situations where neither the lawyer nor the client has an adequate data base, one of two things must occur: either a data base must be obtained from a knowledgeable third person, or the client must be made aware that there are potential consequences, but their likelihood cannot be reasonably predicted.

The Lawyer's Tasks in Identifying and Predicting Consequences

Next, consider the specific tasks which the lawyer should fulfill in the process of identifying and predicting consequences. To insure that all potential consequences are identified and predicted, the lawyer should undertake at least two tasks. Mr. Hanks' case will serve as a useful example. Recall that if Mr. Hanks proceeds to trial there is a 60% chance he will be convicted and a good chance he will be sentenced to jail. To proceed to trial, Mr. Hanks must pay an additional $400 in attorney fees. Should Mr. Hanks choose to plead guilty, the maximum penalty he will receive will be a $200 fine and six months' informal probation. In reviewing the potential consequences of entering a plea of guilty, one task for the lawyer is to predict the legal and nonlegal consequences for which the lawyer has the superior data base. In Mr. Hanks' case, for example, in addition to predicting the legal consequences, the lawyer will be able to point out certain financial consequences. For instance, the lawyer will be able to point out that by being on informal probation, Mr. Hanks will not lose any time from his job.

In addition to pointing out the consequences which the lawyer foresees, a second task for the lawyer is to elicit from the client any consequences the client foresees. Thus, the lawyer will have to ask Mr. Hanks what economic, social, and financial consequences Mr. Hanks foresees or anticipates may arise as the result of a guilty plea. In making these inquiries, the lawyer will typically be concerned with two categories of consequences. The first category will be those consequences which the lawyer, on the basis of his/her experience with previous clients, anticipates the current client might experience. For instance, the lawyer may have had many clients who harbored long-term resentments when they plead guilty while feeling they were innocent. In the light of this experience, the lawyer will probably anticipate that Mr. Hanks may also harbor such resentments. Therefore, the lawyer will want to ask Mr. Hanks whether or not he might experience some long-term resentment should he plead guilty.

The second category of consequences the lawyer should inquire about are those consequences which the lawyer may not have anticipated at all. For example, the lawyer may not have thought to inquire about the social ramifications at Mr. Hanks' place of employment should Mr. Hanks plead guilty. If the lawyer asks Mr. Hanks what consequences he foresees that have not been mentioned so far, this consequence, and probably additional consequences, may be identified by Mr. Hanks.

In sum, the specific tasks the lawyer must perform in the process of identifying and predicting consequences require the lawyer to assume two complementary roles: information provider and information gatherer.

CLIENT–CENTERED DECISION MAKING

Before turning to the technical matter of how the lawyer actually conducts the counseling process, one further issue must be addressed. The issue, in our judgment, is *critical* to all of counseling. It concerns who, between the lawyer and the client, should make the final decision.

The ABA Code of Professional Responsibility, subject to certain exceptions, states that the ultimate decision of whether or not to proceed with, settle, or forego litigation rests with the client.[7] We would

7. ABA Code of Professional Responsibility EC 7–7 states:
   "In certain areas of legal representation not affecting the merits of the cause or substantially prejudic-

ing the rights of a client, a lawyer is entitled to make decisions on his [her] own. But otherwise the authority to make decisions is exclusively that of the client and, if add that this principle of leaving the final decision to the client should usually be applied to auxiliary decisions as well. We will refer to this principle as client-centered decision making.

The ultimate decision regarding which alternative should be chosen should be based upon an evaluation of which alternative is most likely to bring the *greatest client satisfaction*. If a decision is to be made on the basis of maximum client satisfaction, there first must be knowledge of the importance or value which the client attaches to each of the consequences involved. Only when the client's values are known can there be a determination of which alternative, on balance, will provide maximum client benefit. However, it is our belief that, by and large, lawyers cannot know what value clients really place on the various consequences. We therefore conclude that lawyers usual-

made within the framework of the law, such decisions are binding on his [her] lawyer. As typical examples in civil cases, it is for the client to decide whether he [she] will accept a settlement offer or whether he [she] will waive his [her] right to plead an affirmative defense. A defense lawyer in a criminal case has the duty to advise his [her] client fully on whether a particular plea to a charge appears to be desirable and as to the prospects of success on appeal, but it is for the client to decide what plea should be entered and whether an appeal should be taken."

However, the line between what is a decision affecting the merits and what is a tactical one is often hazy. See for example, Linsk v. Linsk, 70 Cal.2d 272, 74 Cal.Rptr. 544, 449 P.2d 760 (1969); D. Mellinkoff, Lawyers and the System of Justice 733–757 (1976); ABA Project on Standards for Criminal Justice, Standards Relating to the Prosecution Function and the Defense Function 162–163 (Approved Draft 1971).

Moreover, even if the decision affects the merits there are exceptions to the notion that the client's decision is binding on the lawyer.

"In his [her] representation of a client, a lawyer shall not:

"(1) File a suit, assert a position, conduct a defense, delay a trial, or take other action on behalf of his [her] client when he [she] knows or when it is obvious that such action would serve merely to harass or maliciously injure another."

"(2) Knowingly advance a claim or defense that is unwarranted under existing law, except that he [she] may advance such claim or defense if it can be supported by good faith argument for an extension, modification, or reversal of existing law."

ABA Code of Professional Responsibility DR 7–102. See also EC 7–5.

Further, what stance may the lawyer adopt when the lawyer believes the client's position is an immoral one? Is it significant that the matter is adjudicatory in nature?

"In assisting his [her] client to reach a proper decision, it is often desirable for a lawyer to point out those factors which may lead to a decision that is morally just as well as legally permissible. He [she] may emphasize the possibility of harsh consequences that might result from assertion of legally permissible positions. In the final analysis, however, the lawyer should always remember that the decision whether to forego legally available objectives or methods because of non-legal factors is ultimately for the client and not for himself [herself]. In the event that the client in a non-adjudicatory matter insists upon a course of conduct that is contrary to the judgment and advice of the lawyer but not prohibited by Disciplinary Rules, the lawyer may withdraw from the employment."

ABA Code of Professional Responsibility EC 7–8.

For an interesting discussion on the limitations which the Code of Professional Responsibility may place on the principle of client decision-making, see Chilar, *Client Self-Determination: Intervention or Interference?*, 14 St. Louis L.J. 604 (1970) [hereinafter Chilar].

ly cannot determine which alternative will provide maximum client satisfaction and that decisions should be left to the client.

Our belief about lawyers' inability to know what values clients place on various consequences is derived primarily from our clinical observations of clients' behavior during the decision making process. Our observations in regard to lawyers' inability to know clients' values include the following:

First of all, clients' values are uniquely personal. For example, the value one client attaches to the consequence of avoiding the strain of trial is generally different from the value other clients would attach to the same consequence. Second, it is often very difficult, if not impossible, for clients to precisely quantify the value they place on specific consequences. Thus, clients cannot usually say, even to themselves, such things as, "On a scale from one to ten, getting $2500 now has a value of plus 5; avoiding the strain of trial has a value of plus 2; however, giving up the opportunity to obtain an additional $5500 has a value of minus 5;" etc. All that clients can usually do is give general statements of the value they place on the various consequences. Thus, clients can sometimes quantify consequences to the extent of labeling them as "very important," "important," "not so important," etc. However, this quantifying process does not usually allow clients to distinguish between consequences which they see as fitting into the same general category of importance. Thus, typically, clients cannot distinguish between two or three consequences, each of which they see as "important," "not so important," etc. This inability to distinguish between consequences is particularly pronounced when the consequences are of different types. For instance, a client typically cannot distinguish between an "important" economic consequence and an "important" psychological consequence. When asked to rank or weigh the relative importance of such consequences, clients will typically say such things as, "I can't say which is more important. Getting an additional $1500 is important, but it's also important that I not be under a lot of stress. My friends say go for the additional money, but they don't have to face testifying in court. I can't say which is more important; they're both important."

Since clients usually cannot precisely identify for themselves what values they place on various consequences, clients generally cannot convey to their lawyers the unique personal values which they attach to the various consequences. Without access to the specific weights clients attach to the various consequences, lawyers usually are not able to decide which alternative, on balance, will provide *maximum client satisfaction.*

Additionally, in our experience deciding which alternative is most likely to provide the greatest benefit involves another unquantifiable self-assessment which generally cannot effectively be conveyed to the lawyer. Inherent in the weighing process is the consideration of the extent to which the client is willing to risk the negative con-

sequences of one alternative in order to gain the positive consequences of another alternative. The willingness to take the risk de-
pends not only on the weights the client attaches to various consequences, but also on the extent to which the client is "a risk avoider."
Even when the odds are the same, and the potential gains and losses
are the same, some people are more willing than others to take the
gamble. However, the specific extent to which a given client is "a
risk avoider," usually cannot meaningfully be conveyed to the lawyer.

In sum, clients are usually unable to communicate a precise description of the weights which they place on the probable consequences and an accurate sense of the degree to which they are "risk
avoiders." In our opinion, without access to this information, the
lawyer usually cannot determine what course of action would be best
suited for the client. We therefore conclude that usually the lawyer
should leave the final decision for the client to make on the basis of
the client's own intuitive weighing process.

The foregoing analysis has been relatively abstract. At this
point, an example may be helpful in illustrating why we have concluded that lawyers generally cannot know their clients' values, cannot know the degree to which their clients are "risk avoiders," and
therefore usually cannot make decisions which provide maximum
client satisfaction.

The example concerns a basic decision of whether to continue
with litigation or settle. The example commences from a point at
which the counseling process has already identified all of the pertinent consequences which the lawyer and client believe bear on the decision.

Arnold White has brought suit against the city for false arrest
and imprisonment. The arrest occurred because a clerk in the local
traffic court failed to note that Mr. White had appeared and paid a
traffic citation. As a result of the clerk's error, a warrant was is-
sued. Pursuant to the warrant, Mr. White was arrested as he left for
work on a Thursday morning. Mr. White was incarcerated until Sunday evening when his family was finally able to raise money for bail.
Before the civil action was instituted, the criminal charges of failure
to appear were dismissed.

After the city filed its answer denying liability, each side served
two sets of interrogatories and took one deposition. Mr. White's attorney fees and court costs to date have been respectively $640 and
$100. The city has now offered $1,000 by way of settlement.

Mr. White's lawyer, Jackie Jones, has carefully analyzed the case
and believes there is a good chance of obtaining a judgment for
$3500. She believes a judgment for this amount is the most probable
result at trial. Additionally she believes there is a small possibility
the judgment could go as high as $5000, or as low as $500. In the
lawyer's opinion, the city will definitely be held liable; the only issue
is the amount of damages the jury will award. The projected additional costs of proceeding to trial, including attorney fees, are $800.

In analyzing the positive and negative consequences of the alternatives of trial and settlement, Mr. White and his lawyer have come up with the following:

SETTLEMENT ALTERNATIVE	LITIGATION ALTERNATIVE
Positive Consequences	**Positive Consequences**
Economic:	Economic:
1) $1000 now.	1) Retain good chance of $3500.
2) No further court costs or attorney fees.	2) Small chance of $5000.
3) No loss of wages for time at trial.	Social:
Social:	None
1) Improved relationship with spouse, who opposes putting more money into the suit.	Psychological:
	1) Avoid feeling of having "chickened out."
Psychological:	2) Retain good chance of having satisfaction of proving city in error.
1) Avoid concern about the trial itself.	3) Satisfaction of having made the best possible effort to obtain reasonable compensation.
2) Obtain satisfaction of having city admit its error.	
3) Avoid concern about ending up with less money than put into case.	**Negative Consequences**
	Economic:
Negative Consequences	1) Give up sure $1000.
Economic:	2) Take small risk of getting only $500.
1) Give up good chance at $3500.	3) Loss of additional $150 in wages to attend the trial.
	4) Cost of additional $800 in attorney fees and court costs.
Social:	
None	Social:
	1) Continued controversy with spouse about proceeding with the litigation.
Psychological:	
1) Feeling of having "chickened out."	Psychological:
2) Feeling of dissatisfaction because not compensated fairly.	1) Retain concerns of going to trial.
	2) Retain concern of ending up with less money than put into case.

[B6278]

Given the foregoing analysis of the positive and negative consequences, can the lawyer determine which alternative, litigation or settlement, would provide Mr. White with the greatest satisfaction? The answer probably must be "no." There is nothing in the listing of the consequences which provides a basis for evaluating which group of consequences, on balance, will give Mr. White the maximum benefit. There is nothing in the list of consequences that speaks about either the actual or relative importance of any consequence. For example, there is no indication of how important it is to Mr. White that he avoid the dissatisfaction of feeling less than fully compensated. Nor is there any information which provides a basis for deciding whether the alternative of proceeding to trial correlates with Mr. White's sense of what is an acceptable degree of risk to undertake.

However, what about asking Mr. White what importance he places on the various consequences? If the lawyer can ascertain from Mr. White what weights he would place on the various consequences, and what constitutes his sense of appropriate risk-taking, could the lawyer then decide which alternative is best for Mr. White? If Mr. White is like most people, any effort to obtain such information will be quite unsuccessful. Our experience indicates that even if Mr. White thinks carefully about the matter, he will not be able to specify what precise value he would place on each of the foregoing consequences. Mr. White may be able to say that certain consequences seem "important" and others "not so important," but he probably cannot attach precise degrees of importance to each specific consequence.

Moreover, though Mr. White may be able to specify the general importance of each of the foregoing consequences, he probably will not, if he is like most people, be able to distinguish between consequences of similar degrees of importance. Assume, for example, Mr. White attaches great importance to "improved relations with his spouse," to "retaining a good chance of recovering $3500," and to "avoiding the feeling of having 'chickened out'." If Mr. White is like most people, he will probably be unable to say whether the value of "retaining the good chance at $3500," together with the value of "avoiding the feeling of having 'chickened out'," are equivalent to, or greater than, the value placed on "improved relations with his spouse."

Similarly, in our experience, although Mr. White may have some general idea of the degree to which he is a risk avoider, he probably will be unable to say whether he wishes to apply his normal degree of risk avoidance in this case.

What clients generally seem to do in making decisions is to try to take into account the positive and negative consequences of each alternative and then, through an intuitive weighing process, decide which alternative, on balance, seems best. In the course of this intuitive process, the client brings into play his/her own values and sense of appropriate risk avoidance. Thus, in a situation like Mr. White's, this intuitive process might occur along the following lines:

> "Well, let's see, I'd hate to chicken out here, but I might end up with only $500 and I really can't afford that. My wife is really going to be mad if I keep going. If I lose it's going to be a mess, the court costs and attorney fees and a lot of aggravation. But there is a pretty good chance of getting $3500. With $3500 I could really do something. Should I gamble? I wish I knew. Um? $3500 sounds good and the chances are good. I guess I'll go for it."

In an intuitive weighing process such as that just described, there is no attempt to quantify the various consequences, nor is there an effort to systematically rank them. The pros and cons are lumped together and weighed, and the risk factor is also somehow included. The final decision rests on some imprecise accounting concept of what factors, on balance, emerge as important to the decision maker. Since decisions are typically made in the manner just described, we conclude that decisions should be left, in the main, to the client.

In our opinion, there is a second reason why decisions should be left to the client. Generally, it seems a client can best live with a decision, and follow through with a decision, if it is one the client has made. This may be true because a client-made decision usually more accurately reflects client values.

Exceptions to Client-Centered Decision Making

Client-centered decision making may not, however, always be possible. Reality dictates that for a variety of reasons some clients will be unwilling to make final decisions. For example, some clients may have an ingrained notion that it is appropriate that the lawyer, rather than the client, should decide. These clients often insist the lawyer make the decision.[8] Other clients, for one reason or another, may feel too busy to bother with decision making, and therefore will turn the decision over to the lawyer. Furthermore, some clients, although willing to make decisions, will feel incapable of deciding. For example, the pros and cons may be so evenly balanced in the client's mind that the client simply will be unable to decide what should be done. Or, perhaps the time within which a decision must be made is so short that the client feels unable to decide. When the client is either unwilling or unable to make a decision, what should the lawyer do?

In these circumstances, if the question involves a basic decision of whether or not to litigate, we believe the lawyer should decide, *provided* the client is willing to let the lawyer do so, and the lawyer

---

8. See Chilar supra note 7, at 608; see also D. Rosenthal, Lawyer and Client: Who's in Charge? 17 (1974) [hereinafter Rosenthal].

has first made a genuine attempt to get the client to decide.[9]   No decision will, in fact, always be a decision.   For example, if the client is unable to decide whether or not to commence a suit, the client's indecision will result in a choice not to institute the action.   Since no decision will always result in a decision, albeit a passive one, the lawyer must either (a) allow the client's no decision to become the decision, or (b) make the decision for the client.   We assume a decision based upon some reasoning is likely to be more appropriate than a decision arrived at by chance or default.   Therefore, when the client is either unwilling or unable to decide, we believe the lawyer should choose, if the client authorizes the lawyer to do so.[10]

At this point, it should be stressed that providing the client with the option of choice by the lawyer should usually be a last resort. For reasons already discussed, the lawyer's decision, no matter how thoroughly the client may have been examined on the importance of the potential consequences, is not likely to fully reflect the client's values.   Therefore, the lawyer's decision runs a fair degree of risk of not providing maximum client satisfaction, and thus probably should be avoided whenever possible.   Chapter Ten will include a detailed discussion of how, as a technical matter, the lawyer might attempt to motivate unwilling or incapacitated clients to make their own decisions.   Chapter Ten will also include a discussion of what actions should be taken to make sure that any lawyer decision accords as much as possible with the client's values.

In closing this discussion of client-centered decision making, one further problem requires discussion.   Suppose the client is quite willing to decide but the lawyer believes the decision is absolutely wrong.   To protect the client's interests, if the lawyer sees the client's decision as erroneous, should the lawyer urge the client to change or re-evaluate the decision?

If the client's decision appears to be erroneous because it is contrary to the values the client expressed when discussing the consequences, the lawyer can call this apparent contradiction to the client's attention.   For example, assume that in discussing the pros and cons of a possible settlement, the client stated the amount offered was of little value to him, and that what was really important was public vindication by a jury.   However, in reaching his decision, the client decided to accept the settlement.   In this situation, the lawyer would want to point out and clarify the apparent conflict between the decision and the client's expressed values.   Once this clarification has occurred, the decision should be left with the client.

9.   Since the final decision is one which the law requires be left to the client, the lawyer must obtain permission if the lawyer is to make the ultimate decision.

10.   For a discussion of the potential applicability of the doctrine of informed consent as it might relate to obtaining the client's permission, see Rosenthal supra Note 8, at 154–161.

However, what about actually urging the client to adopt a different decision? When, if ever, is the lawyer justified in taking this kind of action? Must decisions always be left to the client, since the lawyer can never fully place himself/herself in the client's position? Although it usually will be difficult to know when a lawyer's intervention is called for, we believe intervention is sometimes appropriate. From our point of view, if lawyers always refused to intervene, many overwrought or seriously disturbed clients would make decisions they would long regret. For example, many overwrought clients in dissolution cases would, at the inception of settlement negotiations, give away assets which, in reality, they could not truly afford to part with.

As a general rule, we recommend that lawyers intervene if the client's decision would likely result in substantial economic, social, or psychological harm in return for very little gain. But how is the lawyer to know when this point has been reached? There are no clear-cut answers. In Chapter Ten, we will discuss how the lawyer might determine if intervention is called for. Also discussed will be techniques for intervention.

At this juncture, rather than continuing our abstract discussion of the nature of the counseling process, we will turn our attention to a discussion of techniques for counseling clients.

Chapter Nine

CONDUCTING THE COUNSELING PROCESS

This chapter explores techniques lawyers can use to assist clients in reaching decisions. The discussion proceeds on the assumption that the client is someone who is willing and capable of making a reasonable decision; in Chapter Ten there will be an examination of how the lawyer counsels clients who do not have these characteristics.

We will begin with a description of how the lawyer might proceed with a generally willing client in order to develop a basic counseling model. The model concerns how the counseling dialogue might be organized and conducted in order to help a client reach his/her own decision after a full consideration of all the available alternatives. Our pedagogical theory is the following: If lawyers can learn to be effective with willing clients, it will be easier to learn what adaptations might be made in order to deal with clients who are unable or unwilling to engage in a full consideration of the available alternatives.

In general, our basic counseling model calls for the lawyer first to set forth all the available alternatives and then go back with the client and identify and predict the positive and negative consequences related to each alternative. In setting forth our basic counseling model, we do not mean to imply the model is the only one which can be used to counsel clients. There are undoubtedly various ways of conducting the counseling process. The approach we will outline is one which we have found to be generally useful in a variety of counseling situations.

We will analyze counseling techniques primarily in the context of the basic decision of whether or not to litigate. However, the discussion will be generally applicable to decision making in connection with auxiliary questions as well. Throughout, it will be assumed the client is asking both "What can I and should I do?"

As mentioned in Chapter One, counseling with respect to the basic decision occurs at various times during the course of representation. First, it takes place in connection with an initial decision about whether or not to litigate. If the client decides to proceed, counseling will subsequently occur at various times in connection with making or accepting of settlement offers. The principles of technique developed in this chapter will be applicable regardless of when the counseling occurs.

PREPARATION FOR COUNSELING

Before proceeding to actually conduct the counseling process, it is usually useful for the lawyer to engage in certain preparation. Typically, this preparation will involve thinking through the alternatives to be discussed, as well as the potential legal and nonlegal consequences which bear exploration. Experience indicates that if this kind of planning precedes the actual counseling process, the counseling process itself will usually proceed more smoothly, quickly, and thoroughly. Counseling, like many other tasks, can generally be carried out more competently and efficiently when it has been planned in advance.

In thinking through the legal consequences, the lawyer will want to devote considerable thought to the various sub-predictions which will make up the ultimate prediction about the outcome at trial. This prediction will often be central to the entire counseling process. Typically, only when the client is confronted with the reality of the likely outcome at trial will the client begin to meaningfully think about the corollary economic, social, and psychological consequences which may result.

To prepare for a discussion of the nonlegal consequences, it is often useful for the lawyer to write out a general list of the consequences to be explored. The content of the list can be developed by sitting back and thinking about what economic, social, and psychological consequences might result should this particular client settle, continue with the litigation, etc. Preparing a list in advance will not insure that all relevant consequences are considered. As noted earlier, one task of the lawyer during the counseling process will be to bring out consequences the lawyer has not thought of, but of which the client is aware. However, the development and utilization of such a list will often result in the client having the advantage of being able to consider a wider range of consequences than would be considered if the counseling process were approached on an "off-the-cuff" basis.

IDENTIFYING THE ALTERNATIVES

In our experience, it will frequently be useful for the lawyer to begin the counseling dialogue with a Preparatory Explanation. This explanation typically is similar to the Preparatory Explanation described in Chapter Five. The explanation can include a description of what the ensuing discussion will involve, and emphasize that the final decision will be left to the client. Later in this chapter, we will examine in detail the full content of this Preparatory Explanation. We will begin this discussion of counseling techniques with the assumption that the lawyer has already provided a Preparatory Explanation.

Under our basic counseling model, once the Preparatory Explanation has been completed, the lawyer should focus on the task of setting forth all of the alternatives. The basic alternatives should be set forth before any consequences are examined.

Often the lawyer can best accomplish the task of setting forth all available alternatives by first stating what the lawyer sees as the available alternatives, and then inquiring if the client sees any other options.[1] Should the lawyer fail to make this additional inquiry at the beginning of the discussion, difficulties may arise. If the client already has an alternative in mind which the lawyer fails to mention, the client may believe the lawyer is opposed to this unmentioned option. More importantly, if the client has an unmentioned alternative in mind, the client may not be able to fully concentrate on any analysis of the alternatives mentioned by the lawyer. For example, if the client is thinking about bankruptcy and the lawyer only mentions the alternatives of litigation or settlement, the lawyer is basically wasting time. The client's attention is probably solely focused on the unmentioned option.

The lawyer's inquiry about other alternatives is generally made in the form of an open-ended question such as: "These are the choices I have thought for us to discuss; can you think of other alternatives to be considered? It is important for you to bring up any possibility you see since, in the end, the decision should be one which you find most comfortable."

Not all lawyers, however, begin by articulating the alternatives they see as available and then inquiring if the client sees additional possibilities. Some lawyers begin, particularly with initial decisions about entering litigation, by asking the client what he/she feels or thinks ought to be done. When the client has spoken, the lawyer then articulates other options. In short, some lawyers reverse the process we have suggested. While this approach may reduce the possibility that the client may feel restricted by the lawyer's options, often we find this tack is counterproductive in terms of building client confidence and rapport. When the lawyer begins with a question such as, "What do you think we should do?", the client sometimes has a negative reaction. "What the hell are you asking me for? It's your help I'm paying for." The question sometimes creates a feeling that the lawyer is incompetent. Furthermore, if the lawyer subse-

---

1. When an auxiliary decision is involved and the lawyer has no specific knowledge or expertise to bring to bear on the decision, it might be preferable to begin the dialogue by first asking what options the client foresees. The client's general familiarity with the situation may place the client in a better position to identify potential options. Further, listening to the client discuss what he/she views as the options may cause the lawyer to think of additional options which the lawyer may not have thought of without some initial input from the client. For example, if a client charged with a criminal offense asks, "Should I tell my employer about the arrest?", perhaps it is preferable for the lawyer to begin by asking, "What do you see as the options open to you?"

quently mentions additional choices, the client may feel the lawyer is "playing games." The internal reaction is something like the following: "You started by asking me what I thought, but now you're telling me that perhaps I'm wrong. Why didn't you just tell me what you thought in the first place?"

Still other lawyers begin counseling, not by discussing the alternatives, but by discussing the factors they have been mulling over in reaching their conclusion about the likely legal outcome. The following example is illustrative:

> "Well, Bob, I've been thinking about what we should do. There are several good points. We do have Ms. Herbert who can back up your story, and also we have some bank records. But there are some problems. They do have the letter you signed and it's ambiguous on the point about the price. The cases in the area aren't too clear on how specific the price should be . . . ."

In our experience, this kind of legal analysis at the beginning is usually not terribly helpful, and in many instances may be anxiety-producing. Although most clients ultimately will want to know why their lawyer reached a given conclusion about the likely legal outcome, they usually want something else first. Typically, clients first want to know what their basic options are and what the likely outcome will be if the case proceeds to trial. Once they have heard this information, then they may be able to listen to and evaluate the basis on which the lawyer's analysis was made. Additionally, commencing with an analysis of various legal factors usually results in a dialogue which begins with a detailed discussion of the option of litigation. Perhaps the client would prefer to talk about some other alternative first. If so, why not start where the client wants to begin?

At this point, we will assume the lawyer intends to commence the counseling process by outlining the alternatives he/she sees as available, and then inquiring whether the client sees others. How should the lawyer describe the standard alternatives—litigate, settle, or forego litigation—to the client?

Describing the Alternative of Trial

Consider first how the lawyer might describe the alternative of litigation. In analyzing what result will occur at trial, the lawyer will often conclude that the trial may result in a variety of outcomes. Typically, these outcomes will range from highly favorable to highly unfavorable. In light of these varying possibilities, what is the minimum data which should be presented to the client?

Again, there is no clear cut, easy, or universally accepted answer. Hopefully, our method of approach will result in clients being able to make informed decisions without being utterly confused by too much data. In our judgment, there are as many as five possible results which the lawyer may have to describe to the client.

The five possible results are: (1) the best possible, (2) the best likely, (3) the most probable, (4) the worst likely, and (5) the worst possible. In our view, without these pieces of information, the client often will be unable to fully understand what is potentially involved in the alternative of litigation.[2]

In some instances, certain of the possible results may not exist or may overlap. For example, in a criminal case the lawyer may believe the most likely result of trial will be an acquittal. In such a case, the most probable result, the best likely result, and the best possible result will be identical. A criminal defendant generally cannot obtain a result which is better.[3] Consider another example. Assume the client has instituted an action on a promissory note to recover $1000 allegedly loaned to the defendant. Under the facts of the case, the only conclusion the court can reach is that the full amount of money either was or was not loaned. Under such circumstances, the lawyer will be concerned with only three possible results. These are the best possible, the most probable, and the worst possible. Since, under the facts of the case, the court must render an "all-or-nothing" judgment, there can be no best likely result which is different from the best possible result. Similarly, there can be no worst likely result which is different from the worst possible result.

In some cases, however, a distinction between the five categories of results may be essential to the client's full understanding. Often, without this information, the client will be unable to realistically and meaningfully appraise whether or not he/she wishes to proceed to trial. By way of illustration, consider these examples. In a criminal case, a lawyer believes the most probable result at trial is a conviction. Based upon the lawyer's knowledge of the judge's sentencing practices, the lawyer predicts that if the client is convicted the client will most probably be put on probation. Though probation is the most probable result, the lawyer does recognize there is some possibility that the client could be sentenced to a week or so in the county jail. The maximum sentence allowed under the applicable statute is six months in the county jail. If in talking with the client about the likely result at trial the lawyer omits reference to the likelihood of a week of county jail time, the client will certainly not have full information about the risks involved in proceeding to trial. Though the most probable result is probation, there is some realistic possibility of

---

2. For a discussion of the potential applicability of the "informed consent" doctrine as it might apply to client decisions, see D. Rosenthal, Lawyer and Client: Who's in Charge? 20–22, 154–161 (1974).

3. In California when a defendant is acquitted and the trial judge believes the defendant was "factually innocent," the judge may order that the record of the case and of the arrest be sealed. Thereafter, the defendant may deny being arrested. See West's Ann.Cal. Penal Code § 851.8.

one week of incarceration. Moreover, if the lawyer confines the description simply to the most probable result and the worst possible result—six months in jail—the client will be deprived of full information. Though the worst possible is six months in jail, the client cannot gain a realistic view of the trial alternative if the client is deprived of information that the realistic worst likely result is a week in jail.

Consider a second example. A civil action has been instituted to recover damages for personal injuries sustained in an automobile accident. The complaint seeks damages in the sum of $25,000. The case is now set for trial. In the lawyer's judgment, the most likely result at trial is a recovery of $6500. There is some possibility of recovering up to $12,000, but realistically no more than $12,000 can be expected. On the negative side, the lawyer is practically certain there will be some recovery. Though there is always the theoretical possibility of no recovery, the lawyer believes the worst likely result in this case is a judgment for $3000. Under these circumstances, is there any one of the five possible results which might properly be omitted from the lawyer's description of the litigation alternative? If the client is to be fully informed about the potential consequences of a decision to proceed to trial, we think all five possible results should be mentioned.

Obviously, there are innumerable gradations of result which the lawyer might provide for the client. However, in our experience, there can be such a thing as providing too many possibilities. At some point, the possibilities are so numerous they serve only to confuse. Hopefully, our suggestion about presenting the five possibilities reaches a sound mid-point between the poles of too much and too little information. Of course, whenever possible, the possibilities should be collapsed in order to minimize confusion.

Assuming the foregoing five results are to be conveyed to the client, how should they be described? Should the description of each be couched in the language of percentage chance, or are terms such as, "excellent," "very good," "good," "fairly good," etc., preferable? Certainly some understanding of the degree of chance involved is essential to understanding what proceeding to litigation entails. Lawyers typically use both kinds of descriptions when presenting the litigation alternative to their clients. We have no basis for stating which kind of terminology may be preferable. Obviously, the language used should be selected with a view toward creating maximum client comprehension. But often it will not be possible to know which term "fairly good chance" or "60 percent chance" is most meaningful to the client. Accordingly, it may be best to use both kinds of descriptions. Thus, the client could be told, "I think you have a fairly good chance, say a 70 percent chance, of prevailing."

Assume now that the lawyer has in mind the most probable result, the best possible result, the best likely result, the worst likely result, and the worst possible result. Assume further, the lawyer has decided upon the language to be used in describing the extent to which each of these consequences is likely to occur. How should the lawyer actually outline the situation for the client? In short, how should the lawyer present the litigation alternative to the client? There may be a variety of ways in which this alternative can be meaningfully communicated. What we will describe is a method which our experience indicates is quite successful in communicating this complex predictive information to clients.

The most probable result is set forth as an integral part of the description of the litigation alternative itself. Thus, when the lawyer is listing the alternative of trial, the lawyer says something to the effect of:

> "One alternative is to proceed to trial. If you decide to do this, I would say there is a fairly good chance, perhaps a 70 percent chance, of your recovering $1500."

However, what about presenting the remaining possible results? Under the approach we use, these remaining possibilities are *not* included in the initial description of the alternative of trial. Rather, their description is usually reserved until all the basic alternatives have been described and the lawyer-client dialogue begins to examine the positive and negative consequences of each of the alternatives. Accordingly, at this time we will defer a description of how the best possible, best likely, worst likely, and worst possible results are presented to the client until our later discussion of how the lawyer directs an analysis of the legal and nonlegal consequences of each alternative.

Our approach in deferring discussion of the results other than the most probable result, grows out of our experience in counseling clients. In our experience, what clients typically want at the inception of the counseling dialogue is a succinct statement of their basic alternatives. Although generally clients will want to know of all the possibilities that apply to their case, they usually want the basics first. By following the approach of deferring discussion of the possibilities other than that of the most probable result, the lawyer can usually satisfy the client's desire to obtain the basics first. Additionally, in our experience, proceeding in the manner we have suggested often produces less client confusion, since all the possibilities need not be assimilated at one time. Of course, if the client raises an immediate question about the other possible results, these should be discussed.

Others may have very different approaches than the one outlined in this section. Certainly, these other approaches may also be useful, so long as they provide the necessary predictive information in a non-confusing manner.

Describing the Alternative of Settlement

Consider next how the lawyer might describe the alternative of settlement. Under our approach, when the lawyer is setting forth an offer made by another party, the description simply outlines the offer:

> "One alternative to consider is their offer of settlement; they are willing to pay you $3500 and provide you with a year's free rent."

In setting forth the alternative, the lawyer states the offer but defers any analysis of its pros and cons until all alternatives have been laid out.

If, however, the case calls for the client to consider making an offer or a demand, the situation becomes much more complex. To decide what offer or demand should be tendered, there first must be an analysis of what settlement options are open, and what are the likely consequences of adopting each of the options. Finally, the client must weigh the various settlement options and decide which alternative seems best. In short, deciding what offer or demand to make involves an auxiliary decision to be worked out as a part of, and *in the same manner as*, the basic decision of whether or not to litigate.

Where the settlement alternative calls for the client to make an offer or demand, the lawyer's initial statement about the existence of this option generally will be quite limited. If a lawyer follows the method of approach we suggest, the lawyer usually does no more than the following: The lawyer alludes to the possibility of making an offer or demand, and informs the client that one subject to be discussed during the course of the conference is what offer or demand should be made.[4]

> "One option to be considered is whether or not, at this point, you want to make a settlement offer. Later we can discuss what offer, if any, you might make."

Describing the Alternative of Foregoing Litigation

Insofar as describing the alternative of foregoing litigation is concerned, the lawyer's task is relatively easy. Under our approach, all the lawyer need do is outline the legal consequences of adopting such a decision:

> "Another choice would be to simply do nothing. If you do that, they will recover a judgment against you for $1000. That means you will be legally obligated to pay them $1000 . . . ."

4. In this text, we will not examine the issue of the extent to which clients should participate in decisions about the *strategy* to be employed in making "high" demands or "low" offers. For a general discussion of the benefits of active client participation in the planning and handling of a lawsuit, see D. Rosenthal, Lawyer and Client: Who's in Charge? (1974).

Again, under our approach, analysis of the pros and cons of the alternative are deferred until all basic alternatives have been laid out.

In setting forth the alternatives the lawyer sees as available, should the lawyer always include the option of foregoing litigation? We think not. In some cases, the client's whole manner of presentation and attitude will make it abundantly clear that the possibility of abandonment is not within the realm of consideration. Under such circumstances, to mention the possibility of dropping the matter may indicate to the client that the lawyer has not really listened to what the client has been saying. Moreover, in some instances the mention of the option may be taken as a subtle hint that the lawyer believes the case should be dropped. Again, the lawyer's personal judgment must be used to decide whether or not to mention the possibility.

Identifying Alternatives: A Summary

We will summarize, in terms of technique, how we believe the counseling process might be initiated. We shall do so through an example. Assume the client has been sued for $1220 as the result of an alleged deficiency which occurred following the repossession and sale of the client's automobile. The case is at issue, discovery has been completed, and the plaintiff has offered to accept $500. The case is set for trial tomorrow, and at this point the lawyer is convinced that further negotiation will not be fruitful. The lawyer believes the most probable result at trial is a judgment that the client is not liable at all. The lawyer feels there is about an 80 percent chance that this result will obtain. Under the facts of the case, there need not be an "all-or-nothing" judgment. The lawyer believes the worst likely outcome is a judgment against the client for $800. As for this possibility, the lawyer believes there is less than a five percent chance.

Under these circumstances here is how the lawyer might proceed to initiate the counseling process once the lawyer has provided a Preparatory Explanation.

L.   As I see the situation, Ms. Royce, there are two choices open to you at this point. First, you could accept the plaintiff's offer and agree to pay the $500. The other alternative is to proceed to trial. If you do that, I think there is about an 80 percent chance you will have to pay nothing. At this point, I don't think further negotiations will do any good. So what the situation comes down to is settling for $500 or going to trial, at least as far as I can see. However, maybe there is some other possibility that you can think of. It's important that we consider all the options, particularly other options that you might think of. Can you think of any others?

C.   No, I really can't. I'd like to go to trial, but I'm a little afraid.

L. I can see you're somewhat concerned and that's the kind
    of thing we want to talk about next. We should go over
    each of the two possibilities and try and figure out what are
    the advantages and disadvantages of each. I think when we
    have done that you'll feel more certain about what you want
    to do. Which alternative do you want to discuss first, trial
    or the settlement offer?

In describing the respective alternatives, the lawyer follows our
suggested approach. With respect to the litigation alternative, the legal consequences are described in terms of the most probable result
—80 percent chance of paying nothing. The matter of the worst
likely and worst possible outcomes are deferred for discussion during
the analysis of the consequences. The lawyer also explains that the
typical option of further negotiation is not available. The lawyer
then goes on to inquire if the client can think of other options. The
lawyer's explanation of why further negotiation is not available is
also deferred for later discussion, should the client desire information
on the point. The rationale for reserving this topic is the same as
that for not beginning with an analysis of how the lawyer arrived at
the prediction of the most probable result.

In sum, the lawyer quickly and simply lays out the full range of
available alternatives. The lawyer does so without becoming bogged
down in a detailed analysis of any of the alternatives. Under this approach, the client can quickly see what basic alternatives are available and then choose which he/she wishes to discuss first.

In reviewing this example, it should also be noted how, in the
midst of structuring the examination of alternatives, the lawyer provided an empathetic response. The lawyer used an active listening
type response to reflect the client's fears of going to trial before proceeding with a discussion of the alternatives. As we will discuss in
more detail later, active listening will typically be as much a part of
the counseling dialogue as it is of the interviewing dialogue. Finally,
it should be noted that in the example, the lawyer concludes the discussion of alternatives by asking, "Which alternative do you want to
discuss first, trial or the settlement offer?" When the lawyer desires
to turn the conversation to a discussion of the consequences, this can
be done effectively by asking the client which alternative he/she
wishes to discuss first. Proceeding in this manner has three potential advantages. It may avoid creating the impression that the lawyer favors an alternative because the lawyer selected it first. Also,
allowing the client the choice may help reinforce the message that
the client should feel free to make the ultimate decision. Finally,
giving the client the choice permits the client to start with the alternative which the client feels most comfortable with, or concerned
about.

ANALYZING THE CONSEQUENCES

After the lawyer and client have joined their talents to articulate the alternatives that bear consideration, the counseling dialogue can then be turned to an analysis of the potential consequences of each alternative. In some cases, of course, the parties will, for one reason or another, return to the consideration of additional alternatives. In short, it must be recognized that though the process of identifying alternatives usually will precede the process of analyzing the consequences, the counseling dialogue may go back and forth between these two processes.

The exploration of the consequences should be very thorough so that the client's final decision can be made in the light of all the relevant considerations. Additionally, it is critically important the exploration be conducted in a manner which gives the client a genuine feeling that the client can and should make his/her own decision. The examination must, therefore, be conducted in such a way that the client does not get a feeling that despite what the lawyer says, the lawyer really does have a preference about what alternative is chosen. If a client, particularly a passive client, gets a feeling the lawyer has a preference, this feeling may substantially influence the final decision. In short, the final decision may be made not so much on the basis of the client's values as on the basis of what the client surmises the lawyer thinks is best. Often clients are remarkably sensitive to, and easily swayed by, what they guess their lawyer thinks is best for them. As a consequence, many clients make decisions with which they are not truly comfortable. To prevent this kind of decision making, the lawyer should consciously make every effort to communicate neutrality and the desirability of the client making his/her own decision.

The techniques which the lawyer uses to conduct the process of examining the consequences will have a substantial bearing on both the thoroughness of the process and the client's perception of the lawyer's neutrality. It is to these techniques in light of the goals of thoroughness and neutrality to which we now turn.

In directing the analysis of the positive and negative consequences the lawyer will, as noted earlier, usually perform two tasks. The lawyer will both identify the consequences which he/she sees as probable and also inquire of the client what consequences the client foresees. Thus, the lawyer will both provide information and make inquiries.

Describing the Possible Consequences of Trial

As will be recalled, under our method of approach possible results at trial, other than the most probable result, are deferred for description until all the alternatives have been outlined and the parties have commenced a discussion of the consequences. Accordingly, we are now ready to describe the general method of approach we suggest lawyers use in describing possible results at trial, other than that of the most probable result. Our description will include the four possible results other than that of the most probable result. Recall, however, that because of overlap in some cases, there may be fewer possible results that need to be presented to the client.

Under our approach, the best possible, the best likely, the worst likely, and the worst possible results are generally couched in terms of advantages and disadvantages of going to trial. The best possible and best likely are typically described as advantages. The best likely, for example, would be described in terms similar to the following:

> "If you decide to go to trial, one advantage you'll have is that you'll retain a small chance, perhaps a ten percent chance, of recovering $4000."

The worst likely and worst possible, on the other hand, are described as disadvantages. Thus, the worst possible result would be described in language such as:

> "One disadvantage of going to trial is that you'll be taking a small risk, perhaps a ten percent chance, of recovering nothing."

In addition, these same four possible results may also be described as advantages and disadvantages of settlement. In a choice between settlement and trial, the trial advantage of retaining the opportunity to gain more will typically become a settlement disadvantage if the settlement alternative is chosen. By settling, the client will give up the opportunity to gain more. Conversely, the trial disadvantage of risking less than the settlement offer will become the settlement advantage of avoiding the risk of less than the settlement offer. At this point, the reader may feel somewhat confused by this "crossover concept."

An example may be illustrative of the way in which trial advantages typically become settlement disadvantages, and trial disadvantages typically become settlement advantages. Assume a client has instituted suit to recover damages for fraud in connection with the leasing of a house. The suit seeks damages in the sum of $4000. The defendant has offered $800 by way of settlement. Upon analyzing the case, the plaintiff's lawyer believes the most probable result and the best likely result is a judgment for $1500. The lawyer believes there is a 70 percent chance of such a recovery. The lawyer believes there is only a 10 percent chance of achieving the best possible result—a $4000 recovery. On the downside, the lawyer believes there is only a five percent chance of recovering nothing, and that the worst likely result is $500. The lawyer believes there is only a 10 percent chance of this result.

In these circumstances, the legal consequences of proceeding to trial might look like, and could be described as, the following:

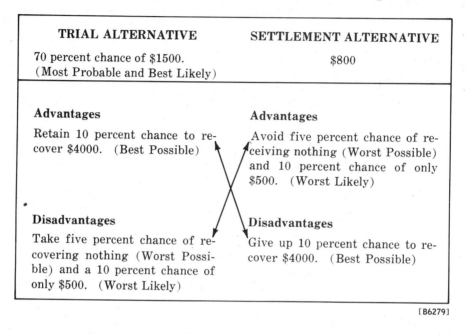

TRIAL ALTERNATIVE	SETTLEMENT ALTERNATIVE
70 percent chance of $1500. (Most Probable and Best Likely)	$800

Advantages

Retain 10 percent chance to recover $4000. (Best Possible)

Advantages

Avoid five percent chance of receiving nothing (Worst Possible) and 10 percent chance of only $500. (Worst Likely)

Disadvantages

Take five percent chance of recovering nothing (Worst Possible) and a 10 percent chance of only $500. (Worst Likely)

Disadvantages

Give up 10 percent chance to recover $4000. (Best Possible)

[B6279]

Inquiring About Consequences the Client Foresees

In addition to providing information about the consequences the lawyer foresees, the lawyer will also want to inquire into consequences the client foresees. Typically, the topics the lawyer will inquire into will come from the lawyer's list of possible consequences. Assume the list of potential consequences which the lawyer developed before commencing the interview [5] includes the topic of the "effect on the client's job." To inquire into such topics, the lawyer might begin with a series of questions initiated somewhat as follows: "Do you think there is going to be any effect on your job if you accept the settlement offer?" If the answer is "yes," but without thorough explanation, a more open-ended question will usually be required to help the client clarify the extent or degree of the effect. "What effect do you foresee?" In general, each topic on the lawyer's list keys a sequence of questions initiated in the manner just described.

The list, of course, will not contain all the possible economic, social, and psychological consequences. The lawyer simply does not

---

5. Of course, the lawyer must prepare the list from a neutral point of view. If the lawyer allows his/her personal sense of what would be best to operate, the list could easily be limited so as to bring about the alternative favored by the lawyer. For a discussion of how a lawyer's personality may influence the choice a client makes, see Redmount, *Attorney Personalities and Some Psychological Aspects of Legal Consultation,* 109 U. Penn.L.Rev. 972 (1961); see also Chilar, *Client Self-Determination: Intervention or Interference,* 14 St. Louis Univ.L.J. 604, 619–623 (1970).

have the ability to sit back and list all potential consequences. Therefore, a thorough exploration of the consequences will have to include an effort to bring out those consequences which the lawyer has not thought about. Generally, this kind of inquiry can be conducted through a sequence of open-ended questions. The questions are generally framed in terms of asking the client to articulate the advantages (pros) or disadvantages (cons) he/she foresees with respect to a given alternative. The following example is illustrative:

No. 1–L   What advantages do you see, if any, to accepting their offer?

No. 2–C   For one thing, it would get the whole mess over with now, and I wouldn't have any more expense.

No. 3–L   What other advantages?

No. 4–C   There are things I could do with that money right now, and I know it would please my husband to have the whole thing over with. He has been against this suit from the start.

No. 5–L   So, as you see it, you'll get the mess over with now, get the money now, and minimize the tension with your husband. Can you see any other advantages of settling?

How long the lawyer might continue to pursue such an open line of inquiry before changing to another topic, such as disadvantages, cannot be stated with certainty. We should note, however, that in using this kind of questioning sequence, it is often helpful to use the summarization technique shown in No. 5. This summary technique can help clarify what has been discussed so far and perhaps free the client to explore additional consequences.

Converting Potential Consequences into Categories of Advantages and Disadvantages [6]

The lawyer's inquiries about consequences sometimes do not call for the client to respond in terms of advantages and disadvantages. The following questions are illustrative:

"How might going to trial affect your job?"

"What effect will pleading guilty have on your family situation?"

"How will settling affect your overall financial situation?"

Clients typically respond to these kinds of inquiries with statements and explanations which do not include the terms "advantage" or "disadvantage." To facilitate the final weighing process, it can be helpful if the lawyer *converts* the client's statement into the language

---

6. In this text, the terms advantages, positive consequences, and pros are used interchangeably as are the terms disadvantages, negative consequences, and cons.

of advantage or disadvantage. When clients can see the consequences in terms of pros and cons, clients seem better able to compare and contrast the available alternatives. The following examples illustrate this conversion process:

Case No. 1:

L.   How might pleading guilty affect your job?

C.   Well, I heard that one guy who had a conviction couldn't get a promotion even though he deserved it.

L.   So, a disadvantage of pleading guilty may be that it could affect your job. This is something we may want to check out.

Case No. 2:

L.   What effect will pleading guilty have on your family situation?

C.   Hard to say for sure, but it could make it rough on my wife. She teaches Sunday school, and if it were to get around that I was convicted, she could be in an awkward situation.

L.   So there could be another disadvantage of pleading guilty. How likely do you think it is that this will happen to her?

Case No. 3:

L.   How will settling affect your overall financial situation?

C.   Well, I'm broke now. Getting only $500 really won't help all that much since I have a whole bunch of bills.

L.   So, there is not too much of an economic advantage to accepting the settlement.

Organizing the Examination of the Consequences

With regard to the matter of thoroughly exploring the possible consequences in a neutral manner, there are a number of issues regarding techniques for organizing the dialogue that bear examination. First, should the dialogue be organized so as to examine one alternative at a time? That is, should the lawyer attempt to focus the analysis on all of the positive and negative consequences of one alternative before discussing the consequences of a second alternative? Additionally, if there is to be a focus on one alternative at a time, should the process be structured to examine the positive and negative consequences as separate units? Perhaps by narrowing the focus in either of the ways just suggested, the lawyer can reduce the likelihood that potential consequences will be omitted from the analysis. For example, if there could be a focus on all the advantages of proceeding to trial before skipping to another topic, perhaps there could be a more thorough exploration of each topic.

Our experience suggests that while this kind of structure may promote thoroughness, it is often too restrictive for the normal thought patterns of most clients. Given that the disadvantages of proceeding to trial are often the advantages of settlement and vice versa, clients will frequently be inclined to jump back and forth between these alternatives. Similarly, the mention of a positive consequence often triggers some thoughts about a negative consequence, and vice versa. For example, mentioning the positive economic consequences of recovering more money if the case proceeds to trial may kindle some thought about possible negative economic consequences such as additional attorneys' fees and court costs. Moreover, in our experience, if the lawyer begins to focus exclusively on one alternative or on one set of positive or negative consequences, the client may get the impression that the lawyer has some unexpressed bias either for or against a particular alternative.

Accordingly, in terms of rigid structure, we believe that if the lawyer is to focus the analysis of consequences exclusively on those of one alternative, or exclusively on one set of positive or negative consequences, the lawyer should do so only after allowing the client initial freedom to jump back and forth between alternatives and pros and cons. Our observation is that if clients are initially permitted some freedom to jump back and forth between alternatives and consequences, they sometimes develop and recognize the need for some assistance in structuring the inquiry into possible consequences. Some clients become so confused and anxious as the result of the jumping back and forth that they begin to appreciate any structured approach the lawyer might impose.

If the lawyer is not to restrict the analysis of consequences to one alternative at a time, should there be an attempt to restrict the number of alternatives that are being considered simultaneously? For example, should there be a simultaneous consideration of the options of litigation, settlement, default, and bankruptcy? Our experience does not lead us to anything approximating a definitive answer. Probably the resolution must come from the lawyer's assessment of the client's capability (and the lawyer's) to consider more than two options at a time without becoming too confused. In our experience, this assessment is critical. When the number of alternatives and consequences become so numerous that the client can no longer keep them clearly in mind, the client will often abdicate the decision-making role to the lawyer.

As noted earlier, in directing the analysis of the consequences the lawyer will usually perform two tasks. The lawyer will both identify potential consequences the lawyer foresees and also inquire what consequences the client foresees. With regard to these two tasks, is it significant which task the lawyer undertakes first? Assume the interview reaches the point where the lawyer believes it would be useful to discuss the potential consequences which the lawyer foresees with regard to the alternative of proceeding to trial. With respect to the potential social consequences, the lawyer knows from prior contact with the client and the client's neighbors (the lawyer's data base) that should the client prevail many people in the neighborhood will think quite highly of the client. Accordingly, in discussing the potential social consequences, the lawyer plans not only to ask what social consequences the client foresees, but also to point out the potential advantage of increased popularity with the neighbors. In terms of providing the client with a feeling the lawyer is truly neutral, is it significant whether the lawyer makes inquiry into the social consequences the client foresees before pointing out the consequence of social popularity, or proceeds in the opposite order? Our observations do not lead us to any general conclusion on this issue. Our intuitive bias is to elicit the client's perceptions first. Similarly, when it comes to inquiring about, or mentioning, positive and negative consequences is it significant which are mentioned first? Again, our observations do not lead us to any general conclusion. Hopefully, in the near future clinical research will begin to provide some factors which can be looked to in resolving these questions.

The Lawyer's Demeanor

Apart from the foregoing questions regarding general organization, there is the *critical* matter of the lawyer's *demeanor*. The lawyer's tone of voice, facial expressions, language, and timing in switching from one set of consequences to another must all be congruent with the verbal assertion of neutrality. If by the force or tone of his/her voice the lawyer emphasizes certain consequences, the client will quickly sense, whether it is true or not, that the lawyer does have a preference. If the lawyer repeatedly calls attention to a particular set of consequences, the same result will often occur. If the lawyer reacts to a client's focus on positive consequences by quickly switching to a discussion of the negative consequences, the lawyer again may be perceived as being less than neutral.

Consider these examples. In which does the lawyer appear to have the most neutral reaction to the client's statement?

Case No. 1:

C.   One real disadvantage I see in going to trial is all this extra expense.

L.   But don't forget what you have to gain if you win. You have to look at both sides.

Case No. 2:

C.   One real disadvantage I see in going to trial is all this extra expense.

L.   But do you see some advantages of proceeding to trial?

Case No. 3:

C.   One real disadvantage I see in going to trial is all this extra expense.

L.   Certainly, that would be a disadvantage. How about advantages of trial, do you see anything there?

Active Listening: Its Importance in Counseling

In stressing lawyer neutrality, we do not wish to imply that during the discussion of alternatives and the analysis of consequences the lawyer should ignore feelings. Quite the contrary. Maintaining lawyer-client rapport throughout the interviewing and counseling processes will be critical. Therefore, empathetic listening should be as much a part of the counseling process as it is of the interviewing process. Generally, unless the client senses he/she is in the presence of someone who has the capacity for non-judgmental understanding, the client may fail to fully explore all of the relevant consequences. Common inhibitors such as ego threat, etiquette barrier, etc., may block open discussion. In particular, our experience suggests that unless the lawyer creates an atmosphere of openness and acceptance, the client may feel reluctant to identify and discuss social and psychological consequences, despite their significance. Instead, the counseling dialogue will tend to focus on the more concrete economic consequences, and thus fail to develop into a thorough exploration of the alternatives. Accordingly, to insure full exploration we wish to emphasize the importance of using active listening and other motivational techniques throughout the counseling process.

Explaining Legal Terminology

Before concluding this discussion of the techniques used in examining consequences, note must be made of the difficulties caused by the use of legal jargon. During the process of reviewing the legal consequences, lawyers often resort to the use of a great deal of legal jargon. Many clients do not understand terms such as writ of execution, judgment, preliminary injunction, probable cause, etc. When the lawyer uses such terms, the client is often too embarrassed to ask what they mean. As a result, clients often decide what to do without fully understanding the legal ramifications of their decisions.

Thorough consideration will usually not be possible until the client clearly understands the meaning of the legal ramifications associated with each of the alternatives. Therefore, the lawyer's task is not only to identify probable legal consequences, but also to clearly explain to the client the meaning and implications of these consequences. Thus, it will often not suffice to tell a client, "If you don't answer, they'll get a judgment against you." What is an answer? How does one answer? What is a judgment against you? What are the ramifications of a judgment against you?

Generally, to explain legal terminology it will be useful to use some combination of simple language, over-simplification, and example. Consider the following illustration:

"If we do not file an answer, they'll get a judgment against you. An answer is a paper signed by you or your lawyer stating why you believe you don't owe them any money. If this paper is not filed, the court will give them a paper, a judgment, which they can take to the sheriff for the purpose of having the sheriff take from you certain property, like your bank account. If you don't want them to be able to do that, then we must file your answer with the court within the next five days."

This example may strike many as unduly patronizing and simplistic. Certainly this kind of an explanation would not be used with a client who has had considerable experience with the law. However, many people, even those who are quite intelligent, do not understand the *meaning and implication* of legal jargon. What explanation might be given to an inexperienced client who is to be told about any of the following?

(1) a set of interrogatories

(2) a deposition

(3) a motion to suppress

(4) a motion for discovery

(5) an appeal

Assume that in the course of deciding whether or not to proceed to trial, the lawyer mentions the possibility of an appeal. In response, the client inquires, "What is an appeal?" Is the following an adequate response? "An appeal means we can have a higher court look at the judge's decision to see if the judge made correct rulings during the trial." If your answer is "yes," consider if the explanation might leave the client with any of the following questions:

(1) "Do I have to testify again?"

(2) "What happens if the higher court says the judge was wrong?"

(3) "What happens to me in the meantime?"

Identifying the Consequences: A Summary

We will summarize the discussion of the techniques involved in the process of identifying consequences through an example. Mary Hicks is thirty-two years of age, divorced, and the mother of one child. She holds a masters' degree in social welfare and is currently employed as the assistant executive director of a very prominent and successful day-care center. Two months ago, Ms. Hicks was arrested and charged with assault on a police officer. Ms. Hicks' lawyer is Martha Reyes. Ms. Reyes is an experienced criminal defense lawyer. Ms. Hicks came to Ms. Reyes on the basis of a referral made by Henry Joffers, who is a member of the board of directors of the day-care center. At the time of the referral, Joffers also contacted Ms. Reyes directly. He told Ms. Reyes that he believed some members of the board knew of the arrest, and would not look kindly on Ms. Hicks should she be convicted.

Trial is set for tomorrow morning. Ms. Reyes has completed her pretrial discovery and believes there is an 80 percent chance that Ms. Hicks will be acquitted. Ms. Hicks asserts the reason she was arrested was that she blew her cool when a police officer who allegedly stopped her for a traffic infraction suggested the whole matter might be forgotten if he had Ms. Hicks' phone number. When the suggestion was made, Ms. Hicks started talking about reporting the officer; at that point the officer became abusive. Ms. Hicks responded and the arrest ensued.

Ms. Reyes believes there is a very good chance Ms. Hicks will be believed because Ms. Reyes has located another woman who has made a similar complaint against the arresting officer. Ms. Reyes believes she can introduce this woman's testimony. All in all, Ms. Reyes believes there is an 80 percent chance of an acquittal. On the other hand, should Ms. Hicks be convicted, Ms. Reyes believes the worst likely result will be a $250 fine and six months' informal probation. The worst possible result would be a $1000 fine and six months in jail. Under the applicable state law, a conviction would not render Ms. Hicks ineligible for any government employment. If the case proceeds to trial, Ms. Reyes expects it will last a day and a half; her fees for this work will be an additional $650.

Ms. Reyes has had a discussion with the prosecutor about dismissing the case. The best "deal" which Ms. Reyes could work out to this point was a plea to a count of disturbing the peace, and a $50 fine with no probation. Ms. Reyes is convinced that at this point there is still a fair chance the case would be dropped if Ms. Hicks would agree to plead guilty to the traffic infraction and stipulate there was probable cause for her arrest. The latter would be required in an attempt to insulate the officer and the city from civil damages.[7]

---

7. The practice of prosecutors insisting upon stipulations or agreements to probable cause in order to foreclose civil suits for false arrest and imprisonment may be widespread. The practice is certainly improper. ABA Code of Professional Responsibility DR 7–105 states that:
"A lawyer shall not present, participate in presenting, or threaten to present criminal charges solely to obtain an advantage in a civil matter."

The practice of demanding such stipulations has been declared unconstitutional. MacDonald v. Musick, 425 F. 2d 373 (9th Cir. 1970). Nevertheless, the practice is still sanctioned by some courts. See Leonard v. City of Los Angeles, 31 Cal.App.3d 473, 107 Cal.Rptr. 378 (1973), and Boyd v. Adams, 364 F.Supp. 1180 (N.D.Ill.1973), both of which claim unconvincingly that MacDonald is distinguishable. See also Dixon v. District of Columbia, 129 U.S.App.D.C. 341, 394 F.2d 966 (1968).

In preparation for a conference with her client, Ms. Reyes has prepared the following list of consequences to be explored in addition to the legal consequences.

Economic	Social	Psychological
Present job	Relations at work	Strain of trial
Future jobs	Social acquaintances	Regret of plea
Attorney fees	Family relationships	
Fine		
Civil damages		

[B6280]

Ms. Reyes intends to point out the financial consequences of the attorney fees and the fine. Insofar as the remaining consequences are concerned, Ms. Reyes does not believe, with two exceptions, she has sufficient data to predict the result. Therefore, with respect to the remainder of the potential consequences, Ms. Reyes intends to confine her role to inquiring of the client what consequences she foresees. The exceptions concern Ms. Hicks' present and future employment. With regard to the present employment, Ms. Reyes plans to add to any data base Ms. Hicks may have by telling Ms. Hicks of the comments of Mr. Joffers. As for the consequences on future employment, Ms. Reyes intends to add to whatever data base Ms. Hicks possesses the information that a conviction would not be an automatic bar from governmental employment.

Our hypothetical picks up at the point where Ms. Reyes begins to outline the alternatives. In the interests of time, we will not attempt to reproduce the full interview.

No. 1–L Mary, as I see the situation, you have three choices. Let me review these and then we can see if you can think of some others. One option is to accept the plea bargain. If you do that, you'll plead guilty to disturbing the peace and pay a $50 fine. There will be no probation.

A second choice is to take the case to trial. If we do that, I think you have an 80 percent chance of being found not guilty. Finally, there may be the possibility of negotiating a slightly better deal. I'm not sure if we can do it. I won't know until right before the trial. The deal would be that you plead guilty to the traffic infraction, and stipulate in court that the police officer had probable cause to arrest you. If you do that, you'll have no criminal conviction, but you may not be able to sue the police officer and the City for damages for false arrest.

	Given these three options, can you think of any other choices?
No. 2–C	No, but I don't understand this probable cause business.
No. 3–L	I can understand that, legal jargon is often confusing. I'll explain probable cause as we get into the possible advantages and disadvantages of each of the choices, and that's what we'll do now. Is there one alternative that you would like to discuss first?
No. 4–C	Well, what about this probable cause situation?
No. 5–L	Okay, let me start by explaining a little more about what is involved. Stipulating to probable cause means that you deny assaulting the police officer but, in effect, you agree the police officer didn't in any sense knowingly act improperly. If you do that, you may not be able to subsequently sue the police officer or the City on the ground that you were falsely arrested. The courts of this state have never ruled on the point, and the courts elsewhere seem to be split on the question of these stipulations for probable cause having any effect on a person's right to damages in a civil action for false arrest. I'd say the chances are pretty good that in this state you could still sue for damages. Accordingly, if you decide on the infraction option, one disadvantage will be that you are taking a risk, say a thirty percent risk, that you may be giving up your rights to subsequently recover damages. Does that give you an idea of what is involved?
No. 6–C	Yes.
No. 7–L	Do you want to pursue the infraction option or shall we discuss something else?
No. 8–C	Actually, I think I'd like to talk about going to trial; damn it, that police officer was trying to take advantage of me and now they are trying to blackmail me. Let's talk about going to trial; that's what I think I'd like to do.
No. 9–L	I can really understand your anger. First, the officer tries to take advantage, and now they are trying to protect themselves by putting you on the defensive. What specifically are the advantages you see in going to trial?
No. 10–C	First of all, I'd get the satisfaction of having that cop know what people really think about him. I'd prove to everyone that what I said was correct.

No. 11–L   From the way you say that, I can see that getting the satisfaction of proving you're correct is quite important to you. What other advantages do you see?

No. 12–C   Well, it wouldn't hurt me at work.

No. 13–L   Can you tell me a little more about that?

No. 14–C   Well, I've been told by the executive director that some people at the day-care center are not too pleased about my being arrested; the wrong image and all that sort of thing.

No. 15–L   Do you think it would endanger your job if you were convicted?

No. 16–C   I don't know. What do you think?

No. 17–L   Well, Mr. Joffers told me that some members of the board of directors are not too pleased with your being arrested. But I really don't know enough about the situation to have a good idea about what would happen to you. You are much closer to the situation than I am. What do you think?

No. 18–C   I really don't know, but it does concern me; that's why the infraction possibility is somewhat attractive.

No. 19–L   Okay, let's talk about that again, but before we do, let me mention a couple of points. First, do you think before tomorrow you could get any more information about whether your job might be in jeopardy? If it might be, then going to trial would have a disadvantage which perhaps you should consider. Okay, what about the infraction possibility? What advantages do you see there?

No. 20–C   Well, for one thing, I'd get this whole mess off my mind. Also, there would be no problem with my job, I'm sure of that.

No. 21–L   What else can you think of that might be an advantage?

No. 22–C   Nothing really, but with that probable cause thing, I would be admitting something I don't believe.

No. 23–L   That the police officer didn't realize he was wrong. I can tell that would really bother you. Do you think it would bother you for a long time?

No. 24–C   I really don't know. What do you think?

No. 25–L   Mary, you know yourself best; I really can't predict how you are going to feel. Only you can know that, and how you feel is what's important because you're going to have to live with the decision. Think about it. Do you think it would bother you for a long time that you had sort of admitted the officer was right when you don't feel that way?

No. 26–C   I think it would.

No. 27–L   Okay, then we have a disadvantage in going the infraction route. Again, keep in mind that I'm not sure I can get them to go for the deal. But let's go back to the positive side of the infraction for a moment. There are some other advantages to that option. First of all, it would be the cheapest way to go. There would be no more attorney fees. If the case goes to trial, my additional fees will probably run about $650.

No. 28–C   I don't give a damn about the money; it's the principle that's important. Do you really think I have an 80 percent chance of winning?

No. 29–L   Yes, I really do. You see, I have discovered that this officer once did this sort of thing before, and the woman is willing to testify. I think that makes your chances very good.

No. 30–C   If she will testify, how can I lose?

No. 31–L   Well, first of all, there is some possibility that the judge will rule her testimony is not admissible. The chance is small, but it's there. Also, in this other case, the woman wasn't arrested. She said nothing at the scene and complained after she paid her fine. The difference may affect the jury. On balance, I'd say you have an 80 percent chance, but there definitely is a risk that you could be convicted.

No. 32–C   What happens then?

No. 33–L   Well, I think what probably would happen, and this seems to me to be the worst that could likely happen, is that you would be fined $250 and be placed on informal probation for six months. Theoretically, you could be sentenced to six months in jail and given a $1000 fine, but this is extremely unlikely to happen. One disadvantage of going to trial, therefore, is taking a 20 percent risk of the conviction and a $250 fine plus informal probation. Also, you'd be out the $650 in attorney fees. So trial involves the risk of the conviction and being out $900. Before we go on, let's kind of summarize where we are. On the positive side of going to trial, we have the matter of your personal satisfaction of proving you're

right. We also have the advantage of probably pre-
serving your right to maintain a civil suit should you
decide to sue. We really don't have an advantage
over the infraction when it comes to your present
job. If you win or if you go the infraction route,
your job is not in jeopardy . . . .

We will now analyze this illustration on the basis of the principles which have been developed earlier in this chapter, and also in
Chapter Eight.

The lawyer initiates the counseling process in accordance with
the model outlined earlier. In No. 1, the lawyer sets forth the three
options she sees and asks the client if the client sees others. In setting out each of the alternatives, the lawyer describes the basic legal
consequences of each. When setting out the alternative of trial, the
lawyer confines the description to the most probable result. She does
not attempt, at this initial stage, to bring out all the possible results,
and she does not go into a lengthy analysis of how she arrived at her
conclusion. She does, however, present her conclusion about the
most probable result. She attempts to describe that conclusion in a
quantitative manner so that the client is given some understanding of
the lawyer's professional estimate of the degree of risk involved.

No. 2 illustrates the point that when discussing legal consequences the lawyer must be careful to explain legal jargon. Remember, many clients won't understand the meaning of terms such as
probable cause, informal probation, etc.

No. 3 illustrates how our suggested approach of first reviewing
the alternatives and then reviewing the consequences must be taken
only as a general guideline. In No. 2, the client asks for an explanation of the "probable cause business." Good relations with the client
probably dictate that the lawyer provide a direct response. The lawyer does not, however, provide an immediate explanation. Rather,
the lawyer attempts to return to our suggested approach by asking
the client which alternative the client wishes to discuss first. In
most instances of this kind, the lawyer should probably deviate from
the general approach long enough to respond to the client's confusion.

Although the lawyer was perhaps not particularly effective in responding to the client's inquiry, the lawyer was effective in using active listening to respond to the client's feeling of confusion. No. 3 illustrates how active listening responses are typically incorporated
into the counseling process.

No. 5 illustrates not only how a lawyer might go about explaining a legal term to a client, but more importantly, how a lawyer
might go about explaining an open or unsettled question of law.
Note how the lawyer includes in the description the degree of chance
involved. The explanation is certainly not complete, but it may be
sufficient for an initial discussion of the alternatives. No. 5 also il-

lustrates how the lawyer can tie the explanation of a possible legal consequence to the concept of advantages and disadvantages. The lawyer first explains the legal consequence of stipulating to probable cause. The lawyer then *converts* this explanation to the language of disadvantage: "Accordingly, if you decide on the infraction option, one disadvantage will be that you are taking a risk. . . . ." As noted earlier, this kind of conversion to the language of advantage and disadvantage may aid the client in the final weighing process.

In No. 7, the lawyer recognizes that once the term "probable cause" has been clarified, the client might wish to discuss another alternative. Accordingly, the lawyer provides the client with the opportunity to change the course of the discussion.

No. 9 is another attempt at active listening. However, does the lawyer go too far? Does the response perhaps approve (judge) the reaction rather than remain confined to demonstrating that the lawyer has heard and understood the client?

No. 9 does, however, illustrate how the lawyer might initiate the examination of the consequences of an alternative which the client desires to explore. Rather than saying anything about how the lawyer sees the situation, the lawyer throws the analysis open to the client. Though the lawyer restricts the client to considering advantages, the inquiry is initiated through a fairly open-ended question. In an overall sense, the lawyer does not seem to be indicating any preference for or against the alternative.

In No. 11, the lawyer keeps the interview focused on the subject of advantages, but again does so in a way which calls for the client's input. Again, no indication of lawyer preference seems apparent.

No. 13 through No. 19 illustrate how a lawyer might go about carrying out the responsibility of making sure a client really does have an adequate data base on which to premise a prediction. Often a lawyer will not have an adequate data base for making a prediction but will have some information which can be useful to the client. This series indicates how a lawyer might add to a client's data base under such circumstances. Finally, this series illustrates how a lawyer might help the client to understand why the client rather than the lawyer is in a better position to make the prediction.

There is perhaps one criticism to be levied against the lawyer. Might the lawyer have gone a little further in No. 19 by helping the client identify where the client might look for information for predicting the effect of a conviction on the client's job? The lawyer does help the client recognize that neither of the parties has a sound data base, and that perhaps more information can be gained from an outside source. Perhaps by asking the client where she might get more data, the lawyer could have given the client some additional assistance: "Who at work might know what effect the conviction might have? Do you think Mr. Joffers could give you some more information?"

Additionally, it should be noted that in this series the conversation shifts from the subject of advantages to the subject of disadvantages. As discussed earlier, this kind of switching is inevitable.

Finally, it should be noted that at the conclusion of the series, the lawyer switches from the alternative of trial to the alternative of a dismissal on a stipulation to probable cause. Given the client's comments in No. 18 about the attractiveness of the dismissal alternative, the switch seems appropriate. The switch reflects the kind of flexibility necessary to maintain rapport. Again, in starting on a new alternative, the lawyer initiates the discussion with an open-ended form of question: "What advantages do you see there?"

No. 21 is another illustration of how the lawyer can use an open-ended question to keep the client focused without indicating any bias in favor of one solution or another.

No. 22 illustrates the normal switching by a client. Ms. Hicks switches the focus from the alternative of trial to the alternative of dismissal with a stipulation to probable cause.

In No. 23, the lawyer uses active listening to respond to both content and feeling. The lawyer then proceeds to make an inquiry which allows the client to clarify in her own mind the long-term significance of the consequence.

No. 25 again illustrates how a lawyer might indicate why the client is in a better position to make a prediction about a particular consequence.

No. 27 illustrates how the lawyer might help the client think about alternatives in terms of positives and negatives. First, the lawyer summarizes the client's conclusion by explicitly pointing out that the consequence is a negative one. Then the lawyer switches the discussion to positive consequences of the same alternative. Absent any indication that the lawyer is somehow trying to favor this alternative, the switch seems appropriate. The switch may help the client obtain a balanced view of the alternative. Note that in switching back, the lawyer does not continue to ask the client about consequences the client foresees. Instead, the lawyer introduces consequences she foresees. In terms of an adequate data base, certainly the lawyer has the superior base of information about the economic consequence of additional attorney fees. Unless the lawyer's demeanor indicates bias, a switch from the role of an information gatherer to the role of an information provider is appropriate.

The lawyer's comment in No. 27 triggers the client to think about the option of trial and hence again initiates a normal switch in the focus of the conversation.   Given that the client makes specific inquiry about the trial option, the lawyer in No. 29 appropriately responds directly to the client's inquiry.   The lawyer responds to the client even though the lawyer apparently was trying to finish the positive aspects of the dismissal option before going to another subject.   While it is appropriate for lawyers to attempt some systematic examination of consequences, flexibility must be maintained.

No. 29 and No. 31 illustrate how a lawyer might explain the basis of the lawyer's prediction about the most probable result at trial. Here the lawyer deals with predictions regarding a disputed question of fact and an open question of law.

No. 33 illustrates five points.   First, it illustrates how a lawyer might explain a prediction about the use of judicial discretion.   Second, it illustrates how a lawyer might explain the worst *likely* result in circumstances where the worst *possible* result is highly remote. However, does the lawyer perhaps go too far in minimizing the worst possible result?

Third, No. 33 illustrates how the worst likely result is converted into the concept of a disadvantage so that it can be weighed in the final decision-making process.

Fourth, No. 33 illustrates how a nonlegal consequence, here the economic consequence of attorney fees, is converted into the concept of a disadvantage so as to aid in the final weighing process.

Finally, No. 33 illustrates how a lawyer might summarize consequences using the terms advantages and disadvantages to help both the lawyer and client keep track of what has been discussed.

WEIGHING THE ALTERNATIVES

The last step in the counseling process involves weighing the alternatives with their respective advantages and disadvantages in order to reach a final decision.   In terms of technique, what can the lawyer do to facilitate the decision-making process?   The examination of the various alternatives and consequences has taken place over a period of time.   How, if at all, can the lawyer help the client assimilate and weigh all the disparate consequences that have been mentioned during this time period?   Remember, the exploration of the consequences has not been a highly structured process.   Indeed, the process of examining the consequences has probably jumped around repeatedly from one alternative to another, and from positive consequences to negative consequences.   In our experience, unless the lawyer can bring about a brief and compact summarization of *all* the consequences which have been identified, most clients find it difficult to reach a decision.

A Written Summary of the Alternatives and Consequences

One technique we have found to be enormously helpful to clients is that of writing down the alternatives and their respective consequences. In our experience, this technique is usually superior to any attempt at verbal summarization.

The technique of listing the alternatives and consequences is one which can be brought into play almost at the inception of the counseling process. When the alternatives are initially presented by the lawyer, they can simultaneously be jotted down on a piece of paper. All the alternatives, including any mentioned by the client, are listed horizontally across the page. Under each alternative, there is a brief description. The description attempts to summarize the essence of the alternative in terms of its legal consequences. For example, the alternative of trial is described in terms of the most probable result: "70 percent chance of conviction." When all the alternatives have been listed across the page, spaces are made beneath each alternative for listing the advantages and disadvantages. As the lawyer and client examine the alternatives, the lawyer jots down each consequence on the sheet of paper as each consequence is mentioned. The consequence is listed as either an advantage or disadvantage.

Assume there is to be an exploration of two alternatives, settling for $3500 or proceeding to trial. The most probable result at trial is a judgment for $12,000. The lawyer predicts there is a very good chance of obtaining such a judgment. After the lawyer and client have discussed what alternatives are available, but before the dialogue has turned to an examination of the consequences, the sheet of paper might look something like this:

TRIAL	SETTLEMENT
Very good chance of $12,000.	$3500
Advantages	Advantages
Disadvantages	Disadvantages

[B6281]

When the sheet of paper is prepared, it is shown to the client and its purpose explained. "What I've done is to write down the two alternatives and left space for listing the advantages and disadvantages of each. As we go through each of the alternatives, I'll jot down the consequences so when we have finished you'll have a fairly complete picture of all the factors that are involved. If you have any questions about what I'm writing down, please ask."

As each consequence is mentioned, it is noted in the appropriate space.[8] In this connection, it should be remembered that many consequences which are the pro of one alternative will be the con of another. Assume the client desired to discuss the option of settlement and the first consequence mentioned was "getting the mess over with." On being asked to clarify this term, the client stated that having the trial to think about was a constant emotional strain. In such a situation, the pro of settlement would be avoiding further strain, while at the same time a con of proceeding to trial would be continued strain. How should the consequence be listed? The choices seem to be three: First, to list the consequence just under the alternative being discussed. Subsequently at some time when the lawyer can appear neutral, the lawyer would point out that the consequence is also a disadvantage of going to trial. Second, to point out the crossover immediately and write the consequence down under both alternatives. Third, to ignore the crossover unless the client mentions it. We do not have enough experience to say which method is preferable. It does appear, however, that with some clients, adopting the third method is unsatisfactory. The approach appears to leave these clients with less than a full understanding of the situation.

Using the hypothetical as an example, if the lawyer's choice were to follow method one, then under the advantage column of settlement the lawyer would list "avoid further strain." At the same time, the lawyer could articulate what was being done. "Okay, so one advantage of settling is avoiding further strain." Similarly, if the lawyer were to use method two, the lawyer would write "experience further strain" under a disadvantage of proceeding to trial. The lawyer would then articulate the crossover to the client.

Obtaining the Client's Decision

If the listing techniques just described are used throughout the process of exploring the consequences, the task of bringing the client to the point where the final decision is to be made is often relatively easy. Taking the sheet in hand, the lawyer can note that the advantages and disadvantages of each of the alternatives have apparently been explored and that a decision is now called for. In this connection, the lawyer can ask the client to look at the sheet of paper and go over the respective pros and cons. As a part of this process, it may be helpful to verbally summarize the information which is on the paper. The following example is illustrative of how the lawyer might bring the client to the point of decision.

---

8. Frequently, it is helpful for the lawyer to sit next to the client so that as the positive and negative consequences are listed the client can observe what is taking place.

"Well, Mr. Franks, I guess we have explored just about all the pros and cons. What you're going to have to do now is decide what you want to do. It will probably be helpful to go over this sheet of paper to try to bring all the consequences together. On the side of settlement we have avoiding further strain, obtaining $1000 now. . . . Take your time in thinking about this. Decide on the basis of what seems best to you. If you have any more questions, please ask, and we can go over the information once again."

Of course, the client will often not immediately reach a decision. Frequently the client will want to discuss the probability of some consequence in greater depth, or the client will want to explore for more consequences. Indeed, the process of going back and rechecking consequences may occur several times before the client will make even a tentative decision. If time permits, it may be useful to have the client "go home and sleep on it." In this event, the client will usually appreciate being given a copy of the paper containing the pros and cons to take home.

Handling Requests for the Lawyer's Opinion

Finally, it must be mentioned that many clients, even if willing to make their own decisions, will want to know what the lawyer would do. Should the lawyer venture his/her opinion? If not, what tack should the lawyer adopt? In the main, we believe that lawyers should refrain from stating what they would do. Given that the lawyer cannot fully know the client's values, and that the client may be unduly influenced by what the lawyer, the "authority figure," would do, we believe lawyers generally should refrain from announcing what they think a client should do.[9]

There are, of course, going to be situations where, because of the lawyer's past dealings with the client, the lawyer will have a fairly good sense of the client's value system. For a similar reason, the lawyer may also know that no matter what the lawyer says, the client will retain an independent decision making capacity. In these circumstances, it may be quite appropriate for the lawyer to comply with the client's request. If the lawyer does so, the lawyer should clearly articulate why the particular choice was made. The lawyer's explanation will at least give the client an opportunity to evaluate whether the lawyer is placing value on the same consequences as

---

9. ABA Code of Professional Responsibility EC 7–8 states that, "A lawyer should bring to bear upon this decision-making process the fullness of his [her] experience as well as his [her] objective viewpoint." In the context of client decision making, is it reasonable to speak of a "lawyer's *objective* viewpoint?" In light of the concept of client values, does the concept of an objective point of view make sense?

those the client considers important. The following example is illustrative:

> "John, given how you could really use the money now and how upsetting you usually find trials, I think that, on balance, I'd settle if the decision were mine."

Generally, however, we believe the appropriate response to the client's request for the lawyer's opinion should be an explanation of why the client should decide. The explanation should point out why the client is in the best position to evaluate the pros and cons, and also that it is the client who must live with the decision. The following is illustrative:

> "Mr. Hawkins, I'm not really in a position to evaluate the situation. You're the only one who can really weigh the consequences. For example, you're the only one who knows whether it's more important for you, in the long run, to have the satisfaction of knowing you did all you could rather than having the $2000 now. I'm not you; I can't know how you actually feel about those two consequences, or any of the others. Only you know what is most important to you, and you're the person who's going to have to live with the decision. I can understand it's difficult to decide, but given I can't know what's most important to you, I think you should make the decision. I'll be glad to explore the consequences with you some more if that will help."

In suggesting the client make the decision, the lawyer must take care to demonstrate that the lawyer is concerned with the client and the client's best interests. Hopefully, the lawyer's genuine concern will be manifested by articulating why the client can best decide, by being empathetic, and by demonstrating willingness to go over the consequences if the client feels confused or uncertain.

In Chapter Ten we will discuss how the lawyer should proceed if the client continues to insist that the lawyer state an opinion.

PROVIDING A PREPARATORY EXPLANATION

Early in this chapter, we suggested the lawyer should begin the counseling dialogue with a Preparatory Explanation. It is to the content of such an explanation that we now turn attention.

Clients come to lawyers with a wide variety of role expectations regarding the function the lawyer will perform in providing solutions. In our experience, though some clients assume they will be the final decision maker, many do not. Many clients expect the lawyer to tell them what to do. If the client expects the lawyer to make the decisions, the client may not participate fully in the counseling process. Believing the lawyer will decide, the client may see little reason to articulate the consequences he/she foresees. Indeed, in some instances the client may feel anxious, frustrated, or even hostile since the client has little idea why the lawyer is asking so many questions rather than telling the client what should be done. If such feelings arise, there will often be resistance to full participation in the counseling process.

Even if the client does expect to make the final decision, difficulties may arise when the client does not know what will actually be involved in the decision making process. Assume the client expects to make the final decision and during the process of exploring the consequences, the lawyer points out particular pros which the lawyer foresees. Given the client's initial expectations, the lawyer's information may make the client feel pressured to make the choice which the lawyer "seemingly" favors. A similar feeling may arise if the client has reached a tentative decision and the lawyer then asks the client to consider the disadvantages of the favored alternative, or the pros of another alternative. Should the client get the feeling that he/she is being pressured, the client may withdraw from fully considering alternatives other than the one which has tentatively been chosen.

To reduce the likelihood of negative feelings and reactions of the type just described, and to encourage full client participation, it is often useful to provide the client with a Preparatory Explanation of what the counseling process will involve.[10] The explanation could cover the following: (1) A statement of the kind of decision to be made and why the decision is required; (2) a description of the process of identifying alternatives and consequences and the roles which the lawyer and client will play in the process; and (3) a statement that the client will make the final decision and an explanation of why.

We will illustrate such an explanation through an example. Assume the client operates an automobile repair business and has been served with an unlawful detainer complaint. The interview has reached a point where the lawyer has made an initial assessment of the client's legal position and believes he/she can make a prediction of the likely legal consequences.

L.   Mr. Waters, I think I now have enough information to discuss with you what might be done. In cases of this type the law allows only 5 days for you to take legal action to respond to the papers which have been served on you. Three of those days have now gone by, so we have to reach a decision rather quickly; otherwise, your landlord will be able to get a court order evicting you without your ever having a chance to contest his claim.

10.   For a discussion of how clients in psychotherapy can profit from an explanation that teaches the client what to expect from counseling and how to behave appropriately during the counseling process, see M. Orne & P. Wender, *Anticipatory Socialization for Psychotherapy: Method and Rationale*, 124 Amer.J.Psychiat. 1202 (1968).

C. Well, I want to contest; that son-of-a-bitch is going to ruin my business. Where could I possibly go?

L. I understand your concern about your business. I can see this really angers you. You've been there a long time and feel you just can't move out. I want to help and that's why I now want to talk about what might be done. Let me explain briefly what we will do to help you make your decision. As I see the situation, you have two options: contesting the matter by going to court or trying to work out a settlement without going to court. There may be other options that you see and we will get to those in a moment. What I'm going to do is explain each of these options to you, and then write each down on this piece of paper. Then, unless you see some other choices, we will go through the two I have mentioned and try to figure out the pros and cons of each approach. As we talk about the pros and cons, I'll jot them down on this sheet of paper; that way you won't have to try to remember them. We will work on this together. Primarily I'll be asking you what you see as the advantages and disadvantages of each approach, but if I happen to see a particular advantage or disadvantage, I'll point it out to you. Because I mention a particular advantage or disadvantage, you shouldn't think I'm for or against one approach or the other. What I want to stress is that although I'm going to explain the legal consequences of the options to you, and although, from time to time, I may point out a particular pro or con, the final decision is going to be up to you. What you decide to do is going to affect a lot of things that only you know about, like your relationship with your landlord and your overall financial picture. Since the decision is likely to affect these matters about which I know nothing, you're going to be in the best position to decide what should be done. Do you have any questions?

C. No, I don't think so.

L. One other thing I'd like to mention before we start is that it is important to consider all the pros and cons before making a final decision. My experience is that it is usually best to wait until the end to make a final decision. Sometimes a person begins thinking he or she already knows exactly what he or she wants to do, but then after weighing the pros and cons, the person changes their mind. Do you have any questions about what we are going to do now?

C. No; I guess not.

L. Okay, let's start by writing down the two choices.

In reviewing the foregoing example, consider the following questions:

1. What modifications, if any, might be made to give the client an increased sense of the lawyer's neutrality?

2. How, if at all, might the statements about the lawyer's role have been modified to provide the client with a greater sense that the responsibility for predicting the consequences lies primarily with the client?

3. What modifications, if any, could have been made to give the client an increased understanding of why the ultimate decision should be his?

4. To what extent, if any, did the description of the purpose of the piece of paper help carry out the objectives of the Preparatory Explanation?

5. Assume the client was sophisticated and experienced. How might the explanation have been modified?

6. Assume the client appeared impatient for a decision. How might the explanation have been modified?

A Preparatory Explanation will not be required in every case. Where the lawyer and client have worked together before, presumably an explanation will not be required. Additionally, for some clients an explanation such as the foregoing may seem unduly patronizing. Apart from what the client may in fact know, the client may believe he/she knows just what to expect from an attorney. In such a situation, an explanation may have the reverse affect of that which is intended. Sensitivity and good judgment must be relied upon to decide if an explanation will make the lawyer appear condescending. If the lawyer senses the client may be affronted by an explanation, then perhaps the parts having to do with the roles of the parties can be conveyed in a piecemeal fashion during the course of the counseling process. A similar tack might be adopted when the client appears to be anxious to get on with the actual decision-making process.

Finally, it should be noted that because the explanation is given at the beginning, one cannot assume there will be no need to repeat it, at least in part, during the subsequent discussion. Frequently, clients will hear only part of what is being said.

In closing this analysis of counseling techniques, we should like to stress one point. The point concerns the importance of time in the counseling process. Clients are often emotionally involved in their problems. They seek the assistance of a lawyer because they are uncertain as to how they ought to proceed. They are often confused about what course of action is best to follow. They cannot weigh alternatives dispassionately. Given this state of affairs, *it is to be expected that it will take the client some time to proceed through the steps of the counseling process.* The lawyer will often form a strong impression about what is an appropriate course of action long before the client does. The temptation to interpose the lawyer's solution will be quite strong. However, the lawyer should remember that it is the lawyer's function to help the client arrive at the client's solution. The lawyer is assigned this role because the solution arrived at by the client will generally be the one which most accurately reflects the client's interests. Accordingly, it is likely to be the decision the client can best "live with" and best follow through on. Therefore, if the lawyer is to truly act in the best interest of the client, the lawyer must facilitate the client's careful evaluation of alternatives and allow time for the decision making process to take place.

Chapter Ten

COUNSELING DIFFICULT CLIENTS

Client-centered decision making, although desirable, is not always viable. In this chapter, we will discuss counseling techniques for helping a variety of clients who do *not* fall within our description of "someone who is willing and capable of making a reasonable decision." Our discussion will include techniques for assisting the following persons:

1. Clients who are extremely indecisive.
2. Clients who insist upon obtaining the lawyer's opinion of what should be done.
3. Clients who have already reached a decision and are not interested in considering other alternatives.
4. Clients who, in the lawyer's judgment, are making extremely detrimental decisions.

Throughout this chapter, unless otherwise noted, the discussion is intended to apply to the basic decision of whether or not to initiate and/or continue litigation, as well as to auxiliary decisions.

THE EXTREMELY INDECISIVE CLIENT

Often, even after the lawyer and client have gone through the lengthy procedure of listing each of the alternatives and their respective consequences, the client will remain undecided. When this situation exists, there are at least three techniques which the lawyer can consider using to break the "log jam" and facilitate a client decision. The three techniques are: (1) clarifying conflicting feelings, (2) rating the consequences, and (3) providing the option of the lawyer's suggestion.

Clarifying Conflicting Feelings

Frequently, the indecision stems from the client's inability to explicitly recognize that no fully satisfactory solution exists. The client fails to appreciate that almost any available alternative will involve some negative consequences. Hence, any solution which is adopted will not be fully satisfying.

There are three basic types of conflicts which seem to impair a client's ability to readily reach a decision: (1) win-lose conflicts, (2) lose-lose conflicts, and (3) win-win conflicts.[1]

---

1. This model of the three basic types of conflicts is drawn from National Drug Abuse Training Center, Training Manual for Counseling Skills (July 1973).

Win-Lose Conflicts:

In win-lose conflicts, the client has both positive and negative feelings about the same alternative.

Client No. 1: "My marriage is bad. I want to get a divorce and be on my own. I feel like I can earn enough to support myself, but I'm really afraid I'll hurt the children."

Client No. 2: "I'll get it over with if I settle, and then I won't have to take any more time off work. That's really important in terms of my future. But if I settle, I'm not going to get what I deserve."

Lose-Lose Conflicts:

In lose-lose conflicts, each available alternative has what the client sees as very negative consequences.

Client No. 1: "I don't know what to do. I could pay the $500 and end the whole thing, or spend $400 just to prove I'm right. Either way, I get 'ripped off'."

Client No. 2: "You mean to say I either have to give up my child or go into therapy with some shrink? Therapy didn't work last time. You call that a choice?"

Win-Win Conflicts:

The client has a choice between two alternatives, each of which is viewed positively. The discomfort comes from trying to decide which of the two rewarding outcomes might be best.

Client No. 1: "Well, all I wanted to do was show that guy he couldn't push me around. Now he either has to pay me $500 in settlement, or go through the aggravation of trial. I can't decide which is best."

Client No. 2: "Since we got this partial summary judgment thing, the only question is how much she has to pay. She is offering $2000 and you say if we go to trial I could get as much as $4000, and probably do no worse than $2000. I never thought I'd get even $500; now, I don't know what to do."

When any of the three types of conflicting feelings are present, a client can often reach a decision if the client is helped to explicitly recognize that the conflict is inevitable. To bring the client to such a recognition, the lawyer can use active listening responses which articulate the inherent conflict. We will now illustrate how active listening responses can be used to help the client recognize that some negative feelings are inevitable.

Win-Lose:

Lawyer: "So you feel if you get a divorce, you are going to gain your independence, but it's going to be at the risk of hurting the children. What the situation comes down to is that you feel you want a divorce, but to go ahead means taking on a risk which you are quite worried about. It seems there may be no way to go ahead with what you want to do without experiencing some worry."

Lose-Lose:

Lawyer: "The situation is that you feel there is really no good choice for you. You're going to feel like a loser whether you pay the $500 in settlement or spend $400 in attorneys' fees to go to court to prove you're right. Either way, you're not going to come out of this feeling very good."

Win-Win:

Lawyer: "Given what you initially expected, you are coming out a winner either way, and yet it's hard to decide which alternative would be best. Whatever choice you make, there will likely be a nagging feeling that it may not be the best choice."

When the lawyer responds by articulating the client's conflict, the client can often, for no precisely explainable reason, return to review the previously articulated pros and cons and reach a final decision. Accordingly, it is generally useful, after clarifying the conflict, to suggest the client re-think the alternatives in light of the clarification.

Win-Lose:

Lawyer: "Given your positive feelings about the divorce, but recognizing that you are going to feel fearful about the children if you decide to go ahead, do you want to think again about the pros and cons of each of the alternatives?"

Lose-Lose:

Lawyer: "Given that you're probably going to feel pretty bad either way, why don't you think about each of the alternatives again. Try to figure out which alternative will make you feel less worse off. Which alternative will minimize your losses?"

Win-Win:

Lawyer: "Given that no matter what you choose to do, you're going to come out ahead; why don't you look at the alternatives again. Whichever one you choose will probably leave you with some feeling of doubt about whether it was the best choice. But at least whatever you choose will put you ahead of where you thought you'd be."

Rating the Consequences

As we pointed out earlier, clients typically do not have the capacity to precisely quantify and rank consequences. Nonetheless, it is often possible for clients to distinguish, in some general way, between "more important" and "less important" consequences. If, after going through the procedure of listing the alternatives and consequences, the client still feels indecisive, the lawyer can sometimes facilitate a decision by helping the client articulate which consequences seem important and which ones do not.

The task of having the client rate the consequences can usually be accomplished if the lawyer structures the dialogue in the following manner. All the lawyer need do is explain what kind of rating is desired, and why. When the explanation has been made, the client can then be taken back over the consequences and asked to assign a rating of importance to each. When this process has been completed, the lawyer can then summarize the situation and ask the client to consider the decision once more. Consider the following example:

L.   Sometimes, Mr. Phelps, it is easier to decide what to do if one first figures out which consequences are important and which ones are not so important. Let's go back over the consequences we have listed here and see which ones you see as really important. Which alternative do you want to talk about first?

C.   Trial, I guess.

L.   Okay, well, the first advantage you saw was the possibility of an additional $2000. How important would that additional $2000 be to you?

C.   Well, it would help, but actually, I don't need it for anything specific.

L.   So it's somewhat important, but not critical?

C.   Right.

L.   Okay, so we'll rate that one as somewhat important. Okay, next, what about proving they were wrong? How would you rate that?

. . .

L.   Well, now it may be a little easier for you to see which alternative seems better. In thinking about trial, you rated having an additional $2000 as somewhat important and rated actually being vindicated in court as not so important. Settlement has the advantage of not having to take any more time away from your work, which you rated as somewhat important.

. . .

L.   Now, Mr. Phelps, with these ratings in mind, why don't you look at the alternatives again and see if you can decide which alternative seems best.

While this kind of rating process may be long and tedious for the lawyer, many indecisive clients apparently benefit from this kind of concrete approach to decision making.

Providing the Option of the Lawyer's Suggestion

When the clarification and rating techniques just discussed prove ineffective, the lawyer can consider offering to make a suggestion about which alternative to choose. This technique, of course, should be employed only as a last resort.

Before making a suggestion, the lawyer typically will want to reinforce the idea that the client should ultimately decide what to do. To accomplish this purpose, the lawyer can indicate that the law usually requires that the client, rather than the lawyer, make the final decision, and that clients who make their own decisions usually feel more satisfied with the choices made. Additionally, the lawyer can point out that the lawyer cannot be certain of what will happen at trial or what, in the long run, will be best for someone else. The client, therefore, should feel free to reject the lawyer's suggestion.

When offering a suggestion, it is important for the lawyer to articulate the reasons for the suggestion. The reasons should be based upon the lawyer's evaluation of which alternative will probably provide maximum client satisfaction. The reasons should be drawn from the lawyer's understanding of the importance which the client places on the various consequences. This understanding should have been developed either when reviewing the consequences, or when the lawyer employed the technique of having the client rate the consequences.

The purpose of having the lawyer articulate the reasons for the suggestion is to provide the client with a basis for evaluating the lawyer's suggestion. If the lawyer articulates the reasons, the client has an opportunity to think about whether or not what the lawyer is saying really accords with the client's value system. If what the lawyer says does not coincide with what the client feels, the client will have an opportunity to recognize the discrepancy and reach an independent decision.

The following example is illustrative of how a lawyer might offer to make a suggestion about what might be done.

L.   Herb, we've gone over this thing several times now, and you really seem to be having trouble making a decision. I can understand that. Given that there is no perfect solution, it is really difficult to decide. One thing you might consider is letting me make a suggestion. I could at least tell you what I think and why. The decision is really yours. It's a decision that you are best off making because I can't really know just how you feel about each of the consequences. On the other hand, if you do nothing, the settlement offer is going to be withdrawn, and what you end up doing is having the City decide that this case should go to trial. You are sort of letting them decide what you should do. Recognizing that I cannot know for certain what will happen at trial and that I may not know exactly what importance you attach to all the various consequences, would you nonetheless find it helpful if I at least told you what I think you should do?

C.   Yes, I really do; at least, I'd like to know what you think.

L.   Okay, but keep in mind that you should feel free to reject my suggestion. After all, I may not see the situation in the same way you do. On balance, I think you probably should settle. Let me tell you why. You indicated that another few hundred dollars, while important, is not critical. Also, you feel that as long as they pay you the $2000, you'll have the satisfaction of knowing you were right. On the other hand, you say going to trial would make you quite nervous and you really don't want to take a week off from work. On balance, it seems to me that you might be best off settling.

THE CLIENT WHO INSISTS UPON THE LAWYER'S OPINION

Many clients will insist the lawyer provide an opinion about whether or not the client should initiate or continue litigation. Here we will discuss how the lawyer might proceed when encountering such clients. Clients will insist upon the lawyer's opinion for a variety of reasons. Some clients will insist upon the lawyer's opinion because they want to crosscheck their own opinion. These clients are willing and able to reach an independent decision; they seek the lawyer's opinion primarily to insure that all factors are considered before reaching a final decision. We will refer to these clients as "independent decision makers."

Other clients insist upon the lawyer's opinion because they believe an appropriate lawyer-client relationship requires the client to obtain the lawyer's opinion. In their view, a proper lawyer-client relationship is one where the client is passive and the lawyer tells the client what the lawyer thinks is best. The client believes that unless the lawyer's opinion is "off the wall," the lawyer's advice should be followed. These clients are therefore unwilling to exercise independent judgment about what should be done. Since these clients have this kind of mind set, they are, for all practical purposes, insisting the lawyer decide what should be done. We will refer to these clients as "passive decision makers."

Another group of clients who insist upon the lawyer's opinion are clients who have no interest in participating in their own case. Their attitude is something like, "Here's my problem, do what you think is best and send me the bill." Typically, these clients turn their case over to their lawyer because they simply don't want to be bothered. In our judgment, clients should have the prerogative to turn cases over to their lawyer when they simply do not want to be involved in their case. Our discussion will not include this group of clients.

A request for the lawyer's opinion from a client who tends to be an "independent decision maker" is not likely to pose problems. The client is simply seeking to obtain maximum information before reaching a decision. By having the lawyer directly state what the lawyer would do, and why, the client can clarify in his/her own mind areas of agreement and disagreement. With this clarification, the client usually can go on to make his/her own decision, even if it is contrary to the lawyer's recommendation.

A request for the lawyer's opinion from a "passive decision maker," however, usually does pose problems. If the lawyer provides his/her opinion, such a client will typically follow it because he/she believes it is proper for clients to follow their lawyers' advice. Unfortunately, these clients often follow their lawyers' advice even when they feel quite uncomfortable with it.

Given that a client may or may not be an "independent decision maker," how should the lawyer respond when a client insists upon the lawyer's opinion? How can the lawyer differentiate between the independent decision maker and the passive decision maker?

Again, ultimate reliance must be placed on good judgment and sensitivity. When the client initially requests the lawyer's opinion, the lawyer often will have little idea of how strongly the client believes it is the lawyer's *duty* to provide an opinion. The client's tone of voice in making the request and passive nature during the earlier part of the interview, may give some indication the client is unwilling to exercise independent judgment. However, since the request will usually come quite early in the counseling process, the lawyer will often be pretty much in the dark concerning how the client feels about reaching his/her own decision. Accordingly, we believe the lawyer should parry the initial request with an explanation about why the decision should be made by the client.[2] When the lawyer makes this explanation, the lawyer should watch the client's non-verbal behavior for indications that the client is quite dissatisfied with the explanation. Does the client's face register understanding and acceptance of the explanation? Or does the client's face indicate dissatisfaction, re-

2. This suggestion is identical with that made in Chapter Nine; see p. 187 supra.

luctance, or resentment? Does the client immediately respond with statements such as, "Gee, I thought you'd tell me what you think."

If the lawyer senses the client understands and accepts the explanation, or if the lawyer is uncertain about the client's position, the lawyer probably should go ahead with the normal counseling process. If the client strongly believes it is the lawyer's duty to advise the client, one explanation of the benefit of client decision making will usually not silence requests for the lawyer's opinion.

If the lawyer feels rather certain the client is unsatisfied with the explanation, our experience indicates it may be useful for the lawyer to proceed in the following fashion. The lawyer should empathize with the client's reaction through an active listening response similar to: "I guess you'd feel better if I gave my opinion?" If the client affirms the lawyer's response—"Yes, I would."—then the lawyer should attempt to put the client at ease by *empathizing with the dissatisfaction or frustration* and providing a further explanation. This explanation can make two points: (1) even if the lawyer were to give an opinion, there will first have to be an examination of the alternatives and consequences, and (2) if, after reviewing the consequences, the client still feels unable to decide without having the lawyer's opinion, the lawyer will provide it. Often, such an explanation will result in the client accepting the idea that the counseling process must precede any decision about what should be done. Upon receiving this explanation, clients are often able to temporarily put aside their anxiety about not having the lawyer's opinion.

The following example is illustrative of how a lawyer might attempt to alleviate the client's concern when it appears the lawyer's initial explanation of the benefit of client decision-making has left the client dissatisfied.

L. Herb, I sense you're somewhat frustrated by not getting an answer right away. I get the feeling that you'd feel much better if I gave you my opinion about what you ought to do.

C. It really would make me feel better; I thought that's what a lawyer did.

L. Okay, Herb, I understand what you're saying. I really do. I know you're facing a difficult decision and it's really frustrating not having an immediate answer. (Pause) As I indicated when we started to discuss what should be done, the decision here is going to have many kinds of consequences. For example, you've already mentioned the possible problem of taking off work to attend the trial. Also, you've expressed concern that if you accept the $2000, you may be left with a feeling that you've not gotten what you deserve. To make any intelligent decision, we are going to have to look carefully at all the consequences. When all the consequences are out on the table, when we have them all listed here on this piece of paper, then we can think about making some final decision. Now, however, it's really premature to think about a final choice. If, when we've gone through everything, you still feel you can't decide and you want my opinion, I'll certainly give it to you then. But right now, neither of us is in any position to make an intelligent choice. So let's go back to looking at the consequences. Okay?

C. Oh, all right.

L. Let's go back to the alternative of going to trial. What other advantages do you see?

However, when this fuller explanation still seems to leave the client dissatisfied, the lawyer is probably left with only two choices. The lawyer can *give an outright promise* to provide his/her opinion at the conclusion of the process of identifying the alternatives and consequences. Or, the lawyer can attempt to proceed with the normal process in the face of the client's apparent dissatisfaction. As to which course of action should be followed, there is no definitive answer.

If the lawyer decides to actually promise to give an opinion, the lawyer can say something like the following:

"Okay, Herb, I sense you're really unhappy not having an answer now. I'll tell you what. When we've gone over the alternatives and the consequences, I will definitely tell you what I think. I need a lot more input from you before I'll be able to say what I think will be best for you. But when I have the information, I'll give you my opinion."

If, at the conclusion of the process of reviewing the alternatives and consequences, the lawyer feels the client really "needs" the lawyer's opinion, or the lawyer has already promised an opinion, then, in our judgment, the opinion should be given. If the client is really a dependent person, no amount of philosophical wishing will make the client feel satisfied by an explanation of why the client will probably be best off by being an independent decision maker. Should the lawyer refuse to voice an opinion, the most likely result will be client dissatisfaction.

When the lawyer voices an opinion, the lawyer should state the reasons for the opinion. The reasons should be based upon the lawyer's understanding of the client's values. If the lawyer articulates the reasons, the client has an opportunity to think about whether or not what the lawyer is saying really does accord with the client's value system. If what the lawyer says does not coincide with what the client feels, the client will have an opportunity to recognize and mention any discrepancy. Perhaps the client will even be spurred to make the final decision.

THE CLIENT WHO HAS ALREADY REACHED
A DECISION

Sometimes a client will enter the lawyer's office with a preconceived idea of exactly what he/she wishes to do. The client's only question is whether or not the action the client desires to take can be legally accomplished. For example, many clients wish only to know whether or not a lawsuit can be instituted. They want to know, from a legal standpoint, if there is a relatively good chance of prevailing in the suit.

The Ethical Considerations of the ABA Code of Professional Responsibility suggest lawyers should not confine their efforts to solely appraising a client's legal position. Rather, the lawyer should attempt to have the client consider all ramifications of the decision. "A lawyer should exert his (her) best efforts to insure that decisions of his (her) client are made only after the client has been informed of relevant considerations. A lawyer ought to initiate the decision making process if the client does not do so." [3]

How, therefore, might a lawyer address a client whose only inquiry is one such as: "The only thing I want to know is whether or not we can fight this?" Once the lawyer has completed the process of ascertaining the client's legal position, the lawyer should attempt to have the client consider all the relevant consequences. Usually, if the lawyer's analysis of the client's legal position *does not* favor the client's preconceived plan, there will be little difficulty in getting the client to engage in a thorough consideration of what should be done. Generally, it is enough to provide the legal analysis, empathize with the client's disappointment, and ask if the client wants to consider other alternatives.

> "Donald, from what you've told me, I think the chances of being successful in a suit against Hero Corporation aren't very good. I'm sure that's disappointing, but that's how I see the situation. But it probably is worthwhile to consider what else might be done. Perhaps some sort of a settlement might be possible. Would you like to consider other possibilities?"

If, however, the lawyer's legal analysis is supportive of the client's preconceived plan, obtaining full consideration of the alternatives and/or consequences will probably be more difficult. Once the client hears the action he/she desires to take is legally feasible, the willingness to consider other possibilities will often be minimal. An inquiry about whether or not the client would like to consider the consequences or other alternatives will often fall on "deaf ears."

3. ABA Code of Professional Responsibility EC 7–8.

Nonetheless, if the lawyer is to comply with the ABA Code of Professional Responsibility, the lawyer should request the client consider the alternatives and consequences. One approach is to begin by providing the client with the lawyer's analysis. At the same time, the lawyer can empathize with the anticipated favorable reaction by the client and acknowledge the client's right to make the final decision. On doing so, the lawyer can go on to request a full consideration by attempting to point out the existence of alternatives and/or consequences the client may not have considered. Hopefully, by demonstrating an understanding that the legal analysis coincides with the client's desires, and by acknowledging the client's independence, the lawyer will prevent the client from feeling that the request for further consideration is an unwarranted rejection of the client's decision. The following example is illustrative of how the client might be approached.

L. Darlene, I'd say the chances of your successfully defending this case are quite good. I guess that given how you feel about this situation, that must be good news.

C. It really is; I really want to show Henderson they can't push us around.

L. I can understand you want them to realize your company's independence must be respected. I know you are the one to finally decide what should be done. Henderson, though, is a big company in your field. Do you think they will try to make trouble for you in the industry if you don't try to work something out with them? Do you think there are other ways of showing them they must respect your rights without becoming involved in lengthy litigation? After all, the litigation isn't going to be cheap.

Note that in this dialogue the lawyer does not directly attempt to point out the possibility of negative consequences. Rather, the lawyer raises this possibility indirectly by employing questions. Perhaps clients will more readily consider the possibility of additional consequences if they "discover" these consequences themselves, instead of having them pointed out by the lawyer.

If this indirect approach kindles the client's interest, the lawyer can then move into the normal counseling process. If, however, the client's reaction is something like, "I've already made up my mind," the lawyer may not be able to do a great deal more. Perhaps, if the lawyer feels it would not seem like an absolute rejection of the client's statement, the lawyer could make one more similar request for reconsideration. In so doing, it might be useful to explain that the lawyer is asking for further consideration only to help the client make sure that, in the long run, the decision is one in the client's best interests.

Lawyer: "I understand your anger at Henderson. On the other hand, as your lawyer, I feel a responsibility to point out a concern I have that you might want to consider before reaching a final decision. I'm still quite concerned that, in the long run, Henderson will cause trouble for you. What do you think?"

THE CLIENT WHO HAS REACHED AN EXTREMELY DETRIMENTAL DECISION

In Chapter Eight, we recommended that the lawyer intervene in the decision making process if the client's decision would very likely result in substantial economic, social, or psychological harm in return for very little gain. Here we will consider what kind of intervention might be appropriate and how the lawyer might address a client who appears to be making an "extremely detrimental" decision.

First, a word or two more about what constitutes an extremely detrimental decision. Although our rule of thumb of "substantial economic, social, or psychological harm in return for very little gain" provides some guidelines, it does not provide a clear description of when intervention is called for. Probably the best it does is to suggest the lawyer should intervene *only* if the lawyer believes severe detriment is likely. Nonetheless, the standard is the best we can come up with. Ultimately, in our opinion, the matter comes down to using good judgment.

The following represent cases which, in our view, call for the lawyer's intervention:

Case No. 1:

The client is accused of the felony of receiving stolen property. The lawyer believes the most probable result at trial is acquittal. In the lawyer's judgment, the chances of this result are 90%. The lawyer knows from experience that there is a fair likelihood that if the client is convicted, his employer will learn of the result and terminate the client's employment. The client has been employed at his current position for 7 years. The client acknowledges that the job is a satisfying one and that finding an equally satisfying job would be difficult. The client admits he has no knowledge of the hiring and firing practices of his employer. He believes, without any basis, that he will not be fired if he is convicted. The client has decided to plead guilty because he wants to avoid "the hassle of trial" and save $200 in additional attorneys' fees. He wants the money for a new tape recorder.

Case No. 2:

The client has been married for 17 years. Her husband has just left her for another woman and has instituted dissolution proceedings. The client refuses to believe her husband really wants to end the marriage. Under local law, the client would be entitled to substantial alimony for approximately 10 years. She has not worked during the course of the marriage and has no immediate prospects for employment. She has instructed her lawyer not to ask for alimony, stating, "I know he'll be back and even if he's not, I want to stay friends. I know if anything happens to me, he'll always provide for me. If I ask for money, it is only going to make things worse."

Case No. 3:

Mr. Henry, age 45, has instituted a $500,000 lawsuit to recover damages for personal injuries sustained in an automobile accident. The injuries suffered were very extensive, and Mr. Henry is now permanently confined to a wheelchair. He presently resides in a convalescent home, from which he will be released in two months.

Mr. Henry is a bachelor and was formerly employed as a construction worker. He has been rendered virtually destitute as a result of the accident. He has no home, no furniture, no family, and no friends. He has no means of transportation.

The defendant's insurance company has offered $100,000 in settlement. Mr. Henry's lawyer believes the maximum likely at trial is $200,000. He believes there is only a 20 percent chance of this result. As for the most probable result at trial, the lawyer believes there is a good chance of a verdict in favor of the defendant.

Every time the lawyer attempts to communicate the lawyer's professional evaluation of the case, Mr. Henry refuses to listen. Whenever the lawyer mentions the settlement offer, Mr. Henry goes into an emotional tirade. He literally shouts, rants, and raves about how those bastards have destroyed his life. He keeps saying, "I won't settle at any figure. They're going to see me there in my wheelchair and realize what they've done! They can't buy me off!"

What Kind of Intervention is Appropriate?

Assume it appears that the client's decision is an extremely detrimental one, how much intervention is appropriate? Should the lawyer merely state that in the lawyer's opinion the client is making a mistake? Or, should the lawyer go so far as to try to convince or urge the client to change the decision? Can the lawyer go so far as to practically command the client to change his/her decision? "Look, Mr. Hefflin, you simply can't reject that offer." If the client refuses to change the decision, can the lawyer seek the appointment of a guardian ad litem?

The question of what degree of intervention is appropriate is not susceptible to easy resolution. So long as the client's mental capacity is such that a court would not appoint a general guardian or conservator, it seems inappropriate for the lawyer to take any major decision affecting the merits of the case away from the client. Thus, so long as the client is competent in a legal sense, it would seem improper for a lawyer to make major decisions or command the client to make the decision the lawyer thinks is the wise one.

At first blush, the ABA Code of Professional Responsibility would seem to suggest that lawyers can make major decisions when the client appears to lack adequate judgment, even if no general representative has been appointed.

> The responsibilities of a lawyer may vary according to the intelligence, experience, mental condition, or age of a client. . . .[4]

> Any mental or physical condition of a client that renders him (her) incapable of making a considered judgment casts additional responsibilities on his (her) lawyer. . . .

> If the client under disability has no legal representative, his (her) lawyer may be compelled in court proceedings to make decisions on behalf of the client. . . .

> If the disability of a client and the lack of a legal representative compels the lawyer to make decisions for his (her) client, the lawyer should consider all circumstances then prevailing and act with care to safeguard and advance the interests of his (her) client. . . .[5]

However, after making the foregoing statements, the Code states:

> But obviously, a lawyer cannot perform any act or make any decision which the law required his (her) client to perform or make, either acting for himself (herself) if competent, or by a duly constituted representative, if legally incompetent.[6]

Under case law, major decisions—decisions affecting the merits of the case—are reserved to the client.[7] Therefore, it would seem that even if the decision is an extremely detrimental one, the lawyer should not intervene to the extent of taking over the decision, unless the client's mental state will justify the appointment of a general representative.[8] If the client's state does justify such an appoint-

---

4. ABA Code of Professional Responsibility EC 7–11.

5. ABA Code of Professional Responsibility EC 7–12.

6. Ibid.

7. Linsk v. Linsk, 70 Cal.2d 272, 74 Cal.Rptr. 544, 449 P.2d 760 (1969); D. Melinkoff, Lawyers and the System of Justice 733–757 (1976).

8. The conclusion that the lawyer should not take over the decision making is consistent with the last sentence of EC 7–12 ("But obviously a lawyer cannot perform any act or make any decision which the law requires his [her] client to perform or make, either acting for himself [herself] if competent, or by a duly constituted representative if legally incompetent."), and EC 7–7 ("[Except for tactical decisions] the authority to

ment, the lawyer should at least request the appointment of a guardian ad litem before proceeding with the case.[9]

However, what about intervention that falls short of actually taking the decision from the client? Assume for some reason the client is making an extremely detrimental decision, but the appointment of a general guardian or conservator is not justified. Should the lawyer go so far as to urge the client to make a different decision? In our opinion, the answer is "yes." So long as the urging does not really start to overwhelm the client's will, we believe this kind of intervention is appropriate. Though some will disagree, we believe that, on balance, more clients will be helped by this kind of intervention than will be harmed by it. Our conclusion is predicated in part by our belief that lawyers do have the capacity and good judgment to exercise appropriate restraint. Lawyers can, we believe, limit their intervention to situations where the decision is likely to be

---

make decisions is exclusively that of the client."). The conclusion is also consistent with the idea that the lawyer is an agent, not a principal. But the conclusion seems inconsistent with some language of EC 7–11 and EC 7–12. EC 7–11 states, "The responsibilities of a lawyer may vary according to the intelligence, mental condition or age of a client . . . ." This language might be interpreted to mean only that the lawyer should be extremely careful in order to make sure there is a full consideration of the alternatives and consequences when counseling clients of the type described, and that a lawyer has a duty to seek the appointment of a guardian ad litem when there is a question of legal competence. Thus, the language need not be taken to mean the lawyer should take over the decision-making function. But EC 7–12 states, "If the client under disability has no legal representative, his [her] lawyer may be compelled in court proceedings to make decisions on behalf of the client . . . . If the disability of a client and the lack of a legal representative compels the lawyer to make decisions for his [her] client, the lawyer should consider all circumstances then prevailing and act with care to safeguard and advance the interests of his [her] client." If tactical decisions are for the lawyer, and decisions affecting the merits are to be made exclusively by the client, to what kinds of decisions does this language of EC 7–12 apply? Does the language contradict EC 7–7?

9. Appointment of a guardian ad litem is sometimes spoken of as a matter lying within the trial judge's discretion. See, e. g. 3A Moore's Federal Practice § 17.26 (1970): "The word 'or' in the last sentence of Rule 17(c) is not to be read 'and'; the subdivision does not make appointment of a guardian *ad litem* mandatory if the court feels that the interests of the infant or incompetent can be as well protected without this action, and if the court has jurisdiction over the person under disability." However, it has been held that even though the appointment of a guardian is discretionary, a trial judge cannot dispense with consideration of the issue of the necessity for the appointment of a guardian ad litem where the facts call for a consideration of the issue, Roberts v. Ohio Cas. Ins. Co., 256 F.2d 35 (5th Cir. 1958). And, usually such an appointment should be made. *Roberts* at 39.

In exercising discretion not to appoint a guardian ad litem, some courts conclude that an incompetent's interests can be adequately protected by competent counsel. See Johnson v. Lambotte, 147 Colo. 203, 206, 363 P.2d 165, 167 (1961). But apparently this is not always the view. See M. S. v. Wermers, 409 F.Supp. 312, 314 (S.D.1976). Furthermore, if the court is considering allowing counsel to serve in lieu of a guardian ad litem, should the court consider potential problems of conflict of interest? See D. Rosenthal, Lawyers and Clients: Who's in Charge? 95–116 (1974).

extremely detrimental. With training and experience, lawyers can learn to recognize the difference between a decision that is extremely detrimental and one that is merely eccentric.[10] Similarly, they can learn to recognize the difference between convincing a client to change a decision and coercing such a change. When lawyers do recognize these differences, many clients can, in our experience, benefit from the reasoned intervention of a lawyer.

Techniques for Intervention

The Temporarily Overwrought Client

Before actually attempting to intervene, it can be useful to consider whether or not the client's decision grows out of some temporary emotional state. Perhaps, if the decision is being made because the client is temporarily overwrought, a client-centered decision can be facilitated by encouraging the client to delay the choice.

By our definition, a client is "temporarily overwrought" when a client is making a decision that the client would not normally make were he/she in a less distressed state of mind. However, how is the lawyer to determine that the client's decision making ability is temporarily impaired because the client is extremely overwrought? Again, there is no easy answer. The following combination of factors sometimes indicate that the clients' "normal" decision-making ability is temporarily impaired:

1. The client mentions a *recent* event which most people would find stressful and begins to focus on a number of problems emanating from the event. For example, a client who suddenly encounters a financial setback begins to discuss the event, and a host of related family and financial problems. *and*

2. Insofar as any decision affecting the case is concerned, the client demonstrates an inability to consider and think about the full range of alternatives, other than the one the client has already chosen. The client seems unable to consider the full ramifications of his/her decision and that other alternatives exist which may be more beneficial. *and*

3. The client's demeanor suggests a high degree of emotionality. The client's behavior is quite volatile. For example, the client is so upset he/she weeps continuously; or, the client is so angry he/she repeatedly interrupts the interview with outbursts such as pounding the desk. At the opposite extreme, the client's behavior exhibits almost no emotion un-

---

10. Although some extremely detrimental decisions may be the result of eccentricity, most eccentric decisions do not result in substantial economic, social, or psychological harm in return for very little gain. Eccentric decisions usually do no more than deviate from standards or norms. For a discussion of eccentricity, see N. Kittrie, The Right to be Different (1971).

der circumstances most people would find quite distressful. Instead, the client exhibits an almost vegetative passivity, withdrawal, and resignation—a sense that it is all so hopeless that there is no point in trying to do anything.

If this combination of factors, or any others, suggests the client is temporarily overwrought, the lawyer might attempt to have the client delay the decision by adopting the following approach:

1. Empathizing with the stress the client is apparently experiencing.

2. Pointing out that, in the lawyer's experience, when clients make decisions while under stress, they often regret them later.

3. Pointing out that, in the lawyer's experience, clients who delay decisions are often glad they waited.

4. Recommending the client delay reaching a decision in order to think things over.

Consider this example:

Lawyer: "Ms. Greenspan, having your husband leave in this way must not be easy. I imagine you're under a great deal of stress right now. My experience has been that when people are in situations like yours, they often make quick decisions they come to regret. Some of my clients, however, have decided to wait and think about things a little more. These people have often found their ideas have changed within a relatively short period of time. Most of them were glad they waited. Right now, you're under considerable stress and I'd recommend you wait before absolutely deciding to give up your right to alimony."

If the client insists upon making an immediate decision, then the lawyer can intervene by suggesting the client change the decision.

Suggesting the Client Change the Decision

Successfully intervening in a client's decision will often require more than explaining why the client may be better off with a different decision. If the lawyer is to be effective in getting the client to change the decision, the client must hear and understand the lawyer's analysis. As a general matter, clients are probably better able to listen to what the lawyer has to say if the lawyer has first demonstrated that the lawyer has heard and understood what the client has to say. Therefore, when suggesting that a client change or reconsider a decision, it is often profitable for the lawyer to use active listening to demonstrate the lawyer understands the client's position. When the lawyer has expressed this understanding, the lawyer can then state what decision the lawyer would make, and why. Consider these examples:

Case No. 1:

No. 1–L   Ms. Greenspan, what you're saying is that no matter what happens, you want to remain on a friendly basis with your husband. You feel that if you ask for alimony your husband will become angry and then for sure he'll never come back.

No. 2–C   Right, and if things really get bad, he'll take care of me. I know he will.

No. 3–L   Having your husband back is the most important thing, and asking for alimony increases the risk he won't come back, is what you are saying.

No. 4–C   Exactly.

No. 5–L   You may well be right, it may increase the risk, but, on balance, I think you're making a mistake. You're giving up your right to alimony when you don't know if he'll be back, and when you don't have a job. You don't know for sure how things will turn out in the future. Right now, you're in a vulnerable position. I think you'd be best off protecting yourself by getting a court order. You can always waive your right to alimony later, but the reverse is not true. Why don't you at least take some time and think this over.

Analysis of Case No. 1:

Note how, in both No. 1 and No. 3, the lawyer uses active listening to indicate understanding of the client's reasons for her decision. Before beginning to suggest the client change her decision, the lawyer obtains (No. 4) the client's acknowledgement that the lawyer does understand the client's position. When stating an opinion, the lawyer supplies the reasons behind the opinion. In concluding his/her statement, the lawyer does not appear to command the client to change her decision. Rather, the intervention is confined to suggesting the client reconsider.

Contrast the foregoing approach with the following:

Lawyer: "Ms. Greenspan, you're making a mistake. You're going to regret waiving alimony. As sure as I'm sitting here, your husband is going to leave you 'high and dry.' Follow my advice and get a court order for alimony."

In this example, the lawyer fails to demonstrate any understanding of the client's position. Also, does the lawyer perhaps go beyond the appropriate limits of intervention? Is the lawyer perhaps commanding the client to seek alimony?

Case No. 2:

Lawyer: "Mr. Bithoff, I understand that thinking about a trial is not pleasant. Most clients don't really want to go to trial, and I really understand how it might seem best to just plead guilty and get it over with. But I think you're not facing up to the fact that your employer is probably going to find out. In my experience, employers usually hear about these things from the police and when that happens the person usually gets fired. Since you like your job, since you know you're not likely to find another you like as well, and since you make good money, it just doesn't make sense to give up a 90% chance of acquittal to save $200. I don't think, for your own sake, you should plead guilty."

Analysis of Case No. 2:

In reviewing this example consider the following:

1. Does the lawyer seem to do an adequate job of demonstrating an understanding of the client's position?

2. Does the lawyer appear to be commanding the client to change his decision?

We have presented one approach for suggesting clients reconsider or change their decisions. Are there, perhaps, other equally effective ways of intervening?

Chapter Eleven

REFERRING A CLIENT TO A MENTAL HEALTH PROFESSIONAL

There are a variety of situations in which lawyers refer clients to mental health professionals.[1] We will discuss two types of situations where referrals are commonly made. In the first type, a referral is made to obtain an evaluation of the client's mental state when the client's mental and emotional functioning is an issue in the case. The referral is made because the lawyer desires to secure a professional evaluation which can perhaps be used as evidence on the client's behalf. In the second type of situation, the referral is unrelated to any legal issue of mental competence. Instead, the client is experiencing difficulty in making decisions about a variety of issues related to the case and typically about a host of matters involving the client's day-to-day living. For example, in an unlawful detainer case the client may have difficulties deciding whether or not to defend the matter and also whether or not to institute a separate action against the landlord for the intentional infliction of emotional harm.[2] At the same time, the client is concerned about whether or not to move, whether or not to get a part-time job or borrow money from relatives to finance the potential attorneys' fees, whether or not to keep the children in the same school if the client does move, etc. Faced with this accumulation of problems, the client is experiencing difficulties making any decision. A referral is made because the lawyer believes the client's difficulties in making decisions about the handling of the case and difficulties coping with day-to-day problems in living would be eased if the client obtained the advice and support of a professional such as a social worker, psychologist, or psychiatrist. We will call the first category of situations Referrals for Evaluation of the Client's Mental State and the second category Referrals for Client Assistance.

REFERRALS FOR EVALUATION OF THE CLIENT'S MENTAL STATE

There is a wide variety of cases in which a lawyer may wish to obtain an evaluation of a client's mental competence. In the criminal

1. The term "mental health professional" refers to psychologists, psychiatrists, social workers, and marriage and family counselors.

2. In many jurisdictions, counterclaims may not be asserted in a summary proceeding to recover the possession of real property. See for example, Lindsey v. Normet, 405 U.S. 56, 92 S. Ct. 862, 31 L.Ed.2d 36 (1971); Erbe Corp. v. W & B Realty Co., 255 Cal. App.2d 773, 63 Cal.Rptr. 462 (1967).

law area, facts may suggest the client was not sane at the time of the commission of the crime. Or, perhaps it may appear the client cannot adequately participate in his/her defense.[3] Perhaps evidence of the client's mental competence or emotional state will be influential in determining what sentence the client receives. On the civil side, many cases raise issues about the client's mental state. Guardianship, conservatorship, and civil commitment all involve issues of the client's current and future psychological functioning. In matters involving the custody of a minor, courts often receive evidence not only about the child's mental state, but also about the emotional strengths and weaknesses of the contesting parties. In the area of torts, a case may involve the issue of traumatic neurosis. The plaintiff alleges that as a result of an accident he/she suffered a psychological trauma.

The Procedure for Making a Referral For Evaluation of the Client's Mental State

There may be a number of ways to facilitate this type referral. There are no clear guidelines, but the following procedures can be helpful.

The lawyer should find a qualified professional who would be willing to accept the referral.[4] Since the referral is being made in order to obtain information that perhaps may be communicated to a court, the lawyer should inform the professional of the applicable legal criteria. For example, when the referral is being made to obtain an opinion of the defendant's sanity at the time of the crime, the lawyer should be prepared to discuss the criteria applicable under the McNaughton Rule or Durham Rule.[5]

In addition, the lawyer should be prepared to provide a detailed description of the client's behavior if it is requested. Some professionals request this information to better prepare for the evaluation of the client or to determine if they have the necessary expertise to handle the case. Others see this kind of information as unnecessary, and perhaps prejudicial. They would rather interview the client

---

3. For a general discussion of problems involved in determining competency to stand trial, see A. Brooks, Law, Psychiatry and the Mental Health System 332–389 (1974).

4. For a discussion of how a lawyer might proceed to locate such a professional, see p. 218 infra. The lawyer needs to find an individual who is competent to evaluate the client and also qualified to testify in court. For a description and review of the many problems involved in the presentation of expert psychiatric and psychological testimony, see A. Brooks, Law, Psychiatry and the Mental Health System (1974); R. Slovenko, Psychiatry and the Law (1973); J. Ziskin, Coping with Psychiatric and Psychological Testimony (2d ed. 1975).

5. The lawyer must be prepared to cope with the reality that lawyers and mental health professionals usually deal with issues of an individual's mental state from very different conceptual frameworks and with very different descriptive language. For a general description of some of these differences, see B. Karpman, *On Reducing Tensions and Bridging Gaps Between Psychiatry and the Law*, 48 J.Crim.L.C. & P.S. 164 (1957).

"blind" and then confer with the lawyer later. Further, the lawyer should ask the professional to describe what the interview or evaluation process will entail. This information will be useful in preparing the client for the referral.

When the lawyer has secured someone who will accept the referral, the lawyer should discuss with the client the need or desirability of the referral and explain what will be involved in the evaluation process. The explanation may help the client feel more comfortable about the referral. Generally, it will be helpful if the lawyer directly arranges the referral. Experience suggests that the client is more likely to accept and follow through on the referral when the lawyer actually arranges the time and place for the initial evaluation interview. The lawyer should arrange a time that is mutually convenient and tell the client how to get to the professional's office.

Making a Referral for Evaluation of the Client's Mental State

In making a referral for evaluation, the precise content will vary from case to case. However, in general it can be useful to explain the following to the client:

1. The issue of the client's mental state either cannot be avoided or may be central to the case.

2. A report from a mental health professional may be advantageous to the client.

3. The lawyer recognizes the client's discomfort with the idea of being evaluated by a mental health professional.

4. The client can expect that the evaluation will consist of certain designated procedures (interviews, tests, etc.).

5. The findings will not be revealed to anyone except the lawyer without the client's consent.[6]

To consider how these points might be communicated to the client, review the following hypotheticals:

Case No. 1:

Mr. Homer is a 74-year-old retired Army colonel. His spouse has instituted proceedings to have herself appointed conservator of Mr. Homer's person and estate. The lawyer representing Mr. Homer

6. There is great uncertainty about the extent to which communication from a client to a mental health professional is to be treated as confidential. Some states recognize that any such communication is privileged, while other states do not. In those states where a privilege is recognized, there are often exceptions to the privilege. In general, see McCormick, on Evidence § 213 n. 9 (2d ed. 1972). In one state, California, it has been held that under some circumstances, a psycho-therapist has a duty to warn intended victims that a patient has indicated an intent to harm the victim. Tarasoff v. Regents of the University of California, 17 Cal.3d 425, 131 Cal. Rptr. 14, 551 P.2d 334 (1976). On the Federal side, there is also uncertainty. In diversity cases, state law is said to govern, whereas in Federal matters, privileges are governed by an as yet uncertain common law. In general, see 10 Moore's Federal Practice §§ 500–501 (1976).

desires to obtain an evaluation in order to acquire an independent professional opinion of whether or not Mr. Homer is competent. In the lawyer's judgment, such opinion is critical for a proper defense of the case.

No. 1–L   Mr. Homer, as you know, what your wife is seeking to do is to obtain an order from the judge that would permit her to have control over you and all of your assets and property. That is, she is trying to get the judge to say that she, rather than you, can say what is to be done with things like your bank account, stocks, and things like that.

What the court is going to be deciding is whether or not you are capable of continuing to manage your own affairs. Your wife is going to present witnesses to the court who are going to say that they think you really don't know what's happening and can't manage things for yourself.

No. 2–C   Dammit. That's ridiculous. I've taken care of myself all my life. She just wants to get my money.

No. 3–L   I can understand your anger, and I want to help. In order to help, we'll need to present evidence that you are perfectly capable of taking care of yourself and managing your own affairs. To do that, what I want you to do is go to someone who can provide us with this information. I would like to get a professional evaluation from a psychologist which perhaps we can use in court. The courts place a lot of weight on this kind of professional evaluation, so it's very important that we get one.

No. 4–C   I'm not going to any damn shrink. In fact, I'm not sure I'm going to any damn court. What's mine is mine. I'm fine, and that's all there is to it.

No. 5–L   Most people feel they don't want to be evaluated un-under these circumstances. I certainly understand your not wanting to. The fact is, however, the court is going to hear evidence about whether or not you're capable. You can't stop the court from doing that. The court will hear evidence whether or not you're present in court. What we've got to do is prepare the best case possible for you, and that's why we'll need you to talk to a professional.

No. 6–C   I just don't want to do it.

No. 7–L   I know, and I can certainly understand your feelings. (Pause) We must prepare the best case possible, and we do need this information. It's a rather simple procedure, and nothing you say will be released to anyone but me without your permission. The psychologist will want to interview you for about an hour to an hour and a half, and then will ask you to fill out a couple of questionnaires. You don't need to prepare for any of this; all you need to do is show up for your appointment. The whole thing will take about half a day. Do you have any questions?

No. 8–C　Yeah, how do I know who to go to?

No. 9–L　I'll arrange for you to see Dr. McBreen. The doctor can see you either Monday morning or Thursday afternoon. Which is better for you?

No. 10–C　Thursday, but how do I get there?

No. 11–L　Dr. McBreen's office is at 48th and Century, Suite 28, on the second floor. I'll call and confirm the appointment and call you if there needs to be any change made. If you don't hear from me, be sure to be there promptly on Thursday at 1:30. I think you're making a good decision here, and we'll get together as soon as I get the doctor's report.

Analysis of Case No. 1:

As this example demonstrates, it usually is not easy to make a referral, even when the issue of the client's mental state cannot be avoided. Where, in the lawyer's judgment, the referral is critical to the case, and the case is very important to the client's welfare, the lawyer will often have to deviate from a client-centered approach to decision making. The lawyer must struggle to be empathetic in order to maintain rapport yet be assertive enough to convince the client that a disfavored course of action is necessary. One explanation of the need and importance of the referral is usually not enough. Note how in No.'s 4 and 6 the lawyer's explanations essentially fall on "deaf ears." The client simply does not want to see a psychologist. The lawyer continues, however, to be empathetic and stresses the importance of the referral (No. 5). Finally, in the face of continued resistance, the lawyer intervenes in the decision-making process and becomes more assertive (No. 7). While being empathetic, the lawyer speaks of the referral as if it were a *fait accompli*. The same assertive stance is adopted in No. 9. When the lawyer intervenes in this assertive manner, most clients will go along with the lawyer's "recommendation." The technique, however, certainly cannot be considered client-centered. After all, the lawyer is at least urging the client to do something the client does not want to do. In so doing, is the lawyer going beyond persuasion? Is the lawyer commanding the client to undertake a certain course of action? If so, can the lawyer's action be justified on the ground that a failure to obtain an evaluation could be "extremely detrimental?" If the lawyer's action cannot be justified on the ground that it is preventing an extremely detrimental decision, can the action be justified on the ground that the client may indeed be legally incompetent?

In terms of the specific content of the explanation, the lawyer's statements in this example seem adequate. No.'s 1, 3, and especially 5, make it clear that the legal issue of the client's mental state cannot be avoided. In No. 3, the lawyer indicates the advantage of obtaining a report by stating that courts place weight on professional opinions.

In No.'s 3 and 5, the lawyer employs active listening to empathize with the client's feelings of discomfort about the referral. In No. 7, the lawyer provides a brief description of the procedures that will be followed and explains the confidential nature of the evaluation.

Case No. 2:

Mr. Parkinson has instituted proceedings to obtain the civil commitment of his wife. The petition alleges Ms. Parkinson is a danger to herself and others. Ms. Parkinson's parents have retained a lawyer to represent her.

Ms. Parkinson, age 36, is employed as a nurse in a local hospital. She has a history of manic-depressive illness, with one prior commitment. At that time, her doctor recommended Lithium treatment. This medication enabled her to function quite adequately for about four years. For some reason, Ms. Parkinson discontinued her medication. At first she went through a period of extreme elation and excitability. She went on long and expensive shopping sprees and signed up for numerous new classes, including flying lessons. Her behavior became quite impulsive and erratic and at one point she disrobed at work and ran naked through the emergency ward. Her employer contacted her husband and complained of her inappropriate behavior.

Ms. Parkinson slowly calmed down, but now she has become quite depressed. She speaks of feelings of despair from having an illness she has no control over. She recently read that manic-depressive illness runs in families. Her husband overheard a telephone conversation in which she told a friend, "I think we'd all be better off dead."

Several nurses and doctors at the hospital where she works believe Ms. Parkinson can function quite adequately. However, Ms. Parkinson's husband took her to the State hospital for an evaluation. Two psychiatrists concluded she was dangerous to herself and others. The proceedings were then instituted to commit Ms. Parkinson. Her lawyer visits her in the hospital and the following dialogue takes place:

No. 1–L   Ms. Parkinson, there is going to be a hearing next week where the judge will decide if you're to be released. As you know, there are two psychiatrists who say you're dangerous to yourself and others. What

I want to do is get another professional opinion that may not agree with this conclusion.

No. 2–C If they already said that about me, it must be true. Why should I bother talking to anyone else?

No. 3–L Look, it's going to be fine. You don't have to worry, just leave that to me.

No. 4–C If I see another psychiatrist, they'll just get more ammunition against me. Why can't people just leave me alone?

No. 5–L Look, I've arranged for Dr. Patrick to see you tomorrow. You're just going to have to do it. Dr. Patrick will be here at 10:00.

Analysis of Case No. 2:

In reviewing this example, consider the following:

1. Is the lawyer's explanation of the need for psychiatric consultation adequately explained to the client? Why or why not?

2. How might the lawyer have expanded upon the potential advantage of participating in the interview?

3. Would the lawyer's response in No. 3 be considered empathetic?

4. Given the facts of this case, do you think the lawyer was overly assertive in the way the appointment was presented to the client? Why or why not?

REFERRALS FOR CLIENT ASSISTANCE

In both criminal and civil cases, the lawyer will frequently be confronted with a client who seeks assistance with a variety of problems, some of which are only at best tangentially related to the case. For example, a client involved in a personal injury action may desire the lawyer's advice not only about whether or not to pay for the services of an investigator but, more generally, about what to do about an entire range of problems which have cropped up since the client was disabled and lost his/her job. The client wants to know whether or not to borrow money from family members, what kind of disability income is available, whether or not it makes sense to move to a smaller home, what kind of job opportunities might be available to a disabled person, etc.

When clients are confronted with a series of problems such as those just described, the clients' day-to-day living often becomes totally consumed with the endless consideration and reconsideration of their problems. These clients often experience severe stress and have difficulty making decisions, not only about what should be done to resolve the legal dispute, but also about what should be done to resolve a host of day-to-day "problems in living." As a result, many clients turn to their lawyers for support and guidance, often because they know of no one else from whom to seek help. Sometimes lawyers can provide the necessary assistance simply by listening in an empathetic manner and making a few practical suggestions. However, in some instances lawyers lack both the time and expertise to provide the assistance that would help reduce the client's stress and resolve the various problems. In these instances, it can be to the mutual benefit of both the client and lawyer to refer the client to a mental health professional. If the client can obtain the help of a counselor, the client may be able to function more adequately. As a consequence, the client may put fewer time demands on the lawyer and may be better able to participate in the legal counseling process.

The Procedure for Making a Referral for Client Assistance

There may be a number of ways to facilitate this kind of referral. As a general guideline, the following procedure may be helpful.

First, the lawyer should find a qualified professional who would be willing to accept the referral. The kind of referral the lawyer will make will vary according to a number of factors, including how severely distressed the client appears, the nature of the problems involved, the client's financial condition, etc. Although the lawyer will often be uncertain about what kind of mental health professional might best assist the client, the lawyer can secure this information. The lawyer can contact sources such as other lawyers, the local university mental health clinic, local or state community mental health centers, or the local welfare department. Often local or state psychological, psychiatric, or social work associations will provide a list of professionals who might be of assistance.

When the lawyer has obtained the name of a specific person or agency, the lawyer should contact the professional and verify that counseling is currently available. Additionally, the lawyer should obtain a description of what the counseling process will entail so the lawyer can subsequently communicate this information to the client.

As in a referral for evaluation, the lawyer should next discuss with the client the need and desirability of the referral. When the lawyer has concluded the explanation of the benefits of professional assistance, the lawyer should directly arrange an appointment. As previously noted, the client is most likely to accept and follow through on a referral when the lawyer actually arranges the time and place for the initial consultation.

Making a Referral for Client Assistance

In making this kind of referral, it can be useful to do the following:

1. Explain the aspects of the client's current situation which indicate a need for referral. This explanation might point out

that the client appears to be under a great deal of stress, the client seems to spend a great deal of time talking about his/her various problems, the client seems to be seeking advice on how to handle these problems.

2. Empathize with the client's current situation and dilemmas, but point out that the lawyer lacks the time and expertise to handle the various problems.

3. Explain that being under stress is not abnormal, and that many people benefit from counseling. In outlining the potential benefits, the lawyer can point out such matters as counseling can reduce stress, the counselor may be able to help the client make decisions, and the counselor may be able to refer the client to other specialized sources of help in the community (e. g., vocational guidance, day-care centers, rehabilitation programs, self-help programs, etc.).

4. Empathize with any client's discomfort about seeing a counselor.

5. Explain what the counseling will entail and that the lawyer can arrange a specific first appointment at a time convenient for the client.

To consider how such an explanation might be communicated, review the following hypotheticals:

Case No. 1:

Ms. Peters is a 37-year-old woman with two children. She has initiated divorce proceedings after 10 years of marriage. Her children are upset about the divorce, and one of the children is currently in trouble at school for fighting and truancy. Her husband's parents are calling her daily and haranguing her. Her housekeeper has just quit, and she has no one to watch the children while she's at work. She doesn't know whether or not to quit her job, or to try to find another housekeeper. Further, she cannot decide what items of personal property she is willing to allow her husband to keep. She talks about her problems incessantly and almost to the exclusion of everything else. She cries often.

She keeps calling her lawyer under the pretext of discussing the case, but then quickly switches to a discussion of her day-to-day problems. The lawyer has tried to be empathetic, but really doesn't have the time or the expertise to advise her on how to handle her child's school problem or her own problem of deciding whether or not to keep working. The lawyer senses that if Ms. Peters could obtain some counseling she might be able to resolve her day-to-day problems, as well as her problems with the property settlement agreement more easily.

No. 1–L   Ms. Peters, it seems you're facing a lot of problems you weren't really expecting. Your child is having problems at school, your in-laws are hassling you, and now the housekeeper has quit. All of these problems seem to be causing you a great deal of stress. Many clients in similar situations have also been quite upset and didn't know where to turn for help. You've called me a number of times, and I only wish I could be of help in some way. Unfortunately, I really don't have the time or training to help you with these problems, but I do know some professionals who do. Many clients have benefited from counseling, and I think it could be helpful for you to talk to someone now.

No. 2–C   I don't think I'm that sick. You know, I don't think there's anything wrong with me. It's just his parents are impossible and won't leave me alone, and now the school is calling about Dennis. I just don't know what to do with all of this and I just can't decide what property I should have.

No. 3–L   You're right. You really do have too many things happening at one time. It's a lot to cope with, and it's very normal to experience a great deal of stress in the face of problems like these. I wish I could offer some helpful suggestions, but I can't. However, Dr. Torres, at the Read Clinic on Broadway, near 6th, has counseled a number of people going through divorces. I think she could help you make some of the decisions you're facing, and also help with Dennis and your in-laws. She specializes in counseling families and children, that's why I thought she'd be the right person for you to talk to. I'm pretty sure I can call and arrange an appointment for you. Shall I go ahead?

No. 4–C   I don't know. I think I should handle these problems myself.

No. 5–L   I can understand how you might want to handle this alone. Many people feel reluctant to seek help from a counselor. I guess I've also seen how upset you've been in the last few weeks and really think that you could benefit from some outside advice and support. Dr. Torres would probably meet with you for one hour per week and you could discuss some of your personal concerns. In addition, she could contact Dennis' teacher and the school counselor. I think she would be quite helpful. Would you like me to call for an appointment for you?

No. 6–C   I guess so, but how much will this cost?

No. 7–L   Dr. Torres sees people on a sliding fee basis. You can discuss your financial situation with her at the first meeting. She will likely set a fee that is quite manageable for you.

Analysis of Case No. 1:

In general, the lawyer seems to adequately follow the guidelines we have suggested. In No.'s 1 and 3, the lawyer articulates those aspects of Ms. Peters' situation that indicate a referral may be called for. In both No. 1 and No. 3, the lawyer expresses empathy for the client's dilemma, but also indicates the lawyer lacks both the time and expertise to provide help for her many problems. In No. 3, the lawyer points out that it is quite normal to experience stress, and that counseling can be beneficial. In No. 5, the lawyer empathizes with the client's discomfort about seeking counseling. Additionally, in No.'s 3, 5, and 7, the lawyer points out the ready availability of counseling, and in No.'s 5 and 7 provides some explanation of what the counseling will entail.

Assume that in this example Ms. Peters said she wasn't interested in getting counseling. Should the lawyer have intervened in the client's decision-making process to the extent of trying to convince the client to see a counselor? Would it have been appropriate for the lawyer to have said any of the following?

1. Ms. Peters, I think you're making a mistake. You've got so many problems now, and the way to straighten them out is to see someone like Dr. Torres. What I'm going to do is call and arrange an appointment for you;
   or

2. Ms. Peters, I'm disappointed to hear you're not interested. You have a lot of problems now, and you're under a lot of stress. Many clients have been helped by counseling, and I think you could benefit from it also. If you change your mind, please call and I'll go ahead and make an appointment for you;
   or

3. O.K., Ms. Peters. I wanted to make the suggestion, but certainly you are free to make your own decision.

There is probably no standard by which a lawyer can determine how strongly to state his/her opinion about the need or desirability for the client to obtain counseling. In making the decision, the lawyer will want to consider his/her assessment of the client's needs and his/her belief in the importance of client autonomy in making decisions.

Case No. 2:

John Harlan was arrested for embezzling funds from the insurance company by whom he was employed. Although he has told his wife about the arrest and the loss of his job, he has been unable to "break the news" to his children. Without income, his debts are mounting. He is determined not to go into bankruptcy, at least until after his trial. The trial is set for 90 days hence. In addition to the concern he feels about telling his children, Mr. Harlan is worred about what to say to his social acquaintances, and how to handle his financial situation. He is considering withdrawing his children from private school. He would like to get a temporary job but has no idea how to do so. He is especially uncertain of how to explain why he now needs a job. He is mulling his problems over continually and has started to drink. He is calling his lawyer at least twice a week, supposedly to talk about the case. However, Mr. Harlan always turns the conversation to the subjects of his children, his lack of a job, and his worries about facing his friends. His lawyer has asked Mr. Harlan to come to the office to discuss the case.

No. 1–L   John, there is something I'd like to discuss with you. You've called me a number of times this past week to discuss your concerns about your family, your job situation, and what to tell your friends. You seem to want to talk about these problems a lot, and they seem to be causing you a lot of stress at this time. I'd like to help with these problems, but they're really out of my area of expertise. It's not just the job, or what to tell the kids, we've been over that. Right now the real problem, as I see it, is all the stress you're under. You've got all of this plus the worry of the trial, so I can understand why you're so preoccupied with your problems. I'd like to make a suggestion. There is a Dr. Bolberg who has an office in this same building. He has counseled a number of people with problems similar to yours, and I think he could help you.

No. 2–C   Paul, look, you know how I feel about shrinks. No way. I know I've been drinking a little too much, but what do you expect? I'll stop being such a pain in the ass, but you gotta admit I'm really in a mess.

No. 3–L   Hey, I knew you wouldn't like the idea of seeing a counselor, but, look, there's really nothing wrong with doing it. One doesn't have to be sick to need some help. You've got enough problems for 2 or 3 people to handle, and counselors often know about resources that I'm not at all aware of. Do yourself a favor, let me call Dr. Bolberg and arrange an appointment. It can't hurt and it might help.

No. 4–C   I fail to see how lying on a couch and going on and on about my mother is going to help me now.

No. 5–L   Listen, you've been watching too much T.V. I'm not talking about psychoanalysis. Dr. Bolberg will meet with you once or twice a week and talk to you directly about the problems you raised with me. Unless you say no, I'd really like to give him a call. I think it would help.

Analysis of Case No. 2:

In reviewing the foregoing example, consider the following:

1. In No. 1, does the lawyer seem to do an adequate job of pointing out the factors indicating a referral may be helpful? Why or why not?

2. In No. 3, is the lawyer empathetic about the client's discomfort about seeing a counselor? Why or why not?

3. Does the lawyer seem to do an adequate job explaining what the counseling will entail? Why or why not?

4. What other things might the lawyer have said to facilitate this referral?

CONCLUSION

Suggesting that the client should consult a mental health professional is often difficult. There is a feeling that merely mentioning the subject will cause the client to become angry, or at least uncooperative. In short, there is a fear, and appropriately so, that the mention of a referral may cause a real break in the lawyer-client relationship. On the other hand, such referrals are often necessary either for successful handling of the case, or because the lawyer's time demands and the client's emotional needs cannot be satisfied without a referral.

We cannot say that the approaches we have outlined will always prevent ruptures in the lawyer-client relationship. We hope, however, that the guidelines will prove to be a useful starting point for thinking about when and how to make a referral.

*

INDEX

RAMBLING
Causes of, 119.
Examples of, 120.
Motivational statements, 119, 120.
Techniques for handling, 119, 121, 122.

RAPPORT BUILDING
See Active Listening; Fabrication; Facilitators; Motivational Statements; Prepratory Explanation.

RECALL
See Perception and Recollection.

RECOGNITION
Defined, 16.
Examples of, 41, 76, 132.

REFERRAL FOR CLIENT ASSISTANCE
Content of, 218, 219.
Defined, 211, 217.
Examples of, 219, 220, 221, 222.
Procedure for, 218.

REFERRAL FOR EVALUATION
Content of, 213, 215, 216.
Defined, 211.
Examples of, 213, 216.
Procedure for, 212.

REFLECTING FEELINGS
See Active Listening.

RELUCTANCE
See Client Reluctance.

REQUESTS FOR CORRECTIVE FEEDBACK, 107

REWARD
See Extrinsic Reward.

ROLE EXPECTATIONS
Defined, 11.
Examples of, 64, 94, 127, 128, 132, 188, 197.

SETTLEMENT
See Alternatives; Consequences.

SIDETRACKING
See T-Funnel Sequence.

T-FUNNEL SEQUENCE
Active listening during, 95.
Examples of, 93, 97, 133.
Nature of, 92.
Sidetracking, 95, 96, 98.
When to use, 92, 99, 193.

THEORY DEVELOPMENT AND VERIFICATION
Checklists, 90.
Nature and purpose of, 54.
Order of conducting, 90, 91.
Planning for, 86, 90.
Using T-Funnel sequence during, 92.

THREE STAGED INTERVIEW
Advantages of, 57.
Exceptions to, 58.
Purpose of, 54.